Truth under attack

Truth under attack

Cults and contemporary religions

Eryl Davies

 EVANGELICAL PRESS

EVANGELICAL PRESS
12 Wooler Street
Darlington
County Durham
DL1 1RQ
England

ISBN 0-85234-266-7

Unless otherwise stated, all biblical quotations are from the New American Standard Bible published by Thomas Nelson, New York (1985).

Other books by the same author:
Condemned for Ever!
The Wrath of God

Printed by the Bath Press, Avon

Contents

	Page
Preface	7
Introduction	9

Section 1: Some churches and movements within Christendom
1.	Protestant churches and modernism	15
2.	Roman Catholicism	29
3.	Quakers: the Religious Society of Friends	46
4.	Seventh-Day Adventists	52
5.	Moral Re-Armament	62
6.	Churches of Christ: 'Campbellites'	68
7.	Unitarian churches	74
8.	'Jesus only': the Apostolic Oneness Movement	80

Section 2: Some established cults
9.	Christadelphians	87
10.	Christian Science or Church of Christ, Scientist	93
11.	Mormons	100
12.	Jehovah's Witnesses	110
13.	Worldwide Church of God	125
14.	Rastafarians	133

Section 3: Some controversial and socially deviant cults
15.	The Unification Church: Moonies	139
16.	The Family of Love (previously called the Children of God)	148
17.	The Way International	153
18.	Scientology	158

Section 4: Freemasonry
19.   Freemasonry   167

Section 5: Some self-improvement groups
20.   EST: Erhard Seminars Training   177
21.   Exegesis   183

Section 6: Some spiritistic groups and the occult
22.   The occult — a general survey and warning   187
23.   Spiritism   193
24.   Theosophy   201
25.   Eckankar   207

Section 7: Some Near-and Far-Eastern movements
26.   The New Age Movement   215
27.   Baha'i   222
28.   Hare Krishna: International Society for
       Krishna Consciousness   229
29.   Yoga   235
30.   Transcendental Meditation   240
31.   Divine Light Mission   247
32.   Rajneesh Foundation   251

Section 8: An outline of major Bible doctrines
33.   The Bible   259
34.   What God is like   263
35.   The Holy Trinity   267
36.   The works of God   273
37.   Man: his creation and fall   276
38.   Man in sin   279
39.   The person of Christ   283
40.   The sacrifice of Christ   287
41.   The exaltation of Christ   290
42.   The Holy Spirit   295
43.   Becoming a Christian   298
44.   The church   301
45.   Death and the after-life   304

Appendices
I.   Humanism   311
II.   Useful addresses and contacts for further reading
       and research   317

References   321
Index   331

Preface

I am grateful to Mr Wyn James and Miss Brenda Lewis, both of the Evangelical Movement of Wales, for their initial interest and encouragement during the writing of this book. I have also appreciated some helpful suggestions made by the directors of Evangelical Press as well as their willingness to publish the work.

Miss Linda Baynham and Mrs Elizabeth Pritchard worked extremely hard in typing most of my original notes; their work was supplemented by Mrs Gill Berry, Mrs Elizabeth Wright and Mrs Tricia Lewis. Mrs Chris Connor kindly retyped some chapters after a final updating and editing of contents. I am unable to repay these ladies for their kindness but assure them that their work encouraged me greatly and freed me to concentrate on ministry and research.

The contents of this book have been carefully researched over a period of sixteen years and I have been assisted by contact with organizations specializing in cult activity and teaching, especially Deo Gloria Outreach. Some organizations helped in rechecking material and I am indebted to them. James Bjornstad, the Academic Dean at North Eastern Bible College, Essex Falls, New Jersey and an authority on the subject of cults, gave me valuable suggestions which I have incorporated in the book. Professor Bjornstad also provided me with materials not available in Britain.

I trust God will bless and vindicate his truth in these pages for the edifying of the church and the salvation of those deceived by false teaching, whether in Protestant/Roman Catholic churches, cults or the more popular movements.

Eryl Davies
Evangelical Theological College of Wales
Bridgend
January 1990

Introduction

I am persuaded that there is an urgent need for a book such as this to serve as a practical handbook for believers on heretical churches, cults and movements operating in Britain today. The book is reasonably comprehensive for, in addition to the cults, I have included groups like Moral Re-Armament and even Freemasonry, as well as churches like the Roman Catholic Church and liberal Protestant churches which have deviated from the Bible.

In addition to serving as a handbook for Christians, the book will also help those who are troubled by false teaching to understand what the Bible actually teaches on important doctrines. Readers, for example, who are anxious to find out what the Jehovah's Witnesses teach about the person of Christ or what the Roman Catholic Church teaches about the mass can quickly turn to the relevant sections and compare their teachings with those of the Bible.

Finally, instead of a bibliography I have included an appendix on organizations specializing in the cults. This list is extensive and covers the groups and organizations currently working in Britain and in the United States to counter and monitor the 'cult explosion'. This information will enable readers to contact specialists in the field and obtain regular, up-to-date information on what is happening in the cult world as well as details of new and helpful publications.

Defining our terms

The terms 'cult' and 'sect' need to be defined briefly at this point. By now the word 'cult' has virtually displaced that of 'sect' previously used to describe Jehovah's Witnesses, Moonies and Mormons, etc. The term 'sect' is regarded as being too restrictive and too closely linked with Christianity.

Sociologically, it is important to distinguish between the categories of a church and a cult or sect. While traditional churches are generally integrated into the prevailing culture, the cults by contrast adopt a more critical and alien attitude towards that same culture. The terms 'sect' and 'cult' are used to describe groups or movements of religious protest against organized religion, secular government and the dominant culture.

For the modern media, the word 'cult' is often a convenient way of referring to the more bizarre groups such as the Moonies and Scientologists. The *Shorter Oxford Dictionary* defines the word as 'devotion to a particular person or thing as paid by a body of professed adherents'. Such devotees are usually sincere, zealous and convinced that they have found the truth. One distinctive feature of the cults is the belief that this 'truth' is found exclusively in leaders who claim to have a special understanding and personal revelation from God. For this reason the cults tend to have an additional authority to that of the Bible. Most Seventh Day Adventists, for example, accept the writings of Mrs Ellen White as comparable in authority to the Bible, while Christian Scientists regard Mrs Eddy's *Science and Health* as an infallible key to the Bible. Similarly, Mormons elevate their book above the Bible and Jehovah's Witnesses do not encourage people to read the Bible without the interpretation provided by the Watchtower.

The word 'cult' has also been used more widely to include self-improvement groups such as Exegesis and EST, but this wide application of the term is unhelpful and confusing. At present, terms like 'movement', 'new religious movements' and 'new religions' are being used increasingly to replace that of 'cult'.[1]

The appeal of the cults

Ronald Enroth, Professor of Sociology at Westmont College,

California, suggests several reasons for the phenomenal growth of the cults in the United States during the past three decades.[2] For example, he observes that the cults developed during times of significant social change and cultural upheaval. They also prosper when there is no single, national issue, such as war or important civil rights problems, to capture people's imagination and loyalty. In an absorbing interdisciplinary study, Irving Hexham and Karla Poewe also draw attention to these social aspects of the 'cult explosion'.[3] The emergence of these cults/movements has also coincided with the decline of church attendance and membership, particularly in the case of young people.

Professor Enroth underlines, too, some psychological factors such as security and a strong dependency feeling which the cults exploit in meeting basic human needs.

You will be wrong if you assume that young people are the only ones to be attracted to the cults. Already in Britain it is evident that many middle-aged and older people have joined cults like the Jehovah's Witnesses, Mormons and Scientology, etc. In America, for example, the Institute of Gerontology at Wayne State University has provided conclusive evidence that the cults are successfully recruiting adherents between the ages of fifty and seventy plus.[4] Some cults in the United States have as many as 20% of their members over the age of sixty while, in areas like Miami, as many as 45% of cult members are over the age of fifty.

Although several cults, including the Moonies, have an anti-semitic bias, many Jews are being recruited. Constituting less than 3% of the American population, Jews form between 30% and 50% of cult members. There are good reasons, of course, why the cults are focusing attention on older people. Some hand over their large incomes to the group while those with fewer resources surrender social security and pension payments. Sometimes their discontent, loneliness and boredom are exploited by cult activists who offer 'instant' answers to personal problems and provide an initial sense of caring for those who feel neglected.

Classifying the cults

The cults have been classified in a number of different ways. Professor Bryan Wilson has distinguished them as world-denying (e.g. Children of God, Hare Krishna), world-indifferent (e.g. The Way International) or world-enhancing (e.g. TM, EST, Scientology).[5] A different classification is given by Professor Ronald Enroth.[6] He classifies them as (1) Eastern mystical, (2) aberrational Christian, (3) self-improvement, (4) eclectic-syncretistic, (5) psychic-occult-astral and (6) established groups including Jehovah's Witnesses, Mormons and Christian Science, etc. These 'established' cults are in contrast to newer cults like the Family of Love and Scientology. Some have gone so far as to describe Scientology, Hare Krishna, the Unification Church (Moonies) and the Divine Light Mission as 'destructive' and not just new cults.

The cults as a challenge

Writing in *Concilium*, John Colemann reminds us: 'The new religious movements represent, world-wide, a challenge to the mainline Christian denominations. They are growing apace. Currently, they comprise 2.2 per cent of the world population, some 96 million. They presently outnumber Judaism and by the year 2000 will approximate to the numbers of Eastern Orthodoxy. Various sociological studies indicate that the new religions in Europe and North America are more successful in recruiting young members and especially in gaining adherents among those whose background is unchurched.'[7]

In the United Kingdom, sixteen of these movements alone had a total of 345,074 members at the end of 1985 with a total of nearly 17,000 leaders/ministers. By 1988, these movements recorded a further significant increase in their numbers.

There is also the challenge to educate Christians in the Bible and at the same time to reach those who have been deceived into accepting error for truth. We need to share with these people *the* gospel of the Lord Jesus Christ.

Section 1
Some churches and movements within Christendom

1. Protestant churches and modernism

2. Roman Catholicism

3. Quakers: the Religious Society of Friends

4. Seventh-Day Adventists

5. Moral Re-Armament

6. Churches of Christ: 'Campbellites'

7. Unitarian churches

8. 'Jesus only': the Apostolic Oneness Movement

1.
Protestant churches and modernism

'I'm confused,' remarked a middle-aged man after attending a Protestant church service one Sunday morning. 'The preacher told us he did not believe in the Bible. He did not even believe that Jesus Christ was God or that he performed any of the miracles recorded in the Gospels.' The man was clearly upset. 'What am I to believe?' he asked. 'Who is right? I was always taught by my family and Sunday School teachers that Christ was God and that he fed the 5,000 miraculously and turned the water into wine at the wedding in Cana of Galilee.' His distress was real indeed. Eventually, however, he shrugged his shoulders and, before going into his house, said, 'I don't like all these new theories.'

Or think of a different situation. A young married couple were watching a religious discussion programme on the television. They were interested in finding out more about Christianity and how it related to their lives. Their reaction, however, was one of astonishment as the three clergymen on the programme proceeded to give their views about God, Jesus Christ, the atonement and life after death. One of them, a bishop, did not believe in the virgin birth of the Lord Jesus and could not accept the fact that the Lord Jesus had risen physically from the dead. The other two clergymen were just as sceptical. 'God is not outside or up there,' one insisted, 'but he is merely the "depth" inside your personality.' Another clergyman was unsure whether there was a heaven or hell after death. 'Perhaps, when we die,' he said, 'we just cease to exist.' At the end of the programme, the young woman turned to her husband and exclaimed, 'I thought those men were supposed to believe all those things, not deny them! Who and what are we to believe?'

The same sad story can be repeated many, many times. The winds of change have blown through many Protestant church denominations causing havoc and confusion concerning the truth. Who or what is responsible? In a word, 'modernism'. The rest of this chapter will explain what 'modernism' is and how it has affected Protestant churches.

What is modernism?

The terms 'modernism' or 'liberalism' are used to describe a critical and rational approach to the Bible which originated in Germany early in the nineteenth century and slowly extended its influence until by the early decades of the twentieth century almost the whole of Protestantism in Western Europe, and more recently Roman Catholicism, had embraced its dangerous presuppositions, methods and conclusions.

The history of modernism

One must really go back to the German philosopher Immanuel Kant (1724-1804), and particularly to his distinction between the phenomenal and noumenal realms, in order to appreciate the rise of modernism. For Kant, knowledge must always be related to what we can perceive by our senses (the phenomenal); but the noumena, that is, objects like God or questions such as immortality and salvation, are beyond the scope of our experience and knowledge and therefore must remain incomprehensible to us or, at best, are matters of faith about which there can be no certainty. The implications of this for biblical Christianity were devastating. For example, Christian doctrines were removed from the spheres of history and knowledge, the verbal inspiration of the Bible was regarded as being impossible, and attention was diverted away from God to the individual and his or her knowledge, so that the door was respectably opened for a thorough-going sceptical and subjective

approach to Christianity. While the Deists[1] of the eighteenth
century had denied all the supernatural elements in the Bible, and
scholars like Lessing (1729-1781) published sceptical accounts of
the life of Jesus which were later to influence Albert Schweitzer and
others, it was Kant and his followers who gave to modernism the
necessary philosophical framework and impetus in order to develop
and win the eventual approval of Christendom.

An important landmark was the *Life of Jesus* written by the
German theologian D. F. Strauss in 1835-36. Strauss's Jesus was a
human, fallible person around whom the early Christians had built
numerous myths in order to project him as a kind of hero-god. In
1863 J. E. Renan published a similar *Life of Jesus* in which Christ
was depicted as a zealous revolutionary with a martyr complex. At
the same time Albrecht Ritschl (1822-1889), the newly appointed
theology professor at Göttingen, whole-heartedly embraced Kant's
philosophy and ridiculed, for example, the doctrine of Christ's
atoning death and the Bible. Near the end of the nineteenth century
the church history specialist, Adolf van Harnack (1851-1930) was
lecturing to enthralled audiences at Berlin University under the
general title, 'What is Christianity?' Once again he viewed Jesus as
an ordinary man but one who was at peace with himself and thereby
able to help others as he proclaimed a moral life of love in the
context of God's fatherhood. In Britain in 1910 Arthur Drews wrote
his devastating book, *The Christ Myth,* in which he claimed that the
entire gospel was fictitious. During this period, Albert Schweitzer
(1875-1965) became popular both as an academic and a missionary,
but his *Quest of the Historical Jesus,* published in 1906, projected
the image of the Lord as a sincere believer who dabbled in politics
and made a mess of things as well. Schweitzer had no time for the
supernatural elements in the Bible. By the end of the nineteenth
century 'higher criticism'[2] of the New Testament was firmly entrenched through the work of men like C. H. Weisse, C. G. Wilke,
B. F. Westcott and H. J. Holtmann, while in the field of Old
Testament study equally disastrous results emerged as Julius
Wellhausen and others subjected the sacred text to a critical and
sceptical analysis. For example, the authorship of most biblical
books was questioned (e.g. the Mosaic authorship of the Penta-
teuch[3]); the historicity of Genesis chapters 1-11 was denied and
Israel's history was interpreted exclusively in terms of man's progressive search for God and for absolute standards.

Protests against modernism

We must not imagine, however, that these radical views were
advocated without protest or opposition. One of the outstanding
Old Testament scholars of the nineteenth century was Ernst
Wilhelm Hengstenberg (1802-1869) who, after his conversion as a
student in Basle, devoted himself to the study and defence of the Old
Testament. Although his writings received little attention,
Hengstenberg answered the critics most competently and wrote
many helpful commentaries which are still in use. In Princeton
Theological Seminary, too, Charles Hodge (1797-1878), B. B.
Warfield (1851-1921) and then Gresham Machen did invaluable
work in expounding and upholding the biblical faith amidst great
opposition. John Urquhart also published an important book in
defence of the Bible in 1895 entitled *The inspiration and accuracy
of the Holy Scripture*. 'Criticism', he affirms in the preface, 'has
reached certain conclusions regarding various books of Scripture.
The older narratives are declared to be mere legends, and the history
generally is described as tradition tinctured by the time when it was
put into writing. Certain books of the Old Testament are said to fall
below even this low level. They are declared to be fictions... and all
these conclusions are placed before the public as genuine scientific
discoveries.'[4] But Urquhart was not content merely to trace the
development of this critical approach and question some of its
conclusions. More importantly he deemed it 'essential to ascertain,
first of all, what the scriptural view of inspiration is. How did
inspired men regard the words which they and others have handed
on to us and, above all, how did our Lord receive them? A clear and
full answer to that question is the need of the hour. Once got, it
would settle this controversy for many.'[5] Concluding his discussion
of the Lord's endorsement of the Old Testament, Urquhart writes,
'If our Master is to be judge in this matter, or if we are to give heed
to the testimony of His apostles and of the Scriptures... doubt is no
longer possible as to the reality or the extent of the Inspiration of the
Bible. The Book has God for its Author. Its every utterance and its
every word are His. But this testimony is openly set aside or silently
ignored by those who claim to be heard as authorities in the
Christian Church. The so-called Higher Criticism sits unchallenged
in our Divinity Halls, our Colleges, and our Universities. It is

moulding the future ministry of every denomination in the land. It is issuing textbooks, commentaries, treatises, and magazine articles in which the public is informed that the former teaching regarding the Bible can no longer be maintained.'[6]

Modernism asserts its stranglehold

Despite the defence of the faith by such competent men, modernism continued to consolidate its stranglehold on Christendom in the first half of the twentieth century. In Britain, for example, men like A. S. Peake, W. R. Inge, Wheeler Robinson, J. Baillie and C. H. Dodd were prominent, while on the Continent theologians such as Paul Tillich and Karl Barth refined the new theology (in radically different ways). Rudolf Bultmann's influence on New Testament studies has been devastating, with his insistence that the Gospels (which he says were glamorized by the early church) must be demythologized before we can discover the authentic meaning of the text. His antagonism to orthodox, biblical Christianity is uncompromising. 'The task of theology,' claims Bultmann, 'is to imperil souls, to lead men into doubt, to shatter all naïve credulity... I often have the impression that my conservative New Testament colleagues feel very uncomfortable for I see them perpetually engaged in salvage operations. I let the fire burn.' When asked who Jesus was and what he was like, Bultmann replied, 'I do not know and do not want to know.'[7]

Tillich, too, rejected orthodoxy in favour of a sceptical, existentialist approach to truth. Deriding the biblical teaching of God's wrath, he wrote that people receive forgiveness in spite of the Saviour's death, not because of it, while the claim that God has become man he regards as not just paradoxical but actually nonsensical. Tillich regards the New Testament narratives of the crucifixion of the Lord as 'contradictory legendary reports' and the resurrection, too, is deprived of all historicity and interpreted in psychological terms as the Lord's restoration to dignity in the minds of the disciples. While pursuing a distinguished academic career, Tillich lived an immoral life and when he was dying he not only spoke at length about the *Tibetan Book of the Dead,* but he refused to have the Bible read to him.[8]

First in a newspaper article and then in a small paperback

entitled *Honest to God,* published in March 1963, the views of Tillich, Bultmann and Bonhöffer were popularized by the then Bishop of Woolwich, Dr John A. T. Robinson. According to the bishop, Jesus was God only in the sense that he gave us insights into God at work, whereas the atonement was the complete self-surrender of Jesus to people, in love, rather than a sacrifice for sin. Similarly he explains prayer away as a 'listening, when we take the otherness of the other person most seriously'. Nor does he believe in the objective commands of God as expressed, for example, in the Ten Commandments. He prefers to advocate 'situation ethics', in which the rightness or wrongness of stealing, adultery, murder etc. must be decided personally in each situation.

Within the mainline churches, the situation has continued to deteriorate, as is evidenced by the publication of books like *The Myth of God Incarnate* in 1977, in which the deity of Christ was again rejected by important church dignitaries. This book was a collection of essays by seven British theologians, edited by John Hick, who also wrote the concluding essay, 'Jesus and the world religions'. Here Hick rejects the traditional Christology of Chalcedon and Nicaea as 'mythical... traditional language'; for Hick Christ was only a man. To be precise, Hick regards Jesus as the largely unknown man of Nazareth. He regards the claim to deity as part of the 'mythical' structure of the New Testament; its true meaning, he says, is not literal but poetic and symbolic.

This argument is really a rehash of what other critical scholars have taught for decades and it evidences Hick's liberal approach to Scripture and his denial of the supernatural. John Hick is now one of the leading proponents of the view that 'God' alone, not Christ, is at the centre of religions, including Christianity. He insists that all religions and 'holy' books are equally valid for they express man's search for the one universal God.

In the late nineteen-eighties the Rt Rev. Dr David Jenkins, the Bishop of Durham, has denied major Christian doctrines including the physical resurrection of Christ. His Easter message in 1989 affirmed that Christ's resurrection was only 'spiritual not physical... It means a spiritual resurrection, a transforming resurrection.' While many Bible-believing Anglicans were outraged over the bishop's remarks, the Bishop of Manchester came to his colleague's defence by saying that Dr Jenkins was not alone in his beliefs. Sadly, modernism is still deeply entrenched and influential in Protestant churches as we enter the final decade of the twentieth century.

Decline in the churches

Modernism has not attracted people to church either in Britain or overseas. Consider, for example, the plight of Canada's largest Protestant denomination, the United Church of Canada (UCC). The head of the sociology department at the University of Lethbridge, Alberta, Reginald Bibby, made a detailed survey early in 1982 of religious life in the country and particularly among members of the UCC (a project supported by the UCC, the Canadian government and the Canadian Broadcasting Corporation). 'Organized religion in Canada is experiencing a dramatic drop-off,' reports Bibby, 'churches are losing many of their once active members and adherents, while failing to replenish such losses...' Only about 40% of UCC members claim to believe in the existence of God and the deity of Christ, and only a small proportion attend church regularly and practise private prayer, while personal Bible-reading is 'virtually non-existent'. The survey shows that whereas in 1956 61% of Canadians said they had attended church during the previous week, only 35% had done so in 1978 and Sunday School attendance slumped from 570,000 to 242,000. A decade later the decline continues unabated. The story is no better in Britain. The steady decline in Protestant church attendance and membership has turned in recent years into a dramatic collapse, with the result that many churches have either closed or are unable to support a full-time ministry. Protestant and Catholic churches have an acute shortage of ministers and an increasing number of churches are grouped together under the pastoral care of a single minister.

Since the early nineteen-seventies many Christians, including pastors, have felt compelled to withdraw from churches and denominations where the Bible is not taught faithfully and a significant number of new evangelical churches have been established throughout England and Wales. In this respect the work of the Universities and Colleges Christian Fellowship among students,[9] the more varied ministry of the Evangelical Movement of Wales,[10] the publishing work of the Banner of Truth Trust and Evangelical Press, and the powerful preaching ministry of the late Dr Martyn

Lloyd-Jones have all had a formative influence in the establishing of Bible-teaching churches and the propagation of biblical truth. However, even amongst evangelicals there is disturbing evidence of a growing departure from orthodoxy and this is reflected in different ways. Some scholars have conceded too much to the critical approach, whereas the charismatic movement tends to affirm the primacy of experience at the expense of biblical doctrine. Others have qualified and redefined the doctrine of Scripture in order to allow for what they consider to be errors and contradictions, while yet others are focusing attention on annihilation rather than the eternal punishment of unbelievers. More than ever before, believers today must 'contend earnestly for the faith which was once for all delivered to the saints' (Jude 3), and this involves rejecting modernism in whatever form it appears.

What modernism teaches	*What the Bible teaches*

God

The notion of divine wrath is rejected as obnoxious and primitive; the major, if not exclusive, emphasis is on divine love.

God's wrath is the controlled and necessary reaction of his holy nature against all sin, necessitating the punishment of sin (Habakkuk 1:13; Romans 1:18-23; 2:5-16). There is no contradiction in the Bible between the love and wrath of God, for even at Calvary, where God's love was supremely manifested, God's wrath also fell upon Christ when he died as our substitute (Romans 3:25-26; Galatians 3:13-14; 1 John 4:10).

By many, God is defined in radical terms as being 'synonymous with the search for human wholeness, for confidence in the ultimate meaningfulness of human existence.'[11] God is the 'God above God', with the result that man can never define or describe him in any objective or absolute way. 'He is the Ground of

Finite creatures like ourselves cannot comprehend the infinite (Job 11:7), yet God has revealed himself to us in his perfections (i.e. power, holiness, love, etc.) in creation and especially in the Bible so that we have an accurate though not exhaustive knowledge of God. To deny this leads inevitably to scepticism and subjectivism.

Being. God is present in all those activities which unite people rather than divide them, which call upon persons to transcend self-interest through brotherhood and sisterhood.[12]

Some accept the orthodox doctrine of the Trinity, but many regard the doctrine only as a symbol originally introduced to safeguard and express man's diverse but unified experience of the Father, Son and Holy Spirit. John T. Robinson, for example, denies any objective validity to the doctrine and interprets it exclusively and subjectively as 'entering into a shared life with others and God.'[13]

See the detailed study of the Trinity in chapter 35.

Bible

A human book, full of mistakes, which describes man's experience of, and thinking about, God.

Because it was written in a cultural context, its statements are relative and personal, being 'the natural by-products of a community's struggle with questions of meaning and faith'.

Reason rather than the Bible is the supreme authority.[14]

'The sum of thy word is truth' (Psalm 119:160).

'Thy word is truth' (John 17:17).

'Men moved by the Holy Spirit spoke from God' (2 Peter 1:21).

Creation

The creation narratives in Genesis 1 and 2 are 'myths' and are not in any sense historical or literal. Man has evolved over billions of years.

'Have you not read, that he who created them from the beginning "made them male and female?"' (Matthew 19:4).

'All things came into being through him; and apart from him nothing came into being that has come into being' (John 1:3).

Person of Christ

A significant number of modernists now question or deny the deity of Christ. Some have used the phrase 'emptied himself' from Philippians 2:7 to suggest that the Lord laid aside his deity so that while on earth he was fallible and frequently in error in his teaching. This is called the 'kenosis theory'.

According to Philippians 2:7 and other Scripture references, the Saviour remained God even after his incarnation. He 'emptied' himself in the sense of veiling his visible glory as God the Son when he voluntarily assumed our human nature and submitted himself to the Father and the law.

Virgin birth of Christ

Untrue and impossible! 'To say that new life was fathered and quickened in Mary by the Spirit of God, is a profound way of expressing an inner truth about Jesus. It is to say that his birth and life cannot *simply* be thought of as biological events: his significance lies much deeper than that...we are not bound to think of the Virgin Birth as a physical event in order to believe that Jesus's whole life is "of God".'[15]

'For nothing will be impossible with God' (Luke 1:37).

'The Holy Spirit will come upon you, and the power of the Most High will overshadow you; and for that reason the holy offspring shall be called the Son of God' (Luke 1:35; cf. Matthew 1:20).

Miracles of Christ

The miracle stories are all 'myths' which teach and remind us of that which 'becomes possible when the power of love is really let loose'.[16]

The healing of Peter's mother-in-law in Mark 1:30-31 is explained in this way: 'She was just fed up with Peter spending all his time going around with Jesus instead of looking after her daughter. But when Jesus came to her house and she saw the sort of person he was, she wanted to get up and do things for people. There's the power of love, overcoming

Three words are used by Luke in Acts 2:22 to describe the miracles of the Lord Jesus. The first word, translated 'miracles', comes from the Greek word *dunamis*, meaning 'powerful works', and emphasizes the extraordinary manifestation of divine power on these occasions. They were not psychological or ordinary happenings in nature.

The second, 'wonders', describes the astonishment of the people when they witnessed these miracles (e.g. Mark 2:12; Luke 5:9; Matthew 15:30-31), whereas the

resentment and the physical protest in which it found outlet. And that's why Jesus saw that so often what was needed was a spiritual miracle — the putting right of a person's whole inner outlook on life.'

Dr Schweitzer explained the feeding of the 5,000 in John 6 as a mere sharing of the boy's food so that all present had at least a crumb or taste of food! John Robinson also calls it the 'miracle of sharing'.[17]

Death of Christ

Apart from expressing God's love and setting an example to us in love and patient suffering, the Saviour's death has no saving value.

The doctrine of salvation through the 'blood of Christ' is regarded as offensive and immoral.

third word, 'signs', emphasizes the purposefulness of the miracles: they had deep spiritual significance and pointed to himself (see Luke 7:22; John 2:11; 3:2; 5:36; 9:35-38).

'Much more then, having now been justified by his blood, we shall be saved from the wrath of God through him. For if while we were enemies, we were reconciled to God through the death of his Son, much more, having been reconciled, we shall be saved by his life' (Romans 5:9-10).

In Genesis 9:4; Leviticus 17:11 and Deuteronomy 12:23 we are told that the blood is the life (of the flesh) so that blood shed is a witness to physical death. In the New Testament the phrase 'blood of Christ' is mentioned nearly three times more often than the 'cross' and five times more frequently than the 'death' of Christ. The phrase, 'blood of Christ', therefore is the most frequent way of referring to the Saviour's sacrifice and it witnesses to the physical, sacrificial death of the Lord Jesus as he bore away our sin (Romans 3:25; 5:9; Ephesians 1:7; 1 Peter 1:18-19; Revelation 1:5; 5:9).

Resurrection of Christ

We can never know what happened to the Lord's body.

Various views are held. For example, Christ arose in spirit only, not bodily or, more radically, he did not rise at all except in the minds of the early believers, so the resurrection narratives need to be demythologized.

Read carefully Luke 24:39-44; John 2:19-22; 20:27-28; Acts 2:23-32; 1 Corinthians 15:4-7.

'If Christ has not been raised, your faith is worthless; you are still in your sins... But now Christ has been raised from the dead' (1 Corinthians 15:17-20).

Ascension of Christ

Christ did not literally and physically ascend into heaven; Luke fabricated the story. 'The truth of the ascension is that Christ after his resurrection is a necessary part of the true idea of God and... controls the entire universe so the ascension is the most political of all Christian doctrines.'[18]

'He who was revealed in the flesh, was vindicated in the Spirit, beheld by angels, proclaimed among the nations, believed on in the world, taken up in glory' (1 Timothy 3:16).

'... who is on the right hand of God, having gone into heaven' (1 Peter 3:22; cf. Acts 1:9-11; 2:32-36).

Salvation

Faith in Christ is not essential to salvation. Atheists and people of all religions will be saved. Missionary work is discouraged or regarded primarily as humanitarian.

'There is salvation in no one else; for there is no other name under heaven that has been given among men, by which we must be saved' (Acts 4:12).

Church

All churches, whatever their beliefs, are equally valid and members and adherents are assumed to be Christians in virtue of their attendance and activities.

'To the church of the Thessalonians *in* God the Father and the Lord Jesus Christ' (1 Thessalonians 1:1) — a people in spiritual fellowship with God, converted (1:9) and examples to others (1:6; cf. 1 Corinthians 1:2; Colossians 1:2-8).

Hell

A revolting, pagan doctrine; God does not punish sinners.

'For the gate is wide, and the way is broad that leads to destruction, and many are those who enter by it. For the gate is small, and the way is narrow that leads to life, and few are those who find it' (Matthew 7:13-14).

'And these will go away into eternal punishment, but the righteous into eternal life' (Matthew 25:46).

Second coming of Christ

It is 'the greatest phantasmagoria in the whole collection of mumbo jumbo that goes under the name of Christian doctrine... The Second Coming... stands for the conviction that — however long it takes — *Christ must come into everything*. There's no part of life from which he can or will be left out.'[19]

'They will see the Son of Man coming on the clouds of the sky with power and great glory' (Matthew 24:30; cf. 1Thessalonians 4:16-17; 2 Peter 3:3-13).

'The Spirit explicitly says that in later times some will fall away from the faith, paying attention to deceitful spirits and doctrines of demons...' (1 Timothy 4:1; cf. 2 Timothy 4:3-5).

Bibliography

The following books have been used as representative samples of contemporary modernist teaching:

Donald E. Miller, *The case for liberal Christianity*, SCM, 1981.

John A. T. Robinson, *The roots of a radical*, SCM, 1980.

Michael Ramsey, *Jesus and the living past*, OUP, 1980.

Christian believing — The nature of the Christian faith and its expression in Holy Scripture and creeds. Doctrine Commission of the Church of England, SPCK, 1976.

John A. T. Robinson, *Honest to God,* SCM, 1963.

John A. T. Robinson, *But that I can't believe!* Collins, 1967.

Peter Kelly, *Searching for Truth,* Collins, 1978.

The Nature of Christian Belief: A statement and exposition by the House of Bishops of the General Synod of the Church of England, Church House Publishing, London 1986.

David Edwards with John Stott, *Essentials,* Hodder & Stoughton, 1988.

2.
Roman Catholicism

'Today for the first time in history a bishop of Rome sets foot on English soil and I am deeply moved at this thought,' declared Pope John Paul as he spoke in Westminster Cathedral on 28 May 1982. *The Times* described this visit as 'Pope John Paul's historic pilgrimage of faith'. It was certainly a historic visit. He was also the first pope to visit Canterbury Cathedral and his agreement with Archbishop Runcie to study and pursue further the union of their respective churches will have a radical impact on the future of inter-church relationships. Again, the celebration of the mass by the pope in Coventry before an estimated congregation of 350,000 was the 'largest known gathering of Roman Catholics in England', and the papal mass in Cardiff on 2 June before a crowd of 100,000 was the largest Roman Catholic gathering ever held in Wales. The tumultuous welcome given to the pope earned him the titles 'the first pop-star pope,' 'the top of the popes' and the 'people's pope'.

In the wake of this historic papal visit, some may accuse me of being ungracious and unfair in including the Roman Catholic Church in this book alongside the more obviously heretical groups of churches such as Jehovah's Witnesses or the Unitarian Church. Such disquiet is expressed in several ways and we must briefly consider two of these objections before we discuss in detail the errors of Rome.

For example, in this ecumenical age when churches are coming closer together, is it right to be critical of Roman Catholicism?

Should we not accept and respect each other's positions and work together in love for church unity?

In support of this objection, one can point to the considerable improvement in church relationships at local and national levels. For example, the British Council of Churches has established more than 300 ecumenical projects in England and Wales where buildings, ministries, Sunday School and day schools are shared by different denominations. Addressing the General Synod of the Church of England in February 1982, Dr Runcie, the Archbishop of Canterbury, called on all Christians to welcome the pope and be optimistic about the prospect for unity and not to give way to prejudice and insularity. 'The pope's willingness to attend the service at Canterbury,' he affirmed, 'has already made a contribution to the seriousness and urgency of our search for unity.' Speaking in Canterbury on 29 May 1982, the pope himself replied in a similar way: 'I appeal to you in this holy place, fellow-Christians and especially members of the Church of England and the Anglican Communion throughout the world, to accept the commitment to which Dr Runcie and I pledge ourselves anew before you today... praying and working for ecclesiastical unity.'

When the pope later met Protestant church leaders in Cardiff he expressed publicly his pleasure in learning of the co-operation between different denominations in Wales, as this bore 'witness to the desire to fulfil God's will for our unity with him and each other in Christ'. Clearly *The Times* was correct in stating that 'The ecumenical movement has been given a boost beyond anyone's expectations because of the pope's visit and because of the way the pope conducted himself while he was here,' and we have entered a new era of openness and of more deliberate and determined plans for the merging of mainline denominations.

Dare we go against the stream, then? Ought we to criticize a church that is seeking closer links with Protestantism? My answer is a positive one. Christian unity is important and it is the duty of the Lord's people to maintain, express and develop the unity which the Holy Spirit has established between believers (Ephesians 4:3). However, such unity must never be sought at the expense of truth. When, therefore, a church is in error concerning key doctrines such as sin, the atonement, justification by faith etc., and thereby propagates a gospel different from that of the New Testament we can neither co-operate with such a church nor support it. Our supreme test here is not sentiment or popular opinion but the Bible.

The objection is expressed differently, too. Are there not radical changes occurring within the Roman Catholic Church — changes both in outlook and in dogma? If this is so then, it is argued, we should not dismiss Rome as being heretical.

Changes are certainly taking place within the Roman Catholic Church and nowhere is this seen more dramatically than in the largest Catholic order, the Society of Jesus, founded originally in 1540 to counter the Protestant Reformation. This society, popularly known as the Jesuits, has a world membership of 26,000 and 600 priests. Their devotion both to the pope and Roman Catholic dogma has been proverbial and exemplary since the Counter-Reformation, but in the past twenty years, particularly since Vatican II, they have led in the more progressive and radical developments within the church by championing such things as new forms of liturgy, liberation theology in Latin America and modernist theology, in which some have even questioned the deity of Christ. Some Jesuits have also adopted a more 'relaxed' sexual life-style and regard celibacy as inappropriate outside the monastery. Jesuits are reported as being active in revolutionary movements in Guatemala, El Salvador and Nicaragua, while in the Philippines a Jesuit priest was accused of plotting to undermine the government. These alarming trends have troubled recent popes, but Pope John Paul II has rebuked the Jesuits and has appointed a man of his own choice, Paola Dezza, as the superior-general of the order with the purpose of bringing its members to heel.

These developments and changes among the Jesuits are reflected more widely throughout the Roman church. The modern critical approach to the Bible, for example, outlawed by the pope in 1907 and in disfavour until the late 1950s, is now openly espoused by the majority of Catholic scholars, while a few, like Hans Küng, now reject the dogma of papal infallibility. There is also a strong charismatic faction under the leadership of Cardinal Suenens, who has helped to accommodate the Catholic charismatic renewal to formal Catholic dogma and polity.

Rather than signalling a return to Bible doctrines, these recent changes and developments within the Roman Catholic Church have served to undermine the Bible and to encourage the reinterpretation

of the gospel in political or sacramental terms. Despite his cha-
risma, the present pope belongs to the conservative or traditional
wing of the church which seeks to propagate, not change, its
unbiblical teachings.

One of our responsibilities as believers in our contemporary
situation is that of contending 'for the faith which was once for all
delivered to the saints' (Jude 3) and distinguishing between 'the
spirit of truth and the spirit of error' (1 John 4:6). For this reason the
teachings of the Roman Catholic Church are here tested by the
supreme standard of the Bible and readers will quickly discover the
error of Rome on many key doctrines. Concerning such important
issues we dare not compromise or be silent, whatever people may
think or say.

When the pope went to Scotland on 1 June 1982 to meet his flock
of 820,000 he was welcomed in the courtyard of New College,
Edinburgh by the Moderator of the Church of Scotland and the brief
ceremony took place under the shadow of the statue of the Scottish
Protestant Reformer, John Knox. Was that significant? Certainly.
The gospel preached by John Knox was thoroughly biblical, apostolic and Christ-exalting but radically different from that which the
pope brought to Britain. Sadly, however, such differences are no
longer important to many Protestants in Britain and are regarded as
ancient and irrelevant disputes. Is the Roman Catholic Church in
error? Are these differences of secondary importance? Read the
following section carefully and discover for yourself what God
declares in his infallible Word, and then make the Bible your
supreme standard by which you judge truth and error. Do not be
afraid of being thought narrow. 'Yes,' writes Dr Martyn Lloyd-
Jones, 'we *do* think that we are right; but we are not alone. The great
stream of evangelical witness runs down through the centuries of
Church history. The gates of hell have not prevailed and will not
finally prevail against it. We believe as our evangelical forefathers
did, and we must be prepared for the reproaches of "intolerance"
and "bigotry" which they also bore... The charge of intolerance is
a compliment. For, surely, if your position is that in which God has
ordained His elect should stand, we must necessarily be intolerant
of all that would divert us from it. We believe and hold to it. We must
be prepared to sacrifice everything for it. We must be like Martin
Luther when he stood alone against the authority of the Roman
Church...We must be like the Puritans, who were prepared to

forsake their emoluments rather than to compromise on such principles. We must be humbly aggressive in propagating the true faith, and patiently adamant in the true gospel's defence — if need be, to the utmost degrees of sacrifice.'[1]

What Roman Catholicism teaches	*What the Bible teaches*

Bible

The Bible *plus* the fifteen books of the Apocrypha and tradition as interpreted by the Roman Catholic Church are equally authoritative. The ultimate standard of truth then is the church which, it is claimed, gave birth to the Scriptures and tradition.

1. The sixty-six canonical books of the Bible are a sufficient revelation of God to man and sufficient for all matters of faith and conduct (cf. 2 Timothy 3:15-16; Luke 16:29; Acts 17:11).

2. Whenever the Lord Jesus spoke of tradition, he condemned it and warned his people against it (see Matthew 15:3,6,9; Mark 7:8-9, 13; cf. Deuteronomy 4:2; Colossians 2:8; Revelation 22:18-19).

3. The church both in the Old and New Testaments submitted itself to the Word of God proclaimed by the prophets and apostles.

4. Concerning the Apocrypha note:

    a. There is no record of Christ quoting from or referring to it. This is surprising as he would have known about the existence of at least some of these writings.

    b. There were two versions of the Old Testament in circulation at the time of the Lord's earthly ministry, namely, the Hebrew Old Testament (without the apocryphal books) and the Greek translation of the Hebrew Old Testament made in Alexandria and called the Septuagint, which included twelve or more apocryphal books. While this

'Septuagint' translation was popular in Palestine yet the Lord did not endorse the apocryphal section or refer to it.

c. It was almost 2,000 years after the completion of the Old Testament that the Roman Catholic Church (at the Council of Trent in 1546) 'added' the apocryphal books to the Old Testament. Several members in this council disagreed with the decision.

d. The apocryphal books are inferior in content, style and reliability, and teach unbiblical ideas such as purgatory and salvation by works.

Everywhere in the Bible the sufficiency of the Old and New Testaments is assumed — they alone are authoritative, final and adequate, thus determining all matters of faith and conduct so that no extra-biblical tradition is required.

Pope

The pope (from the Latin *papa* meaning 'father') is regarded as the vicar of Christ on the earth, taking the place of Jesus Christ in the world. He is also viewed as the ruler of the world and supreme over all.

It was the evil emperor Phocas in A.D. 604 who first used and applied the title of 'pope' to Gregory I. While Gregory established the power and supremacy of the Bishop of Rome, he refused to accept the title 'pope', but a successor, Boniface III, accepted it and it has been used ever since to describe the Bishop of Rome.

Vatican I in 1870 claimed

1. The Lord Jesus warns us not to call any man 'father' — that is, in a spiritual context.
2. The position of a pope as an overlord ruling over all believers is forbidden in 1 Peter 5:3.
3. Concerning the apostolic succession of bishops, the Bible teaches: firstly, the uniqueness of the apostles as eye-witnesses of the resurrection (Acts 1:21-22); secondly, apostolic succession means believing and teaching only what the Lord and the original apostles taught. The test is doctrinal and biblical (Galatians 1:8-9; Ephesians 2:20; 1 Timothy 6:3-5; 2 Timothy 1:13-14).

supreme authority and infallibility for the pope in all aspects of faith and morals, particularly when he speaks *ex cathedra,* that is, officially. Vatican II, in its decree on the constitution of the church called the *Lumen Gentium,* modified the authority of the pope somewhat, claiming that when the bishops as successors of the apostles act together to define questions of faith and morals they thus teach infallibly. At present some Catholic scholars, like Hans Küng in his book *Infallible?,* are questioning this traditional doctrine of papal infallibility.

Peter

On the basis of Matthew 16:13-19, they wrongly claim that Christ appointed Peter as the first pope and Bishop of Rome.

'And I also say to you that you are Peter, and upon this rock I will build my church...' (Matthew 16:18).

While the Greek word 'Peter' here is masculine (*Petros*) and refers to a person, the word 'rock' (*Petra*) is feminine, referring not to Peter but to his confession that Jesus is 'the Christ, the Son of the living God' (v. 16). Christ builds his church not upon a man but on the truth that Peter confessed (cf. 1 Corinthians 3:11; Ephesians 2:20).

'I will give you the keys of the kingdom of heaven; and whatever you shall bind on earth shall have been bound in heaven, and whatever you shall loose on earth shall have been loosed in heaven' (Matthew 16:19).

According to verses 1 and 18 in Matthew 18 this authority was given to all the disciples, not only to Peter. The authority our Lord speaks of here is that of opening the kingdom of heaven to people *through the preaching of the gospel.* This was not an absolute power to exclude or admit people to heaven but a declarative power only, that is, authority to proclaim the conditions on which God is prepared to forgive and save sinners. In Acts 2:14-42 (see especially v. 21) Peter did this through preaching, and later in Acts 10:34-43 he had the privilege of preaching the same gospel to Cornelius, thus opening the door to the Gentiles, but such authority, or 'keys', was given to *all* the apostles, then to others like evangelists and pastors.

Note also:
1. Peter nowhere claims in the Bible to be a bishop or pope in Rome (see 1 Peter 1:1; 5:1-3; Acts 10:25-26).
2. Paul was called to be an apostle independently of Peter (see Galatians 1) and that Peter was not more important than Paul is evident in 2 Corinthians 12:11 and Galatians 2:7, 11-14. Again, it was not Peter but James who chaired the church council in Jerusalem in Acts 15.
3. There is no evidence that Peter was ever in Rome, and even Paul's letter to the Romans includes no reference at all to Peter, which would have been strange if Peter was a bishop there.
4. Neither are the words, 'Strengthen your brothers,' in Luke 22:31-32 unique to Peter, as Rome teaches. Luke uses the words to describe Paul's work in Acts 14:22;

15:32, 41; 18:23.

Similarly, the command to 'feed the flock' in John 21:15-17 was not exclusive to Peter, for Paul uses one of the words in describing the work of elders at Ephesus in Acts 20:28.

Priests

The priest is a special person who, by the sacrament of ordination, receives special grace and authority to act in the place of Christ, communicating spiritual life and grace to people. He is able, for example, to hear confession and forgive sins, to offer Christ as a sacrifice in the mass, to baptize and hereby make children or adults Christians. He also has the task of administering 'extreme unction' before individual Catholics die.

Without the help of the priesthood, salvation is impossible and the church would be unable to fulfil her divine mission.

In the New Testament there is *only one* priest, namely, Jesus Christ, the great High Priest who offered himself as the sufficient and final sacrifice for sins (Hebrews 7:17, 24-27; 10:12-14). Christ is, therefore, the only mediator between God and men (1 Timothy 2:5), so there is no need for priests to mediate for us.

The Old Testament priesthood, like the system of sacrifice and temple worship, was temporary. It pointed to, and found its fulfilment in, Christ, so after the Lord's incarnation and sacrifice the priesthood was abolished.

Church officers are never described as 'priests' in the New Testament and even the apostle Peter described himself as a 'fellow-elder' (1 Peter 5:1) and not as a priest. While the book of Acts, for example, refers to the establishing of many Christian churches, there is no reference at all to a sacrificing priesthood. The Swiss Catholic theologian, Hans Küng, has shown convincingly that the theory of the Roman priesthood emerged and developed between the fifth and thirteenth centuries.

According to 1 Peter 2:5, 9 and Revelation 1:6, *all* believers are priests and have the privilege of direct access to God through Christ

(Hebrews 10:19; 4:16), the right and duty of praying for others (Ephesians 6:18) and offering, not an atoning sacrifice, but spiritual sacrifices of praise (Hebrews 13:15), monetary gifts (Hebrews 13:16) and themselves in service to God (Romans 12:1).

This biblical truth of the priesthood of all believers was rediscovered in the Protestant Reformation of the sixteenth century and needs to be re-emphasized today.

Transubstantiation

This doctrine, first formulated in the ninth century and officially accepted in 1215, refers to the communion when the priest claims to change the bread and wine into the physical body and blood of Christ; even individual particles of bread or drops of wine become the entire Christ.

1. The Lord was still present in the flesh when he spoke the words, 'This is my body', so there could have been no literal identification of the bread with his own body (Matthew 26:26).
2. Many other sayings of the Lord, such as 'I am the door', must be interpreted symbolically, not literally.
3. Even after Jesus said, 'This is my body', he still regarded the wine a few moments later only as wine and certainly not as his literal blood (see Matthew 26:29; Luke 22:18).
4. Nor does John 6:33 support the teaching of Rome, for in verse 63 the Lord stresses that the words have a spiritual meaning. To eat and drink is to trust Christ, as in verse 35.
5. Before Christ ascended to heaven he promised to come to us not in the sacrament of the mass but by the Holy Spirit (John 16:7), but at the end of the world he will return personally and visibly to the world (Acts 1:11). In the Lord's Supper, therefore, we proclaim the

Saviour's death 'until he comes' (1 Corinthians 11:26).

6. At the Council of Constance in 1415 it was agreed to withhold the cup from the congregation lest the wine — or, for the Roman church, the literal blood of the Lord — be spilt. This was not, however, the practice in the New Testament. Our Lord told his disciples, 'Drink from it, *all of you*' (Matthew 26:27), and Mark records, 'They *all* drank from it' (14:23). The Corinthian believers also all drank of the wine (1 Corinthians 11:25-29).

Mass

The most important part of Roman Catholic worship is the mass when the priest is supposed to offer Christ as a sacrifice to God the Father on behalf of the living and the dead. It is the same sacrifice as Calvary but offered differently.

1. The Lord's Supper must be observed 'in remembrance' of Christ (1 Corinthians 11:25) and *not* as a sacrifice for sin.
2. At the Last Supper, our Saviour was not offering a sacrifice through the bread or wine but giving the bread and the wine to the disciples as symbols of his own body and blood to be broken and shed on Calvary.
3. The significance of this ordinance is explained by Paul in 1 Corinthians 11:26 as 'proclaiming' or 'heralding' the death of Christ; there is *no* sacrificing of Christ in it.
4. The Lord's sacrifice was final and perfect and he died 'once' and 'once for all' (Hebrews 9:12; 10:10, 12, 14, 18). The mass implies the inadequacy of the Saviour's sacrifice and the need to repeat it indefinitely, but his cry from the cross, 'It is finished!' (John 19:30), means that the work of our salvation was accomplished at Calvary, so that the mass is both unscriptural and unnecessary.

Christians

Children and adults are made Christians in water baptism by the power of the Holy Spirit operating through an authorized priest.

Penance

Rome distinguishes between greater or 'mortal' sins and lesser or 'venial' sins. Examples of the former include the breaking of the Ten Commandments and also pride, lust, anger, sexual offences and failure to attend mass. Speaking hastily or being slothful in doing one's religious duties are examples of venial sins.

In Roman Catholic confession, a distinction is also made between 'attrition' and 'contrition'. The motive in the former is the fear of sin's consequences, such as shame, imprisonment or hell, etc. While this is regarded as adequate for 'lesser' sins, 'contrition' is required for greater sins and such contrition or repentance includes a resolve to confess to a priest as soon as possible.

Confessing sin before a priest in order to obtain pardon is a sacrament binding on all Catholics. The priest, they argue, does more than declare God's forgiveness; he actually has the power also to forgive or retain sins and impose penance as a means both of testing the genuineness of the person's confession and of making a satisfaction to God for that sin.

'He who believes in him is not judged; he who does not believe has been judged already' (John 3:18).

'Believe in the Lord Jesus, and you shall be saved' (Acts 16:31; see also John 1:12).

The Bible does not distinguish between 'mortal' and 'venial' sins.

Only contrition is true repentance and a good example of this is seen in Psalm 51.

There is a need at times to confess, not to a priest, however, but to fellow believers if we sin against them (James 5:16), but as a general practice sin must only be confessed to God (1 John 1:9), for God alone has the power to forgive (Mark 2:7-10).

Furthermore, no good works we do by way of penance will ever satisfy God, but sinners can be accepted and forgiven on the sole ground of Christ's sacrifice,

Indulgences

The punishment of sins is met partly by penance and partly by sufferings in purgatory after we die. For this reason, Rome teaches, indulgences are necessary for they reduce the temporal punishments for sin imposed by God. Indulgences are available because the Roman church claims to have a great wealth of unused merit accumulated through Christ's sufferings and also through the holy, unselfish lives of Mary and the saints who did more than God's law required of them.

Mary's perpetual virginity

After giving birth to the Lord, Mary continued as a virgin for the rest of her life.

through which alone the justice and wrath of God against sin have been satisfied (Romans 3:25; Ephesians 2:8-9; 1 John 2:2).

Church discipline sometimes demands suspension of an individual from communion but the church can reduce or remove this discipline when there is evidence of repentance. This, however, is not an indulgence nor an action of merit or satisfaction to God (see for example, Matthew 18:15-18; 2 Corinthians 2:6-8).

It is impossible for any human being to obey God more than is necessary. The Lord says, 'When you do all the things which are commanded you, say, "We are unworthy slaves; we have done only that which we ought to have done"' (Luke 17:9-10; 1 Corinthians 15:10; 1 Timothy 1:15).

See Matthew 1:24-25. We are not told here the reason why Joseph and Mary abstained from sexual intercourse until after the birth of the Saviour. Was it meant as additional, irrefutable evidence that the child was conceived miraculously by the Holy Spirit and not by man? But notice the following details of Scripture which contradict Rome's teaching of Mary's perpetual virginity.
1. We read in Matthew 1:25 that Joseph 'kept her a virgin *until* she gave birth to a son,' i.e. full physical union began and continued after the Saviour was born.
2. Our Lord had brothers and

sisters, according to Mark 6:3.

3. Jesus is described as Mary's 'first-born son' which suggests that she had other children (Luke 2:7).

4. Marriage is a divinely ordained ordinance within which sexual intercourse is legitimate.

Immaculate conception of Mary

In 1854 the pope declared, 'The most holy virgin Mary was, in the first moment of her conception, by a unique gift of grace and privilege of Almighty God, in view of the merits of Jesus Christ the Redeemer of mankind, preserved free from all stain of original sin.'

Although Genesis 3:15 is used by Rome in support of the immaculate conception, the verse actually teaches that the 'seed of the woman' (Christ), not the woman herself, will overcome Satan. Luke 1:28 is also misused, especially the words, 'Hail, favoured one!', or as in the NIV: 'Greetings, you who are highly favoured!'

'Hail' was a word of greeting commonly used (Matthew 26:49; 28:9; Acts 23:26), whereas the word translated 'favoured' is also used in Ephesians 1:6 to describe the elect people of God, who are far from being sinless! This verse does not therefore teach or imply the sinlessness of Mary.

But what of the words in Luke 1:42, where Elizabeth says of Mary, 'Blessed among women are you...'? Certainly Mary was greatly privileged to be chosen as the mother of the Lord, but this does not mean she was sinless. Later, in verse 45, Elizabeth shows it was Mary's faith that marked her out as being blessed: 'Blessed is she who believed that there would be a fulfilment of what had been spoken to her by the Lord.'

Two other details provide conclusive evidence of the error of Rome at this point. Mary calls the Lord 'my Saviour' in Luke 1:47 (cf.

Matthew 1:21), and after the Lord's birth she obeyed the Old Testament law of purification by making a sin-offering (Luke 2:22; Leviticus 12:6-8). If she had been perfect, there would have been no need of this offering. In fact, Mary is included with all other people in the statement of Romans 3:23.

Bodily assumption of Mary

This dogma, formally announced as recently as 1950 by Pope Pius, maintains that at the end of her life Mary's body and soul were taken directly to heaven.

There is no biblical support for this erroneous teaching.

Mary, queen of heaven

Mary is enthroned in heaven as queen where she prays for her church. Her special relationship to Christ makes her prayers valuable and effective.

Recent popes have gone on to claim: 'Nothing... comes to us except through Mary... nobody can approach Christ except through the Mother...' Mary dispenses 'all gifts which Jesus has acquired for us by his death and his blood...'; she is 'the mediatrix with God of all graces'.

Christ invites sinners to go directly to him as Saviour: 'Come to me, all who are weary and heavy-laden...' (Matthew 11:28; cf. John 7:37).

Again, Christ is the *only* mediator, as verses like 1 Timothy 2:5 and John 14:6 teach. We have only one advocate in heaven, namely, 'Jesus Christ, the righteous; and he himself is the propitiation for our sins...' (1 John 2:1-2), and he is certainly sympathetic in his intercession for us (Hebrews 4:15).

Worship of Mary

A distinction is made between the 'adoration' of God, the 'veneration' of saints and the 'special veneration' given to Mary.

This distinction is not found in the Bible and, clearly, only God should be worshipped (Matthew 4:10). Both Peter (Acts 10:25-26) and Paul (Acts 14:15) refused to accept veneration or worship from people, while the wise men worshipped the Lord Jesus, not Mary (Matthew 2:11).

Roman Catholics tend to give as much, if not more, honour to Mary as to the Lord himself. The rosary, for example, which was invented in 1070, demands the reciting of the Lord's Prayer and the *Gloria* fifteen times each, but there are 150 Hail Marys. In other words, there are ten times as many prayers to Mary as there are to the Father, and not one prayer to Christ.

In Luke 11:27-28 a woman was so impressed by the Lord's teaching that she exclaimed, 'Blessed is the womb that bore you, and the breasts at which you nursed.' But Christ did not allow any special veneration of Mary, for he went on to say, 'On the contrary, blessed are those who hear the word of God and observe it.' Mary's blessedness consisted primarily in the fact that she received and obeyed the divine Word.

Purgatory

While some distinguished and 'holy' people in the Roman Catholic Church go directly to heaven after death, and non-Catholics or unbelievers go to hell, the majority of Catholics go to purgatory where their venial and mortal sins are purged and punished.

Some of the verses appealed to in support of purgatory are:

1 Corinthians 3:13. Here the reference is to ministers of the gospel and their responsibility to do their work well in view of the scrutiny of their work in the Final Judgement. There is no reference at all here to purgatory.

1 Peter 3:19. The 'disobedient' here refers to the unbelieving people in the days of Noah to whom Christ preached through Noah before the Flood. Again, there is no reference to purgatory here.

Matthew 5:21-26. William Hendriksen summarizes these verses most helpfully: 'It is as if Jesus were saying, "Be not surprised about the urgency of my command that you be reconciled; for, should it be that you were to pass from this life with a heart still at variance with your brother, a condition which you have not even tried to change, that wrong would testify against you in the day of judgement. Moreover, dying with that spirit of hatred still in your heart, you will never escape from the prison of hell."'[2]

Rather than going to purgatory, the Bible teaches that believers go directly to heaven when they die (Luke 16:19-31; 23:43; John 5:24; Philippians 1:21; Revelation 14:13), and unbelievers go immediately to hell (Luke 16:22-23); there is no intermediate or preparatory place such as purgatory.

Bibliography

In addition to newspapers and periodicals/journals, I have consulted several books, including:

H. M. Carson, *Dawn or Twilight?*, IVP.

Giuseppe Alberigo, (ed.), *The Reception of Vatican II*, Burns and Oats, 1987.

Herbert McCabe, *The Teaching of the Catholic Church: A New Catechism of Christian Doctrine*, Catholic Truth Society, 1985.

3.
Quakers: the Religious Society of Friends

You may be surprised that the Quakers are included in this book, and if so I understand your reaction. For example, the Quakers are usually very kind and sincere people; some are converted and love the Lord Jesus Christ deeply. In the United States, some of the Quaker groups are more thoroughly biblical and evangelical. These facts I gladly acknowledge as well as their valuable humanitarian work throughout the world.

What we are concerned with in this book, however, is the Bible. To what extent do Quakers still adhere to the Bible and the foundational truths which the Bible teaches? Sadly, their distinctive conviction concerning the inward illumination and authority of the Spirit has led many Quakers to a more open and less biblical position on important truths. Their strong biblical heritage is now being eroded.

Who are the Quakers? How did they begin? What do they believe? These questions will be answered in this chapter.

How did they begin?

Whatever picture is conjured up in your mind by the name 'Quaker', you need to remember that it was originally a nickname given to the followers of George Fox in the middle of the seventeenth century. The nickname was given partly because some members 'quaked' in meetings, and partly because of a joke made by a judge in 1650 when George Fox faced a charge of blasphemy. When Fox told the judge he should 'tremble at the word of the Lord', the judge proceeded to call Fox and his followers 'Quakers'. The official title of the movement, however, is 'The Religious Society of Friends' but members are still popularly referred to as 'Quakers' or 'Friends'.

At the age of nineteen the founder of this society, George Fox (1624-1691), was invited to a drinking party by some religious friends. He was disgusted at their behaviour at the party, and as a result turned away from the recognized churches in his search for truth and spiritual reality. Three years later he had a conversion experience in which he claims that Christ was revealed directly to him by means of an 'inner light'. Within a year Fox began his public ministry and the first Quaker community was established in Preston Patrick in 1652, while by 1654 there were groups in London, Bristol and Norwich. A strong missionary zeal helped to spread the Quaker message quickly as far as Germany, Austria, Holland, the West Indies and America.

The effects of persecution

Until freedom of worship was introduced by Parliament in the Toleration Act of 1689, Quakers as well as other Dissenters were persecuted severely. Unlike most Congregationalists and Presbyterians, they refused to meet secretly and consequently about 400 Quakers died in prison during this period and many more were impoverished by heavy fines. To escape from such suffering and poverty, many emigrated to America when William Penn offered them a home in his new colony in Philadelphia in 1681. One writer estimates that between 4,000-5,000 'Friends' left their native Wales for America and numbers in Britain fell so much that the Yearly Meeting for Wales (1797) appealed regularly for their numbers 'not to run away to America'.[1] In the late eighteenth and nineteenth centuries it was nonconformity, signally blessed by God with numerous outpourings of the Holy Spirit, which won many of the British people, including some Quakers, to the kingdom of Christ.

Today the world membership of the Society of Friends is approximately 203,000; the membership of the London Yearly

Meeting in England, Scotland and Wales in 1987 was only 18,587. To this figure must be added the 6,104 who, while not in the formal membership, attended the meetings regularly.

The 'inward illumination'

Fox and his early followers felt that they had rediscovered primitive Christianity and that 'Christ had come to teach his people himself', directly. Despite a powerful conversion to Christ and a deep love of the Bible, Fox tended to emphasize the inward illumination and authority of the Spirit at the expense of the Bible. In the late seventeenth century, one of the society's most illustrious members, William Penn, could write, 'It is not opinion, or speculation, or notions of what is true, or assent to, or the subscription of articles or propositions, though never so soundly worded, that makes a man a true believer...' We can concur whole-heartedly with this statement, but when Penn goes on to describe a believer as one who lives 'according to the dictates of this Divine principle of light and life in the Soul',[2] we must disagree, for he has now abandoned the objective and supreme authority of the Bible. This subjective emphasis has gradually led the Quakers away from biblical truth. While Quakers in the United States are still evangelical, nevertheless the society has become more liberal and unorthodox in its teaching.

'Concern' and practice

Another strong Quaker conviction is that their 'concern' must be translated into practice, and this concern is channelled, for example, into the Samaritan movement, the Marriage Guidance Council, the Local Council of Churches and, more especially today, into various peace and international organizations like the United Nations Association and Amnesty International.

What non-evangelical Quakers teach	What the Bible teaches

God

'Friends' are cautious about using the name of God, partly because it has been misunderstood and used, often exclusively, as an intellectual concept. They have no official or formal doctrine of God. The Quaker awareness of God 'is discovered in response and commitment to the deep meaning of life'.

'Who is like thee among the gods, O Lord? Who is like thee, majestic in holiness, awesome in praises, working wonders?' (Exodus 15:11).

'Now to the King eternal, immortal, invisible, the only God, be honour and glory for ever and ever' (1 Timothy 1:17; cf. 1 Chronicles 29:11-12; Psalm 96:4-10).

Bible

The Bible is 'a remarkable collection of writings covering the history and experience of countless ordinary, fallible men and women... who had a great capacity to reflect upon the inwardness of this experience and to interpret it to their fellows in such a way as to command respect for their insights... These insights were expressed in the thought forms and assumptions of the day.'

'For no prophecy was ever made by an act of human will, but men moved by the Holy Spirit spoke from God' (2 Peter 1:21).

The authority of the Bible does not rest on an external and infallible guarantee of its truth but 'on its ability to arouse the response and trust of men'.

'Jesus answered, "It is written..."' (Matthew 4:4, 7, 10; cf. John 17:17).

Among modern 'Friends' the Bible, while still greatly treasured, is not as widely known as in previous generations, but 'Where some of the time previously given to the study and devotional use of the Bible is spent on other sources of religious insight, the life of the Society will be enriched.'[3]

'Let the word of Christ richly dwell within you, with all wisdom teaching and admonishing one another...' (Colossians 3:16; cf. Deuteronomy 6:5-7; 2 Timothy 3:15).

Jesus Christ

'Friends' vary in their views but the more common position is that the historical Jesus was an outstanding religious teacher whose absolute trust and commitment to love give us 'a window into God' for, 'In his life the love that is God is most clearly seen.' The biblical account of Christ's person is unimportant: 'What matters is the greatness of his personality and his spiritual insight.'

'Have this attitude in yourselves which was also in Christ Jesus, who, although he existed in the form of God, did not regard equality with God a thing to be grasped...' (Philippians 2:5-8; cf. John 1:1; Colossians 1:15-19).

Death of Christ

No atonement was necessary. The Jews killed Jesus because they were afraid of him, but the Lord's creative attitude of love and forgiveness radically changed this act of human wickedness into an event that releases love and forgiveness into the world. Such love can overcome evil and this knowledge has freed many people to live meaningful lives.

'And according to the Law, one may almost say, all things are cleansed with blood, and without the shedding of blood there is no forgiveness... So Christ also, having been offered once to bear the sins of many...' (Hebrews 9:22-28).

Resurrection of Christ

Many 'Friends' are sceptical about the New Testament accounts of the physical resurrection of Jesus. They would agree that the essential meaning behind the Easter story is 'that death could not destroy all that was of real value in the earthly life of Jesus'.

'If Christ has not been raised, your faith is worthless; you are still in your sins... But now Christ has been raised from the dead' (1 Corinthians 15:17-20).

Man

Man is a unique and individual person, made in the image of God. 'That of God in every man' is a

'God created man in his own image, in the image of God he created him' (Genesis 1:27).

popular Quaker phrase and means that each person has the capacity to experience 'mystical awareness' and the 'inward light'.

Man is essentially good.

'For all have sinned and fall short of the glory of God' (Romans 3:23).

Death

Life has a timeless quality and death cannot destroy love. Quakers do not dogmatize about what happens after death. Some are convinced there is an after-life, while others believe death is the end of our existence.

'It is appointed for men to die once, and after this comes judgement' (Hebrews 9:27).

'... having the desire to depart and be with Christ...' (Philippians 1:23; cf. Job 19:25-27).

4.
Seventh-Day Adventists

The story of this movement begins in America with a military captain named William Miller (1782-1849), who left the army in 1812 to work as a farmer. He was not a Christian at this time but was determined to study the Bible thoroughly. His resolve was somewhat weakened by some cynical friends but in 1816 he was converted, joined the local Baptist Church and reapplied himself diligently to the study of the Bible, using only *Cruden's Concordance* as an aid. Prophecy soon absorbed his interest and after two years he was convinced that the coming of Christ was imminent and that the Lord would set up his kingdom in America. Anxious to find out when this would occur, Miller made the serious error of date-fixing. By misusing certain verses in Daniel and Revelation he announced publicly in 1831 that the Lord's return would take place on 10 October 1843. For months before the specified date there was great excitement amongst his followers. When the Lord's return did not occur on this date, Miller blamed himself for making an error in his calculations, so 22 October 1844 was then proposed as the correct date.

Several weeks before this date many of the 'Millerites' left their jobs and there was considerable anticipation of the Lord's return. In one shop-window in Philadelphia the following message was displayed: 'This shop is closed in honour of the King of Kings, who will appear about the 22 October. Get ready, friends, to crown him Lord of all.' Needless to say, the Lord did not return and Miller acknowledged his mistake, remarking that 'To contend that we were not mistaken is dishonest. We should never be ashamed frankly to confess our errors.' Until his death in 1849 Miller remained a keen Bible student and a godly believer.

His successor in the movement was Mrs Ellen White, a 'prophetess' who frequently claimed to have visions and revelations directly from God. She was convinced even as a seventeen-year-old that Miller was right in his prediction regarding the date of the Lord's return. When on the morning following 'the great disappointment', she saw in a vision the heavenly sanctuary in need of cleansing and Christ standing there, she regarded this as the revelation explaining the true significance of Miller's prophecy. Christ *had* come in 1844, but he had come to his heavenly, not earthly, sanctuary! Mrs White exercised a great influence on the development of Adventism and since her death in 1915 her writings are frequently appealed to as authoritative and divine expositions of Scripture.

A chequered history

Seventh-Day Adventism has had a chequered history. The early years, 1844-1888, were difficult years characterized by a failure to appreciate and accept justification by faith. 'The almost universal position' in this period was, according to Australian researcher G. J. Paxton, that 'Acceptable righteousness before God is found through obeying the law with the aid of the Spirit of God.'[1]

1888 was a watershed in the movement's history. Talks given by E. J. Waggoner and Mrs White at the General Conference Session of 1888 in Minneapolis helped to re-establish the doctrine of justification by faith to a position of prominence in the movement. They stressed the impossibility of human obedience satisfying the law of God and also underlined the necessity of a mediator who was both God and man to satisfy the law on behalf of sinners. Only through faith, they added, could this righteousness be received.

There was opposition to this new emphasis in the conference and subsequently some leaders were strongly criticized by Mrs White for their antagonism to the doctrine of justification by faith. The years 1901-1920 witnessed expansion and consolidation of the movement despite a crisis over the teaching and influence of pantheism, i.e., the theory that the world and God are identical.

In subsequent years the controversy over the meaning and importance of justification and its relation to sanctification deepened and the decade of the seventies was a period of profound crisis with differing emphases and interpretations.

Adventist scholars like Desmond Ford, Geoffrey Paxton and Robert Brinsmead argued strongly for the Reformation principle of justification by faith alone; they insisted that sanctification is not the basis of salvation. Others, however, like Hans K. La Rondelle, disagreed. As the debate continued in the late 1970s, an official committee was appointed to study the question. Sadly, this committee issued an ambiguous, compromising statement which did little to clarify the official Adventist position concerning the crucial doctrine of justification by faith. La Rondelle, for example, had rejected the Reformation gospel as the norm for the Adventists' understanding of the apostolic gospel, while Fritz Guy affirmed, 'One of the most important elements in our Adventist heritage is the notion of "present truth" — truth that has come newly alive and has become newly understood and significant because of a new experience, a present situation. What is important, then, theologically and experientially, is not whether our understanding is just like that of the Reformers; what is important is whether our beliefs are *true*.'[2]

With the establishment of Adventist research centres in the 1960s and 1970s, attention also focused on the nature and authority of Ellen White's writings. As a result of this historical research, three points were established. First of all, Ellen White borrowed a lot of her material from other sources; secondly, she was fallible and also conditioned by late nineteenth-century American culture.

Recent controversy

In September 1980 church leaders disciplined one of the movement's leading theologians, Australian Desmond Ford, removing him from ministerial and teaching posts within the movement. Having gained his doctoral degree in New Testament studies in Manchester under Professor F. F. Bruce, Ford had been head of the theology department of the Adventists' Avondale College in New South Wales, Australia for sixteen years. Ford challenged some of the most cherished Adventist traditions, including the status of Mrs White's writings and the 'Investigative Judgement'. He claims, 'You can't find the investigative judgement in the Bible. You can get it out of Ellen White. The fact is, she got it out of Uriah Smith, an early Adventist writer.'

Prior to his dismissal, Desmond Ford was given a six-month leave of absence in order to research the question of the 'sanctuary' doctrine and other related issues. Ford published the findings of his research in the summer of 1980 in a manuscript called *Daniel 8:14, The Day of Atonement and the Investigative Judgment*.[3] In this lengthy document, Ford denied the traditional Adventist teaching that Christ entered the Most Holy Place in 1844 to start upon his work of investigative judgement. Ford then underlined the biblical truth, namely, that Christ has been interceding for his people as High Priest since his ascension. What then, according to Ford, was the significance of 1844? It was the time, he declared, 'when God, in heaven and on earth, raised up a people to whom he entrusted his last, everlasting gospel of righteousness by faith in Christ, for the world'.[4]

The official Adventist response was disappointing. In numerous articles and editorials in the *Adventist Review* it was argued that the traditional sanctuary doctrine was an essential article of faith. Richard Lesher, for example, insisted: 'These landmark doctrines are to be received and held fast, not in formal fashion but in the light of divine guidance given at the beginning of the movement and made our own. Thus we become part and parcel with the movement, and the beliefs that made the original Seventh-day Adventists make us Seventh-day Adventists too.'[5]

Ford's manuscript was then studied by the 'Sanctuary Review Committee', where the majority of members decided that the 'Adventist tradition was the norm for interpreting the Bible, rather than the Bible for tradition'.[6]

A few weeks later the General Conference recommended that Ford should be disciplined and the Australian Division took the appropriate steps. Almost immediately, however, a new magazine called *Evangelica* was launched to defend and propagate Ford's teaching. Ford's influence on Adventism both in America and Australia has been extensive. One Adventist reported that in the U.S.A., 'There is a vast youth movement in the church identifying with the evangelistic gospel [as a result of Ford]. There's a renewed

excitement about the cross.'[7] Some, like John Toews, the Califor-
nian pastor, withdrew their churches from the movement; Pastor
Toews renamed his church the South Bay Gospel Fellowship. 'We
feel,' he explains, 'we want to move into the mainstream of
Christianity now because we feel that Adventism is very definitely
way off to the side.'[8] He predicted that many more pastors would
resign.

Evangelicals and Adventists

Many evangelicals, however, now insist that Adventism should be
regarded as a Christian church rather than a cult.

A dialogue was held in 1955-6 in America between leading
evangelicals like Donald Grey Barnhouse (a Presbyterian minister
in Philadelphia and editor of the influential evangelical magazine
Eternity) and Adventists.

Walter R. Martin had also been commissioned by Zondervan to
write a book exposing Adventism as a cult, but after his discussions
with Adventist theologians he concluded they were Christians and
that Adventism was not a non-Christian cult. Dr Barnhouse and his
son agreed with Martin and their conclusion was reported in
Eternity. Martin then wrote a book called *The truth about Seventh-
Day Adventism*.[9] In this book he demonstrated how Adventists
believe all the crucial biblical truths which are necessary for
salvation. Areas of disagreement, too, were pinpointed by Martin,
including Adventist teachings on conditional immortality, the
seventh-day sabbath, the investigative judgement, the heavenly
sanctuary and the claim that Ellen White was a divinely appointed
messenger of God. In his conclusion, Martin wrote, 'We trust that
evangelical Christianity as a whole will extend the hand of fellowship to a group of sincere, earnest fellow Christians, distinguished
though they are by some peculiar views, but members of the Body
of Christ and possessors of the faith that saves.'[10]

The issues are important and clearly defined. If Adventism
wants to be within the Reformation tradition and be accepted as
evangelical, it must make its supreme appeal only to the Bible, and
embrace the biblical doctrine of justification by faith which, as
Calvin observed, is 'the hinge on which all true religion turns'.

The movement in the world today

Official statistics reveal that there are over 3,500,000 Adventists spread over 189 countries. A breakdown of this figure in terms of geographical location is interesting. 76% of the total membership live in Third World countries, 16% in North America, 6% in Europe and only 1% in Australia and New Zealand. By 1980 almost half of Adventist missionaries came from the Third World. Adventists maintain 433 hospitals or health-care institutes, fifty publishing houses and have the largest Protestant school system in the world. They have also been active in Britain since 1878 and now have 420 workers here. Their membership in Britain in 1970 was 12,145 and this increased to 16,831 in 1987, with an estimated membership of 23,000 expected by A.D. 2000. It was the Adventists who first used the Dial-a-Prayer for the lonely and Five-Day Clinics for those wanting to abandon smoking; these clinics have been used now in over 100 towns and cities in Britain. They also run Britain's leading health-food company, Granose, and are involved in several health-food retail businesses. In addition, they maintain old people's homes at Oulton Broad, Norfolk and Lundin Links, Fife and a large nursing home in Crieff, Perthshire, seven junior schools, a secondary school and a college which prepares students for the degrees of B.A. and M.Div. Their British headquarters stands in a large area of parkland near the Watford exit of the M1 and they also own the New Gallery Theatre in 123 Regent Street which they use, among other things, as an evangelistic centre. They also have or use numerous conference or youth camp centres in various parts of Britain.

As a movement the Adventists are using their wealth to establish an extensive network of interests throughout Britain in order to evangelize the people as effectively as possible. Despite the fact that many Adventists may be born again and orthodox concerning the doctrines of Scripture and the Trinity etc., they nevertheless present a challenge to us in view of their confused thinking over the doctrine of justification by faith.[11]

| *What Seventh-Day Adventists teach* | *What the Bible teaches* |

Adventists accept the orthodox biblical teaching concerning the Trinity, the deity and incarnation of the Lord Jesus, including his virgin birth, the Lord's bodily resurrection and ascension to heaven, and the prospect of his personal return to earth in glory.The sinfulness of human nature, salvation through Christ alone and the necessity of the new birth are also affirmed by them.

There are, however, some deviations in their teaching, as set out below.

Death of Christ

Disappointed that Christ had not returned personally in 1844 as William Miller had predicted, a teenage disciple of Miller claimed she saw Christ in a vision that same year entering the heavenly sanctuary to cleanse it from sin.

A distinction is then made between receiving forgiveness here and the ultimate, final blotting out of sins from our records in heaven. Apart from Daniel 8:14, this view is based on Leviticus 16:14, namely, that on the Day of Atonement the sin-stained blood was taken into the Holy of Holies, but there was still need for sin to be removed by the blood which, Adventists claim, Christ has been doing in heaven since 1844.

They regard the goat sacrificed on the Day of Atonement as a type of Christ and his sacrifice,

Hebrews 9:11-12 indicates the sufficiency and finality of what Christ did on the cross (cf. v. 26).

Christ entered heaven not in 1844, but in his ascension, 'to appear in the presence of God for us' (Hebrews 9:24).

'And the blood of Jesus his Son cleanses us from all sin' (1 John 1:7). It is not past sins only that are forgiven, nor a partial forgiveness, that is obtained at Calvary.

While Hebrews 8 teaches that there is a heavenly sanctuary where Christ is the priest, it also shows that Christ has sat down there, having completed the work of atonement. Even if 'Azazel' in Leviticus 16:8 refers, as Adventists claim, to Satan or an evil spirit, this does not prove that the scapegoat is Satan.

whereas the other goat sent into the wilderness is regarded as a picture of Satan, who will be punished as the originator of the world's sins.

Their 'sanctuary' teaching detracts from the sufficiency and finality of the Saviour's sacrifice. For example, they speak of the Lord entering the inner sanctuary of heaven in 1844 to finish his work of atonement for sin. This is called his 'investigative judgement', that is, examining and revealing the life records of people to the Father and blotting out the sins that are still recorded against the believers in heaven.

Justification by faith

As we have seen, conflicting views are held by Adventists on this major doctrine. The tendency is to make salvation dependent ultimately on our obedience to divine laws, including the observance of the sabbath. While the Lord Jesus Christ has purchased redemption for us and this is accepted by personal faith, we are then put on probation to see if we are worthy of eternal life.

Sanctification

Laws must be observed and the keeping of the traditional Jewish sabbath, that is, the seventh day, is 'the sign of sanctification' and its disregard has been regarded by some as 'the unpardonable sin'.

A state of sinless perfection obtainable here on earth is also implied.

According to verses 20-22, after atoning for his personal and then for the nation's sins, Aaron as high priest put his hands on the goat while confessing the sins of Israel. These sins are symbolically laid on the head of the second goat which is then sent into the wilderness, never to return. The symbolism is deeply significant. Through the death of the first goat a full atonement for the people was made, typifying the sacrifice of Christ, while in the sending away of the second goat they are shown that the curse upon us due to our sins is removed for ever (see Isaiah 53:6; 2 Corinthians 5:21; Galatians 3:13).

'To the one who does not work, but believes in him who justifies the ungodly, his faith is reckoned as righteousness' (Romans 4:5).

'A man is not justified by the works of the Law but through faith in Christ Jesus, even we have believed in Christ Jesus, that we may be justified by faith in Christ, and not by the works of the Law; since by the works of the Law shall no flesh be justified' (Galatians 2:16).

'Therefore let no one act as your judge in regard to food or drink or in respect to a festival or a new moon or a Sabbath day — things which are a mere shadow of what is to come; but the substance belongs to Christ' (Colossians 2:16-17).

'If we say that we have no sin, we are deceiving ourselves, and the truth is not in us' (1 John 1:8).

Perseverance of believers

Believers can fall from grace and be eternally lost.

'I give eternal life to them, and they shall never perish; and no one shall snatch them out of my hand' (John 10:28; cf. John 6:37-40; Romans 8:35-39; Philippians 1:6; 1 Peter 1:5).

Death

Between death and the resurrection the souls of believers 'sleep'.

'We... prefer rather to be absent from the body and to be at home with the Lord' (2 Corinthians 5:8).
    '... having the desire to depart and be with Christ, for that is very much better' (Philippians 1:23; cf. Psalm 73:24; Luke 16:22-31).

Future state of unbelievers

Satan and unbelievers will be annihilated.

'And these will go away into eternal punishment, but the righteous into eternal life' (Matthew 25:46).
    'They will be tormented day and night for ever and ever' (Revelation 20:10).

Sabbath

Mrs White claimed that in a vision she saw the ark and the Ten Commandments in heaven, but a halo of light surrounded this fourth commandment. She concluded that this was a message to stress a commandment which had been greatly neglected. On studying the history of the sabbath she concluded that Sunday observance was 'the mark of the beast' (Revelation 13), the beast being the pope.

The fourth commandment is part of God's abiding moral law although it includes temporary elements applicable to Jews to whom it was first given. Even Adventists acknowledge they are unable to keep the Jewish sabbath in all its original detail.
    In the New Testament there is a change from the seventh day to the first day of the week as the Christian sabbath, largely because on this day the Lord rose from the dead (John 20:1), and his resurrection appearances to the disciples occurred on this first day also (John 20:19, 26; cf. Acts 20:6-7; 1 Corinthians 16:2; Revelation 1:10).

Second coming of Christ

When Christ has finished his 'investigative judgment' in the heavenly sanctuary, he will return personally to the world. Believers who are alive then will be taken into heaven while the believing dead will be resurrected to join the church in heaven. The millennium will be spent then in heaven, not on earth. During the millennium in heaven, the earth will be desolate and the punishment of unbelievers decided, then, after the millennium, Christ will return to earth with the believers and eternity will be spent on earth, while the wicked will be destroyed.

Note: Miller decided on his first date, 1843, by using Daniel 8:14 and assuming the 2,300 days here to be years. 2,300 years would elapse then before the sanctuary would be cleansed at his return. The 'seventy weeks' reference in Daniel 9:24 was interpreted as seventy weeks of years, that is 490 years before the Messiah would die in A.D. 33. Working back 490 years Miller arrived at the date of 457 B.C. and he then added the 2,300 years of Daniel 8:14 which gave him A.D. 1843!

1. Date fixing is wrong: 'But of the day and hour no one knows, not even the angels of heaven, nor the Son, but the Father alone' (Matthew 24:36). 'Therefore be on the alert, for you do not know which day your Lord is coming' (Matthew 24:42).

2. For descriptions of the Lord's second coming read Matthew 24:30-31; 25:31-46; 1Thessalonians 4:16-17; 2 Thessalonians 1:7-10.

5.
Moral Re-Armament

The superintendent of a hospice in Philadelphia, U.S.A., found himself at variance with his committee, who felt he was being extravagant in the quality and amount of food he gave to the destitute boys in his care. Appointed to this post in 1904 by the Lutheran Church of Pennsylvania, Frank Buchman had used most of his $600 a year salary to furnish the hospice more adequately but now, three years later, a crisis had arisen. Buchman was now ordered to give his boys less food. In October 1907 he wrote, 'They refused to let us have good butter. What they provided was rancid. The fish was not fresh. You can't run a Christian institution that way...' There was no alternative for the superintendent but to leave the hospice and, feeling extremely bitter towards the committee and exhausted, he was advised by his doctor to go on a Mediterranean cruise. The cruise, although enjoyable, did not meet his deep personal need and in the summer of 1908 this dejected and embittered young man arrived in the Lake District in time for the Keswick Convention. He derived no help at all from the main convention meetings but, while walking alone on the Sunday, he noticed a small chapel where a service was in progress. Buchman joined the small congregation and heard a woman preacher, Mrs Penn-Lewis, who was a close friend of the Welsh revivalist Evan Roberts, preaching about the death of Christ. God spoke to him through the message. 'A doctrine which I knew as a boy,' he remarked later, 'which my church believed, which I had always been taught, that day became a reality for me. I had entered the little church with a divided will, nursing pride, selfishness, ill-will. The woman's simple talk personalized the cross for me that day, and suddenly I had a poignant vision of the Crucified. With this deep experience of the love of God in Christ... I wrote to the six committee men in America against whom I had nursed the ill-will and told them of my experience, and how at the foot of the cross I could only think of my own sin. At the top of each letter I wrote this verse:

When I survey the wondrous cross
On which the Prince of Glory died,
My richest gain I count but loss
And pour contempt on all my pride.

'It wasn't difficult to write the first three lines of that hymn, but to write the fourth line was like writing in my own blood.'

Buchman was now determined to share his faith with others and generally to help people. Returning to America, he accepted the post of YMCA secretary in Pennsylvania State College and it was here, through the visit of F. B. Meyer, that Buchman was again challenged. Observing him hard at work, Dr Meyer told him that he should listen more to God than to telephones and make personal interviews more important than the organizing of meetings. He immediately acted on the advice. 'It was then,' Buchman writes, 'I decided to devote an hour, from 5 a.m. to 6 a.m. every morning before the telephones would begin to ring, to listen to the Voice of the living God, in a daily time of quiet. Everything is so different when the Holy Spirit is a daily reality.' This practice of silence or a Quiet Time in which he listened to the inner voice of God is one of the distinctive features of Moral Re-Armament.

The movement spreads further afield

Evangelistic work in India, China and Japan, then a new appointment in Hartford Theological Seminary, provided Buchman with numerous opportunities for helping people. While in Hartford, he travelled regularly to Yale to hear Professor Henry Wright lecture on the relevance of Christianity and it was from Wright that Buchman learned to use the four moral standards of honesty, purity, unselfishness and love, as well as the triangle — God, myself, my neighbour.

In Cambridge in 1921 the thought suddenly came to him: 'I will use you to remake the world' and for the next ten years his centre of operations was Oxford, where he gathered over 100 students together under the name of the Oxford Group. Slowly other groups were established in South Africa (1928), Canada and the U.S.A. (1932), Switzerland (1935), Holland (1937) and Scandinavia in 1938.

He was troubled in the spring of 1938 by the recurring thought: 'Moral and spiritual re-armament. The next great movement in the world will be a movement of moral re-armament for all nations.' This thought gripped Buchman and his followers. After being known by such names as the Oxford Group, Buchmanism, the New Groupers and the First Century Christian Fellowship, it was now decided to rename the movement as Moral Re-Armament (MRA) to mark their leader's sixtieth birthday.

There followed seven busy years in the United States for Buchman before he left in 1946 with 150 helpers to work in post-war Europe. One of the most important developments was the purchase of a mountain hotel in the fashionable Swiss village of Caux. During the Second World War the hotel sheltered Jewish and Italian refugees as well as British and American escaped prisoners of war. Renamed 'Mountain House', the hotel has become the MRA international centre for conferences and reconciliation work, providing 'a common ground for people of all faiths, and people of no faith, to work together to build a new world'. When Buchman died in 1961 at the age of eighty-three, the work of MRA was both influential and international.

The movement today

There is no formal membership of the movement but people from different church denominations, as well as those without any faith, are involved in the MRA. In Great Britain there are 400 full-time workers, who are active in industry, education, inner-city and multi-racial communities, etc. In addition, they have an English conference centre in Tarporley, Cheshire, and considerable use is made of plays and films as a means of communicating the message of moral and spiritual renewal. The Westminster Theatre in London, for example, is owned by the MRA.

It is generally assumed, especially in the light of Buchman's passionate and fearless love of Christ and the movement's high moral and spiritual aims, that Moral Re-Armament is unquestionably Christian and biblical. That there are Christians within its ranks and positive Christian elements in its work I readily concede. Much of this is work which Christian churches should have been doing, but sadly the failure of Christendom has highlighted the need for MRA. However, when we assess MRA teaching, although it has no official creed, we find that some of its beliefs are at variance with the Bible and, sadly, I must draw attention to these differences here.

What Moral Re-Armament teaches	*What the Bible teaches*

Mankind

Buchman saw the line of division in the world lying not between Christians and non-Christians, or between the world religions, but between men whose allegiance is to God and spiritual values (whatever their religion) and those who are dedicated to their destruction. Embracing people of all religions, MRA is not specifically Christian.

The Bible divides mankind into two basic categories only: those who trust in Christ and enjoy eternal life, and those who are without Christ and without hope (cf. John 3:15-18, 36; 10:9; Galatians 2:16; Ephesians 2:11-13).

Conversion

A basic conviction of MRA is that the revolution we most need is the change in human character itself. 'Human nature can change. When men are freed from the control of forces like self-interest, hatred, pride, fear or lust, a passion gets liberated in their hearts which issues in social, economic and national change.'

While Buchman and others have known genuine conversion to Christ, 'change' for the MRA is not specifically Christian conversion.
1.   It wrongly stresses man's ability to change himself (cf. John 3:3-8; Romans 7:18; Ephesians 2:8-10).
2.   It wrongly suggests that deep spiritual change can take place

How do people change? It involves five stages:
Conviction: awareness of personal sins;
Contrition: being sorry for sin;
Confession: telling God and people we are sorry;
Conversion: living differently and better, then trying to keep the four absolutes of honesty, purity, unselfishness and love;
Continuance: persevering in this new life of obedience and love.

Christian life

An individual must express his change of life in a striving to keep the four absolutes — absolute honesty, absolute purity, absolute unselfishness, absolute love. These absolutes can be attained by means of four principles:
Sharing in the confession of sin and temptation;
Surrender of one's whole life to God;
Restitution to people who have been wronged;
Guidance in listening to and obeying God's 'inner' voice.

Guidance

'When man listens, God speaks. When man obeys, God acts,' wrote Buchman. But how does God make known his will? 'Through friends,

apart from Christ and faith in him (cf. John 6:44; 2 Corinthians 5:17; Galatians 4:4-7).
3.   While there is a strong pietistic strand in MRA writings, the work of the triune God in our salvation is minimized (cf. Titus 3:4-7; 1 Peter 1:2).

Buchman borrowed the four absolutes from Robert Speer's book *The Principles of Jesus* (1902), in which the author claimed that these absolutes were the standard of the Sermon on the Mount. Buchman also heard these same absolutes from Professor Wright in Yale.

Three observations must be made here:
1.   The four absolutes are a hopelessly inadequate summary and statement of the Sermon on the Mount.
2.   It is not the four absolutes but the whole revealed will of God in the Bible which is the standard of life for believers (cf. 2 Timothy 3:16).
3.   Not even the four absolutes can be kept perfectly (cf. 1 John 1:8, 10.)

It is true that the Bible teaches the fact of God's guidance and providence (Psalm 32:8; Isaiah 58:11; Daniel 4:34-35; Matthew 6:26-33),

the Scriptures and the teachings of your faith, even through circumstances.' Such guidance may come as a compelling thought or insistent conviction or whisper, but if heeded the consequences may be far-reaching. For this reason a 'quiet time' each morning when one is able to meditate, listen, pray and read is invaluable. 'Inner guidance' wrote his biographer Theophil Spoeri, 'became the determining force in Buchman's life.'

the importance of praying to God (Jeremiah 33:3; Luke 11:2-13; 1 Thessalonians 5:17), and reading and then obeying the Scripture (Psalm 119:97; Colossians 3:16; James 1:21-25), but the MRA account of guidance is excessively subjective and lacks the objectivity and supremacy of the Bible. Guidance comes from God through the Bible ultimately and not from within oneself.

6.
Churches of Christ: 'Campbellites'

Recently, some Christians and churches, both in Britain and the United States, have expressed concern about the beliefs and practices of churches known as the Churches of Christ. Generally, Christians have lacked reliable information about the 'Campbellite' churches, so they have been unable to substantiate the charge of heresy in relation to them.

In Britain concern was expressed soon after the founding in London in 1982 of the Central London Church of Christ, which now calls itself just the London Church of Christ (LCC). There are other Churches of Christ in London, but at present the LCC claims over 800 members and it is in the process of establishing other branches in Britain. For example, the Central Birmingham Church of Christ was founded in 1988. The LCC in turn was the product of a missionary initiative taken by the Boston (U.S.A.) Church of Christ; the latter is only ten years old.

Causes for concern

Four areas of concern have surfaced in Britain of late concerning the LCC. First of all, *the LCC has concentrated its work among students in the colleges*. The church has set up Bible-study groups in a number of colleges and halls of residence, sometimes without identifying themselves clearly to the students. Some college chaplains and leaders of Christian Unions in the London area have been unhappy about the Bible-study groups but in some cases LCC members have also joined in the activities of CUs without revealing their motives and affiliation. Due to this intense activity within the student population, a high proportion of LCC members are, or have been, students.

Another area of concern relates to *the demands which the LCC makes upon its members.* They are expected to attend several meetings each week and also to engage in evangelistic activity as well as personal Bible Study and memorization of Scripture. There are claims that this pressure has caused examination failures and nervous breakdowns. While LCC leaders deny encouraging students to give up their studies, a number proceed to full-time work for the LCC immediately after completing their studies. INFORM know of a medical student who does not plan to do his 'house-jobs' year and will therefore fail to register as a doctor. There is also a tendency for members to withdraw from outside friendships and contacts.

A third area of concern is *the degree of supervision exercised over LCC members.* INFORM refer to a student who recently joined LCC and was telephoned each day during a three-week vacation. Similarly, there are members who left the movement but were persistently telephoned over several weeks afterwards. Some ex-LCC members have talked freely about their decision to leave the movement and mentioned reasons such as leadership pressure, the level of time commitment involved, etc. These people have shared too the attractions of the LCC and have referred to factors such as the style of worship, commitment to Bible study and the friendliness of the members.

The final area of concern has been *the extent to which the LCC resembles genuine evangelical churches.* For example, the LCC appeals to the Bible as its only source of authority and emphasizes the importance of group/personal Bible study, while it actively seeks to evangelize and recruit new members. However, the LCC and other Churches of Christ are not sound in biblical theology and cannot be regarded as evangelical. One INFORM worker reports that an LCC leader spoke to him in a derogatory manner of evangelicals. What is even more important are some of their distinctive beliefs which are erroneous. The LCC and similar churches, for example, deny major gospel truths by insisting that baptism is essential for salvation and that salvation is never in fact certain in this life. They also regard doctrines such as original sin, predestination, and once saved always saved as 'false doctrines' which made 'their official debut in' the fifth century.[1] Sadly, young students and even older Christians are often ill-taught themselves and are unable to discern between truth and error in the teachings of the LCC and related churches.

The historical background

We must be careful how we use the term 'Campbellites' in relation to the LCC and other Churches of Christ. Historically the term 'Campbellites' is associated with the Christian Church (Disciples of Christ) which began in the early 1800s in America with three ex-Presbyterian ministers, namely, Thomas and Alexander Campbell and Barton Stone. The Campbells were Irish but educated in Scotland and, while they were Presbyterian, they had been influenced by Free Church attitudes towards state churches and on matters such as creeds, liturgies and lay-oriented leadership. Within weeks of his arrival in America and joining the Philadelphia Synod of the Presbyterian Church, Thomas Campbell's name was removed from the rolls of the church in May 1807 because of heresy. Thomas then established the Christian Association of Washington (Pennsylvania) and was joined by his brother, Alexander, who broke his links with the Scottish Presbyterians.

Various congregations were founded by the Campbells and for seventeen years from 1813 they joined the Red Stone Baptist Association. This was a formative period for the Campbells in which their main doctrines were developed and articulated. However, some of these doctrines conflicted with Baptist principles and there was consequently a break with the Baptist Association in 1830. Alexander was by now teaching a sharp distinction between grace and law as well as the opposition between the New and Old Testaments. Both brothers now aimed to restore New Testament Christianity and one result was that they condemned any structure which impinged on the independence of local churches.

In 1832 Campbellite churches merged with those of Barton Stone and they were commonly described as the Christian Church and Disciples of Christ. By 1849, these churches had grown rapidly.

Regional fellowships were arranged, colleges established and a publishing programme was launched. A convention was held in 1849 which adopted the name 'American Christian Missionary Society' and for the following sixty years it facilitated the work of church extension and overseas mission. Since 1849 several divisions have taken place over details of doctrine and practice so that there are now several factions of the Churches of Christ in the United States and Britain.

Current divisions

Many of these groups acknowledge a link with the nineteenth-century 'Campbellites', but it is difficult to ascertain how many of these groups use the name 'Campbellite' to describe themselves. The situation is complex and this is illustrated in relation to Britain. For example, a representative of the Fellowship of Churches of Christ in Britain commented recently, 'We are of course Campbellites in origin.' This FCC represents only thirty-seven Churches of Christ; previously there had been about seventy in the fellowship. Nearly half of these churches in the FCC joined the United Reformed Church in 1980, so the FCC was depleted. It is interesting that in the 1989/90 edition of the *U.K. Christian Handbook*[2] the Churches of Christ which left the FCC are included under the United Reformed Church and named in a footnote as the Reformed Association of Churches of Christ.

To illustrate further the complexity of the situation, there is another separate group of churches called the 'Old Paths Churches', numbering as many as ninety, which split from other Churches of Christ in the 1920s. It is this latter group which is closest to the LCC; in fact, in 1987 the LCC was listed in their directory but omitted from it in 1989.

Despite all these divisions, there are basic doctrines which all these groups have in common, namely, the necessity of baptism for salvation, the possibility of losing one's salvation and a strictly congregational form of church government. A major reason for past divisions relates to the departure of some Churches of Christ from congregational principles by the establishing of a structured organization threatening to exercise authority over local churches.

An FCC representative adds that the London Church of Christ

differs from them not in important points of doctrine but rather in methods and organization. In fact, the mainline Churches of Christ in the United States have repeatedly criticized the Boston Church of Christ for its authoritarianism. One major difference between the older and newer Churches of Christ is the more aggressive missionary zeal of the 'new' churches and a tendency to adopt a more authoritarian structure and approach. In the United States, some Churches of Christ have become quite liberal in theology and practice.

What the Churches of Christ believe	*What the Bible teaches*

Predestination

This is a 'false doctrine' invented in the fifth century A.D.

'And whom he predestined, these he also called...' (Romans 8:30; cf. 9:11-18).

'...just as he chose us in him before the foundation of the world...' (Ephesians 1:4).

'God has chosen you from the beginning for salvation...' (2 Thessalonians 2:13).

Original sin

A misleading and false teaching invented in the early centuries of the church.

'Behold, I was brought forth in iniquity, and in sin my mother conceived me' (Psalm 51:5).

'Through the one man's disobedience the many were made sinners, even so through the obedience of the One the many will be made righteous' (Romans 5:19).

Baptism

This ordinance must be observed as a condition and means of salvation.

'References to baptism in the patristic literature abound! It is extremely clear that for the first few centuries everyone was in agreement that baptism was for the

'For by grace you have been saved through faith; and that not of yourselves, it is the gift of God' (Ephesians 2:8).

Salvation is planned, accomplished and applied to us by the Lord; faith is the means by which

forgiveness of sins, and was the only way to be saved.'[3]

we receive this salvation as we rest upon the Lord Jesus (Romans 5:1; 1:16).

Believers' baptism is an act of obedience on the part of the believer to Christ and is an outward sign of an inner spiritual change and of entry to the church. Baptism has no efficacy in itself (Matthew 28:19; Acts 2:41).

Falling from grace

Salvation is never secure in this life and members can be lost again even after baptism and a reasonable life of commitment.

'And I give eternal life to them and they shall never perish; and no one shall snatch them out of my hand' (John 10:28).

'He who began a good work in you will perfect it until the day of Christ Jesus' (Philippians 1:6; cf. Romans 8:35-38; 1 Peter 1:3-5).

7.
Unitarian churches

While all Unitarian churches are autonomous, they are linked together by means of a General Assembly, which was established in 1928 to give encouragement and cohesion to the work. In 1987 there were 237 congregations and fellowships in Great Britain, including four in Scotland. The majority of the churches in England are in the Midlands, Lancashire and the London area. The Non-Subscribing Presbyterian Church in Ireland, with its thirty-two congregations, including two in the Republic, also co-operates closely with the British Assembly. The first avowedly Unitarian Church, which was opened in London in 1774 by Theophilus Lindsey, is now the site of the Assembly's headquarters.

In Britain and the Commonwealth countries of Australia, New Zealand and South Africa there are an estimated 15,000 Unitarians, whereas there are about 150,000 in the United States and Canada. Romania (where organized Unitarianism began under the Unitarian Prince Sigismund in 1568 at the Diet of Torda), Hungary, Czechoslovakia, Western Germany and the Khasi Hills of Assam, India, all have Unitarian churches, with an approximate total membership of 20,000.

The religious affiliations of the Unitarian General Assembly in Britain are both revealing and disturbing. For example, it is an associate member of the British Council of Churches and also of the World Congress of Faiths.

In one of its official publications the Assembly defines

Unitarianism as 'a liberal religious movement arising out of Christianity, expressing itself largely but not wholly in Christian forms and terms, and in the spirit of the man Jesus. It is liberal in rejecting the idea of a unique and final revelation of truth and in trusting men to discover and believe as much as they can for themselves; it is a religious movement inasmuch as it has churches and a ministry and ways of worship... It is glad to remain Christian where it can but glad also to discover other truth and beauty and goodness in other faiths and other lives. Unitarians know of no better man in religion than Jesus of Nazareth but they believe that there have been others like him in the past, and that there will be others like him again.'[1]

It is significant that Unitarianism did not take root in North Wales during the latter part of the last century. Its influence never extended beyond places like Lampeter and Ciliau Aeron and although meetings were held regularly in Aberystwyth from the autumn of 1902, the cause remained extremely weak and services were finally suspended there on Sunday, 14 March 1976. The main factor, of course, in checking the progress of Unitarianism especially during the last century was the vigorous and fruitful preaching of the gospel under the power of the Holy Spirit. There were numerous outpourings of the Holy Spirit upon churches, communities and counties at regular intervals, with the result that large numbers of people were converted and the truth of God's Word was vindicated. This is a salutary lesson for us in our contemporary situation, namely, that despite our evangelism, apologetics and social involvement, nothing but the outpouring of the Holy Spirit upon the church will radically alter our situation and cause the truth to prevail in our land.

What Unitarians teach	*What the Bible teaches*

God

They deny the Trinity, affirming that in God there is only one personality, namely, God the Father. Even when referring to God as Father they feel human language is inadequate to define what is beyond definition. For this reason	'God said, "Let *us* make man in *our* image"' (Genesis 1:26; cf. 11:7). '... in the name [the one name, yet including three persons] of the Father and the Son and the Holy Spirit' (Matthew 28:19).

some find it more helpful not to use the word 'God' at all.

They usually reject miracles, believing that the natural order of the universe is never broken or superseded.

Bible

In contemporary Unitarianism the individual conscience, guided by human reason, is the source of what is believed. While the Bible is respected as a 'helpful guide' containing religious insights, it is rejected as the Word of God. God continues to reveal himself in life, in the order and beauty of nature, in moral standards, spiritual desires, human aspirations and in the love of what is pure and good. Thus they teach 'universal inspiration'.

'To the law and to the testimony: if they speak not according to this word, it is because there is no light in them' (Isaiah 8:20, AV).

'Thy word is truth' (John 17:17).

'Where is the wise man? Where is the scribe? Where is the debater of this age? Has not God made foolish the wisdom of the world? For since in the wisdom of God the world through its wisdom did not come to know God, God was well-pleased through the foolishness of the message preached to save those who believe' (1 Corinthians 1:20-21).

'But a natural man does not accept the things of the Spirit of God; for they are foolishness to him, and he cannot understand them, because they are spiritually appraised' (1 Corinthians 2:14).

Person of Christ

Jesus was only a man and as such should not be worshipped. He was an example and has shown us what man's life can be like when he obeys God's will and co-operates with the Spirit. Jesus is one of the many great spiritual leaders of the world.

'Thou art the Christ, the Son of the living God' (Matthew 16:16).

'For this cause therefore the Jews were seeking all the more to kill him, because he not only was breaking the sabbath, but also was calling God his own Father, making himself equal with God' (John 5:18).

'I and the Father are one' (John 10:30).

Death of Christ

Modern Unitarians do not believe that men and women need a mediator to approach God. Therefore Christ's death was not sacrificial or substitutionary.

Not all Unitarian churches observe the communion; those who do regard it as a mere remembrance of the life, works and teachings of Jesus Christ.

Resurrection of Christ

Most Unitarians interpret our Lord's resurrection as his deeds and thoughts living on in the lives of others in history. There was no physical or spiritual resurrection of the Lord.

Holy Spirit

The Holy Spirit is regarded in several ways: for example, as the influence of Christ's teaching on people; as God's way of revealing himself in the whole of life; or as the 'Power' beyond us.

He is *not* regarded as a person in the Godhead co-equal with the Father and since man is basically good there is no need for his regenerating and sanctifying work in people.

'I am the way, and the truth, and the life; no one comes to the Father, but through me' (John 14:6).

'Because by the works of the Law no flesh will be justified in his sight' (Romans 3:20).

'But now in Christ Jesus you who formerly were far off have been brought near by the blood of Christ' (Ephesians 2:13).

'For through him we both have our access in one Spirit to the Father' (Ephesians 2:18).

'For Christ also died for sins once for all, the just for the unjust, in order that he might bring us back to God' (1 Peter 3:18).

'Why do you seek the living One among the dead? He is not here; but he has risen' (Luke 24:5-6).

'He was buried, and ... he was raised on the third day according to the Scriptures' (1 Corinthians 15:4).

'If I go, I will send him to you' (John 16:7)

'Why has Satan filled your heart to lie to the Holy Spirit?... You have not lied to men, but to God' (Acts 5:3-4).

'Because you are sons, God has sent forth the Spirit of his Son into our hearts, crying, "Abba! Father!"' (Galatians 4:6).

Man and sin

Unitarians assert their belief in man and his essential goodness. Although people are capable of great cruelty, this is regarded as a falling away from their essential goodness, which is best displayed in babies.

'Behold, I was brought forth in iniquity, and in sin my mother conceived me' (Psalm 51:5).

'For out of the heart come evil thoughts, murders, adulteries, fornications, thefts, false witness, slanders' (Matthew 15:19).

'There is none righteous, not even one' (Romans 3:10).

'All have sinned and fall short of the glory of God' (Romans 3:23).

Salvation

All religions are regarded as equally valid schemes of salvation and Jesus belongs to the class of the great saviours of mankind. No mediator is needed to approach God and no special requirement is needed on man's part to attain salvation.

'I am the door; if anyone enters through me, he shall be saved' (John 10:9).

'And there is salvation in no one else; for there is no other name under heaven that has been given among men, by which we must be saved' (Acts 4:12).

'Believe in the Lord Jesus, and you shall be saved' (Acts 16:31).

Future state

They believe that the process of dying is one of the processes of life and their aim is to approach it without fear. There are three general Unitarian positions here:
1. Those who believe in personal immortality;
2. Those who believe their deeds and thoughts survive only in the memory of other people;
3. Those who don't know.

'I know that my Redeemer lives, and that in the end he will take his stand upon the earth. And after my skin has been destroyed, yet in my flesh I will see God' (Job 19:25-26, NIV).

'And these will go away into eternal punishment, but the righteous into eternal life' (Matthew 25:46).

'For an hour is coming, in which all who are in the tombs shall hear his voice, and shall come forth; those who did the good deeds, to a resurrection of life, those who committed the evil deeds to a resurrection of judgement' (John 5:28-29).

'It is appointed for men to die once, and after this comes judgement' (Hebrews 9:27).

Prayer

True prayer aims at effecting a change in ourselves so that, by our example, we may change others. For many Unitarians private prayer has been equated with honest work rather than with the devotional life, and there is a general dislike of petitionary prayer. Believing that man has direct access to God in prayer, they do not pray 'through Jesus Christ'.

'"For I know the plans that I have for you,' declares the Lord, 'plans for welfare and not for calamity to give you a future and a hope."' While God's purpose was clear, prayer was one of the means he decreed through which he would accomplish his purpose, so he continues, 'Then you will call upon me and come and pray to me, and I will listen to you' (Jeremiah 29:11-12).

'If you shall ask the Father for anything, he will give it to you in my name' (John 16:23).

'Pray without ceasing' (1 Thessalonians 5:17).

'If we ask anything according to his will, he hears us' (1 John 5:14).

8.
'Jesus only': the Apostolic Oneness Movement

What's
Wrong
With the
Name
JESUS
?

These were the words on the front page of a leaflet circulated to homes in the Cardiff area some years ago. The leaflet was published and distributed by the First United Pentecostal Church in Llanrumney, Cardiff. After reading the leaflet, people began to ask questions such as, 'Who are these people?' 'What do they believe?' No one seemed to know very much about the group but the leaflet was clearly misleading and heretical.

It was at this point that a friend asked me to investigate the First United Pentecostal Church. I soon discovered that the group was not Pentecostal at all but one of a number of groups which denied the doctrine of the Holy Trinity. Their 'Jesus only' teaching is popular today even among some evangelicals; in some reasonably orthodox churches and also in a few charismatic and house-church fellowships one hears talk of being baptized in the name of 'Jesus only'. Clearly these Christians and churches are often unaware of the historical background to this teaching and its theological implications, not only for baptism but for the doctrine of the Holy Trinity.

This chapter may help to clarify the issues for Bible-believing Christians.

The historical background

During the second decade of its history, American Pentecostalism was plunged into a major doctrinal controversy concerning baptism in the name of Jesus. It began in 1913 at a world-wide Pentecostal meeting at Arrayo Seco, Los Angeles, when R. E. McAlister preached from Acts 2:38 on 'baptism in Jesus' name', in which he claimed that all baptized believers in the apostolic age were baptized in the name of Jesus Christ alone, rather than in the name of the Father, Son and Holy Spirit.

There was opposition to McAlister's message, but men like Frank J. Ewart and John C. Scheppe were won over to his side. Within a short time, Ewart was confirmed in this view, especially when he felt that answers to prayer resulted from his praying in the name of Jesus. Verses like Matthew 17:8; John 10:30; 14:13; Philippians 2:9-11 and Colossians 3:17 were wrongly used by Scheppe and others to support a 'modalist'[1] theory of the Trinity. While the much earlier heresy of Sabellius had taught that the Father alone was God and that he had manifested himself as the Son and then as the Holy Spirit, these 'Pentecostal' leaders regarded Jesus, not the Father, as the only one God. For them, Jesus manifested himself in the 'form' or 'office' of Father, Son and Holy Spirit at different times.

Along with evangelist Glenn A. Cook, Ewart led this new movement, assisted by some prominent leaders of the Assemblies of God like G. T. Haywood, E. N. Bell and H. A. Goss, who all played a key role in propagating the new teaching. A magazine was published and edited by Ewart under the title of *Meat in due season* which had the dubious distinction of being the first 'oneness' periodical.[2]

As members of the Assemblies of God were the most vocal in advocating the new theology, they were disciplined by their denominational General Council meeting at St Louis in 1916. The council strengthened its trinitarian theology and thereby expelled many of its assemblies and as many as 146 ministers. Those expelled from the Assemblies of God gradually organized themselves into 'oneness' churches of various shades, but they held in common certain distinctives such as a 'modal' view of the Trinity, the insistence that baptism by immersion was essential to salvation and that such baptism should be carried out only in the name of Jesus. They also retained a 'Pentecostal' position concerning the gifts and Spirit-baptism.

Some of the 'oneness' Pentecostal churches active today include the Apostolic Church of Jesus,[3] Apostolic Faith (Hawaii),[4] Associated Brotherhood of Christians,[5] Assemblies of the Lord Jesus Christ,[6] Pentecostal Assemblies of the World,[7] Jesus Church,[8] Apostolic Overcoming Holy Church of God,[9] Church of Our Lord Jesus Christ of the Apostolic Faith,[10] Bible Way Church of Our Lord Jesus Christ World Wide, Inc.,[11] New Bethel Church of God in Christ (Pentecostal),[12] The Apostolic Gospel Church of Jesus Christ,[13] and the larger United Pentecostal Church.[14] Altogether there are well over seventeen such denominations which share in common the 'Jesus only' teaching.[15]

I now want to pinpoint the main errors of this teaching.

1. The 'Jesus only' teaching denies the biblical doctrine of the Holy Trinity.

2. Baptism in the name of Jesus is an expression of non-trinitarian theology.

3. The movement has an unbiblical doctrine of salvation.

What the 'Jesus Only' movement teaches	*What the Bible teaches*

Holy Trinity

The Father, Son and Holy Spirit are only different expressions or 'manifestations' of the one true God, who is Jesus. A United Pentecostal Church radio speaker confirms this error: 'I want to tell you what the great truth is. We do not believe in three separate personalities in the Godhead, but we believe in three offices which are filled by one person.'[16]	1. The Father is *not* the Son (John 12:49-50; 14:23, 28-31); the Son is *not* the Spirit (John 16:7-14), and the Spirit is *not* the same as the Father (John 14:16-17). 2. Passages like Matthew 3:17; 17:5; 26:39; John 14:26; 16:7, 13-14; 17:4; Luke 23:34, 46 are meaningless if Jesus alone is God. For example, how do you explain the Father's voice at our Lord's baptism? Was the Lord Jesus praying

to himself when he prayed? Did the Lord really submit to the Father's will in Gethsemane or was it play-acting?

3. The Bible teaches that there are three distinguishable but co-exis-tent, co-equal and co-eternal per-sons designated God (see, for ex-ample, 1 Corinthians 8:6; John 1:1; Acts 5:3-4) and in the unity of the Godhead they constitute the 'one God' (1 Timothy 2:5). In the words of Jim Beverly of Atlantic Baptist College, 'These three are Persons and yet the "one God". Only this position does justice to the teaching of the New Testament.'[17]

Baptism

'Oneness' Pentecostals insist that all believers must be baptized in the name of Jesus *only*. In support of this view they use texts such as Acts 2:38; 8:16; 10:48 and 19:5. Fur-thermore, they argue that 'the name' of Matthew 28:19 is the same as 'the name of Jesus Christ' in Acts 2:38; their conclusion is that Jesus is the Father, the Son and the Holy Spirit!

1. The trinitarian formula of baptism given by the Lord Jesus Christ in Matthew 28:19 must govern our theology of Christian baptism.

2. The phrase, 'in the name of Jesus Christ', may have the pri-mary meaning of baptisms being carried out under the authority and command of Jesus Christ, the head of the church. In Acts 2:38, for example, Peter would have been conscious of complying with the Great Commission recorded in Matthew 28:19-20.

3. Significantly, the phrase 'in the name of Jesus' in relation to baptism is used only sparingly in Acts and then only at strategic moments to mark the extension of the church amongst the Jews (2:38), the Samaritans (8:16) and the Gentiles (10:48).

4. Calvin maintains that the words of Acts 2:38, 'in the name of Jesus Christ', are not a formula to

be used in baptism but rather a declaration that all the efficacy of baptism is found in Christ alone. 'Christ is the mark and end whereunto baptism directs us,' stresses Calvin, 'wherefore, everyone profits in baptism as he learns to look to Christ ... for we are both made clean by his blood, and also we enter into a new life by the benefit of his death and resurrection.'[18] This is part of the significance of the same phrase used in Acts 19:5.

The use of these New Testament texts by 'oneness Pentecostals' is therefore both irresponsible and unbiblical.

Salvation

Baptism by immersion in the name of Jesus alone is essential for salvation. Some groups, like the United Pentecostal Church, also believe that 'speaking in tongues' is necessary for salvation.

While baptism is commanded by Christ and richly significant, it is not essential to salvation (see Luke 23:42-43; John 3:14-17; Acts 16:31; Ephesians 2: 8-9).

Concerning speaking in tongues, we are not told anywhere in the New Testament that all Christians spoke in tongues; rather Paul's question in 1 Corinthians 12:30 shows clearly that this was not the case.

Section 2
Some established cults

9. Christadelphians

10. Christian Science, or Church of Christ, Scientist

11. Mormons

12. Jehovah's Witnesses

13. Worldwide Church of God

14. Rastafarians

9.
Christadelphians

Although originating in America during the mid-nineteenth century, this cult was founded by an Englishman, John Thomas. He was born in London on 12 April 1805 and his father was a Congregational Church minister. In 1832, after qualifying as a medical doctor at St Thomas's Hospital, London and obtaining the MRCS degree there, he sailed for America, intending to develop his medical career. His plans, however, were abruptly changed when, after surviving a shipwreck *en route* to America, he felt he should give his entire life to the service of God.

After his arrival in America he practised medicine for a few years, but he immediately became a zealous student of the Bible and he was particularly fascinated by the book of Revelation and some of the more difficult parts of the prophetical books. His views became increasingly more unorthodox and intolerant; he insisted, for example, that salvation depended on the acceptance of his views. In order to publicize his views more widely, he published *The apostolic advocate* and, ten years later, *The herald of the future age*.

1848 was another significant milestone in his life. Not only was he awarded an American medical degree (MD), but he visited England in order to propagate his teachings. For two years he travelled and preached extensively throughout England and wrote his famous *Elpis Israel — an exposition of the Kingdom of God*. When he returned to England a second time in 1862 he discovered numerous small groups called Thomasites meeting in various towns and cities. The more flourishing groups were in Birmingham, Nottingham, Aberdeen, Halifax and Edinburgh. Initially the groups met in members' houses for the breaking of bread but soon the Birmingham group emerged as the most influential group, providing guidance and speakers for the group network. On this second visit, Dr Thomas wrote a large commentary on the book of Revelation, entitled *Eureka*, in which he claimed to have solved all the problems of interpretation!

The movement expands

The growth of the movement was slow. In 1865, for example, the number of adherents throughout the world only numbered about 1,000 and most of these were from Britain. There was a gradual increase in membership and by 1868 there were four assemblies in Wales, twelve in Scotland and twenty-five in England. It was Robert Roberts, an early convert of Thomas, who led the British branch of the movement and he published a magazine entitled *The ambassador of the coming age*, but when Thomas made his last visit to England in 1869 he renamed it *The Christadelphian* (meaning 'Christian brothers'). On Thomas's death on 5 March 1871, Roberts assumed the leadership of the cult. One of the basic textbooks of the cult is *Christendom astray* and it was written by Roberts with the purpose of criticizing orthodox Christian doctrines and vindicating Christadelphian views.

Christadelphianism remains one of the smaller cults and continues to receive more support from Britain than from any other country. They do not believe in ordained ministers and the administration of the local *ecclesia* is the responsibility of all male members. Christadelphians had an estimated United Kingdom membership of 20,000 in 1987, compared with 22,000 in 1980 and 25,500 in 1975.

Rejection of basic biblical doctrines

While there are significant differences, nevertheless their doctrines are similar to those held by Jehovah's Witnesses. Both groups, for example, reject the Trinity, the deity of Christ, the personality and deity of the Holy Spirit, and justification by faith; both teach the annihilation of unbelievers.

One thing is certain. Despite their study of the Bible, they have rejected many basic Bible doctrines. Although they are 'always learning', yet they are 'never able to come to the knowledge of the truth... these men also oppose the truth...' and are 'men of depraved mind, rejected as regards the faith' (2 Timothy 3:7-8). During 1987 there were encouraging reports of some Christadelphians being converted and leaving this cult.

What Christadelphians teach	*What the Bible teaches*
God	
The orthodox Bible teaching concerning God is rejected. There is no Trinity of persons in the Godhead and Christadelphians accuse Christians of believing in three gods. (This is a failure to understand the Trinity for we do not teach there are three gods but rather that the one God eternally exists in three persons.) They regard the Son and Spirit as creations of the Father and believe only God the Father existed before the man Christ Jesus.	'Go therefore and make disciples of all the nations, baptizing them in the name of the Father and the Son and the Holy Spirit' (Matthew 28:19). See also Isaiah 63:8-10 and 'Before Abraham was born, I am' (John 8:58; cf. John 17:5). For a fuller treatment of this subject see chapter 35.
Bible	
They profess to believe the whole Bible as the Word of God and sometimes refer to themselves as 'Berean Bible Students'. Great emphasis is placed upon the study of the Old and New Testaments but their diligence and zeal in Bible study have led them into error. There are several reasons for this,	'And you do not have his word abiding in you, for you do not believe him whom he sent. You search the Scriptures, because you think that in them you have eternal life; and it is these that bear witness of me; and you are unwilling to come to me, that you may have life' (John 5:38-40).

such as the emphasis on certain scriptures to the neglect of others, wrong principles of interpretation, but particularly the absence of the Holy Spirit's illumination of the Word.

'For to us God revealed them through the Spirit' (1 Corinthians 2:10; cf. Psalm 119:18).

Person of Christ

For Christadelphians, Jesus was not the eternal Son of God, nor did he exist at all prior to his birth by Mary. Jesus was not perfect nor was his birth miraculous. He is regarded as a mere expression of God the Father in human form and is not to be worshipped on the same level as the Father.

'No man has seen God at any time; the only begotten God, who is in the bosom of the Father, he has explained him' (John 1:18).
'All may honour the Son, even as they honour the Father. He who does not honour the Son does not honour the Father who sent him' (John 5:23).
'Before Abraham was born, I am' (John 8:58)'
'...who committed no sin, nor was any deceit found in his mouth' (1 Peter 2:22).

Work of Christ

There was no atoning purpose nor value in the Lord's death. He died to express his Father's love and *not* to remove the wrath of God from sinners.

'But he was pierced through for our transgressions, he was crushed for our iniquities...' (Isaiah 53:5).
'The Son of Man did not come to be served, but to serve, and to give his life a ransom for many' (Matthew 20:28).
'Much more then, having now been justified by his blood, we shall be saved from the wrath of God through him' (Romans 5:9).

Devil

No personal devil exists. The devil is explained away as the sin which is committed in the flesh and the name 'devil' is simply a personification of sin.

'Resist the devil and he will flee from you' (James 4:7).
'He [the devil] was a murderer from the beginning, and does not stand in the truth, because there is no truth in him. Whenever he speaks a lie, he speaks from his own

Holy Spirit

They deny that the Holy Spirit is a divine person but regard him as some kind of invisible power or energy proceeding from the Father. Believers are not indwelt by the Spirit.

nature; for he is a liar, and the father of lies' (John 8:44; cf. Job 1:6-12; Matthew 4: 1-11; Acts 5:3; Revelation 20:1-3).

'And I will ask the Father, and he will give you another Helper, that he may be with you for ever; that is the Spirit of truth, whom the world cannot receive, because it does not behold him or know him, but you know him because he abides with you, and will be in you' (John 14:16-17).

'But the Helper, the Holy Spirit, whom the Father will send in my name, he will teach you all things...' (John 14:26; cf. John 15:26; 16:7-13).

'But one and the same Spirit works all these things, distributing to each one individually just as he wills' (1 Corinthians 12:11).

Salvation

They deny the biblical doctrine of salvation by grace. In their view salvation is achieved by baptism (by immersion, administered by their own leaders) plus obedience to Christ's commandments. There is no guarantee of salvation but after baptism the person begins a life of probation and his ultimate destiny depends on his character and performance after baptism.

'For God so loved the world, that he gave his only begotten Son, that whoever believes in him should not perish, but have eternal life (John 3:16).

'For by grace you have been saved through faith; and that not of yourselves, it is the gift of God; not as a result of works, that no one should boast' (Ephesians 2:8-9).

Future State

Extinction at death, not eternal punishment in hell, is God's punishment of sinners, while believers have their sphere of glory on earth alone (not heaven) after the general

Hell. 'But rather fear him who is able to destroy both soul and body in hell' (Matthew 10:28; cf. Luke 12:4-5).

'And these will go away into

resurrection. Between physical death and the resurrection of the dead, even believers are in an unconscious state but their eternal life is experienced as a result of the resurrection and then enjoyed on the earth.

All the Jews will return to Canaan. The ancient kingdom of Israel will be restored and Jesus will return and reign on the earth. After a new temple is built then the offering of sacrifices will be resumed. Christadelphians will be raised and given immortality while the wicked will be annihilated.

eternal punishment' (Matthew 25:46; cf. Luke 16:19-31; Revelation 20:10-15).
Heaven. 'Today you shall be with me in Paradise' (Luke 23:43).

'...to be absent from the body and to be at home with the Lord' (2 Corinthians 5:8; cf. Philippians 1:21-23).

'Then we who are alive and remain shall be caught up together with them in the clouds to meet the Lord in the air, and thus we shall always be with the Lord' (1 Thessalonians 4:17).

The priesthood as well as the sacrifices and temple of the Old Testament have been fulfilled in Christ and will never be reinstated (Hebrews 9:12; 10:12). In the New Covenant all believers are priests and enjoy direct access to God (1 Peter 2:9; Revelation 1:6).

10.
Christian Science or Church of Christ, Scientist

The founder of this cult, Mary Baker-Eddy, reacted strongly against the Calvinistic views of her parents and when she joined the local Congregational Church at Tilton at the age of twelve she had already rejected doctrines like predestination. Born in 1821 at Bow in New Hampshire, U.S.A., the youngest of seven children, Mary suffered constant ill-health and her life was a most unhappy one. A spinal complaint, unpleasant stays with friends and relatives, three marriages and her deliberate estrangement from her only child, born in 1845, just weeks after her first husband died — all caused her considerable pain and anguish. Her second marriage in 1853 to a dentist, Daniel Patterson, was an extremely unhappy one and she eventually obtained a divorce on the ground of desertion in 1873. Before this divorce two events of major significance occurred in the life of Mrs Baker-Eddy.

First of all, she was 'healed' in a Portland Hotel by Phineas Quimby who, convinced of the power of auto-suggestion, mesmerized her. On waking up, she claims that all sickness had left her body. Despite official 'Christian Science' denials, the movement's founder became an ardent admirer of Quimby's abilities and views although there was no religious base to his approach. In fact, a great deal of 'Christian Science' teaching originates with Phineas Quimby.

The second major event in this period occurred in 1866 when Mrs Baker-Eddy fell on a frozen pavement. There are many conflicting reports as to the extent of her injury, but she claimed that the principles of healing were revealed exclusively to her at this time and, applying them to herself, she was immediately healed. After this she began to publicize her views, giving both private and more public instruction. For a course of twelve lessons, for example, she charged $300. This high fee certainly helped to make her rich and her estate was worth three million dollars when she died in 1913. Despite her view that suffering and death were mere illusions of the mind, when she was in great pain herself she turned at times to dentists and physicians for relief. She received many pain-killing morphine injections and wore glasses as well as dentures. Calvin Frye, the long-serving personal secretary of Mrs Baker-Eddy, acknowledges this as one example of the inconsistency between her teaching and her actual practice.

In 1875 she published the first edition of her *Science and Health* with the *Key to the Scriptures* (this work was revised several times until 1907) and with a small group of friends the 'Christian Scientists' were formed. Two years later she married a former student of hers, Asa Gilbert Eddy, but he died five years later in 1882.

Mrs Baker-Eddy claimed to be the only agent of revelation, the custodian of the key to the Scriptures and the woman of Revelation 12, being 'the God-appointed messenger to this age'.

When we compare the teaching of this sect with that of the Bible, it is obvious that it is neither Christian nor scientific.

The movement today

According to Constant Jacquet, editor of the National Council of Churches' (USA) *Yearbook,* membership of this movement dipped from the peak of 300,000 in the mid-1930s to about 200,000 in 1979. Officials in the Christian Science headquarters in Boston concede that in the last ten years 257 branch churches and ninety-seven reading rooms have been closed and that their famous newspaper, *Christian Science Monitor,* is losing between five and six million dollars annually, with a fall in circulation from 300,000 to 190,000. To add to the seriousness of their plight, some ex-members have grouped themselves together as United Christian Scientists and insistent demands are being made that the finances and activities of Christian Science at its $82,000,000 offices should be investigated.

In the United Kingdom, there was a 2.1% fall in membership in 1985 (13,500) compared with a total of 15,000 in 1980. In 1985 Northern Ireland only had 170 members, Wales 285, Scotland 625 and England 12,420. Membership fell further by 1987 to 12,000 and it is estimated that this figure will almost be halved by A.D. 2,000.

Amongst even some faithful adherents there is a preference for competent medical treatment, even though official policy condemns the use of drugs such as aspirins and antibiotics, although it allows immunizations, obstetric care at childbirth and treatment of broken bones. To replace medical treatment they advocate 'prayer and mental renewal' and, for a charge varying from two to fifteen dollars a day, they provide their own 'practitioner' to encourage people to think properly and avoid reliance on medics. The news item entitled 'Christian Science may be sick, dying'[1] in a responsible American Christian monthly may not be very wide of the mark.

What Christian Science teaches	*What the Bible teaches*
God	
God is substance and the only intelligence in the universe. He is the All-in-all and there is no reality or existence outside of him. God is also divine Mind and mind is all that exists.	'Behold, heaven and the highest heaven cannot contain thee' (1 Kings 8:27).
This teaching is pantheism, namely, the theory that the universe is God and God is the universe. The Trinity is also rejected.	'Before the mountains were born, or thou didst give birth to the earth and the world, even from everlasting to everlasting, thou art God' (Psalm 90:2).
	'Even they will perish, but thou dost endure; and all of them will wear out like a garment; like clothing thou wilt change them, and they will be changed. But thou art the same, and thy years will not come to an end' (Psalm 102:25-27).

Bible

While they claim to take the inspired word of the Bible as their 'sufficient guide to eternal life', in practice they only accept the Bible as interpreted by Mrs Eddy, and her *Science and health, with key to the Scriptures* is their ultimate authority. Furthermore, the Bible is thought to have errors, whereas the writings of Mrs Eddy are 'unerring and divine'.

'For I trust in thy word' (Psalm 119:42).

'Thy word is very pure... Of old I have known from thy testimonies, that thou hast founded them for ever' (Psalm 119:140, 152).

'To the law and to the testimony: if they speak not according to this word, it is because there is no light in them' (Isaiah 8:20, AV).

'Scripture cannot be broken' (John 10:35).

Providence

God, having no existence apart from the universe, cannot plan or decree events or govern the world.

As neither God nor bread exist independently of each other, they deny the validity, for example, of the petition, 'Give us this day our daily bread.' Using her 'key' to reinterpret the petition, Mrs Eddy explains it as 'Give us grace for today; feed our familiar affections.'

'I have rejected him as king over Israel... I will send you to Jesse... I have selected a king for myself among his sons' (1 Samuel 16:1).

'The king's heart is like channels of water in the hand of the Lord; he turns it wherever he wishes' (Proverbs 21:1).

'He does according to his will in the host of heaven and among the inhabitants of the earth' (Daniel 4:35).

'According to his purpose who works all things after the counsel of his will' (Ephesians 1:11).

Man

To say, 'Matter does not exist' means in relation to man that he has no body. Belief in bodies is an error of the mortal mind. Man is spiritual and the reflection of God.

In denying man's fall into sin they also teach that evil, sin and matter are unreal, so when we think we sin or see others sin we are being deluded by our mortal minds. If, then, man has no separate mind from God, it means that man is a

'Then the Lord God formed man of dust from the ground, and breathed into his nostrils the breath of life; and man became a living being' (Genesis 2:7).

'Then the dust will return to the earth as it was, and the spirit will return to God who gave it' (Ecclesiastes 12:7).

'Therefore, just as through one man sin entered into the world, and death through sin, and so death

part of God and the distinction between creature and Creator is rejected.

Person of Christ

A distinction is made between *Jesus*, a merely human man who lived in Palestine nearly 2,000 years ago, and *Christ*, which is the name for the divine idea. Christ, then, is not a person, but only an idea, and this idea continues in the teaching of Christian Science!

Death of Christ

Jesus did not actually suffer or die. His death was only apparent and during his three days in the tomb he was alive. Thus his physical resurrection and ascension to heaven are denied.

Regarding sin as unreal, they view as abhorrent the teaching that the Lord atoned for our sin by the offering up of himself as our substitute on the cross. Rather he came to demonstrate a divine idea and his crucifixion demonstrated goodness and affection. His work was essentially that of providing us with an example to follow.

spread to all men, because all sinned...' (Romans 5:12).

'If we say that we have no sin, we are deceiving ourselves, and the truth is not in us' (1 John 1:8).

Jesus (Saviour) is the personal name of the Lord, whereas Christ ('anointed one') is his official name as Messiah.

'Behold, a virgin will be with child and bear a son, and she will call his name Immanuel, which translated means "God with us"' (Isaiah 7:14; Matthew 1:23).

'And the Word became flesh, and dwelt among us' (John 1:14).

'For I did not speak on my own initiative, but the Father himself who sent me has given me commandment, what to say, and what to speak' (John 12:49).

'For in him all the fulness of deity dwells in bodily form' (Colossians 2:9).

'O foolish men and slow of heart to believe in all that the prophets have spoken! Was it not necessary for the Christ to suffer these things and to enter into his glory?' (Luke 24:25-26).

'Christ died for our sins according to the Scriptures, and ... he was buried, and ... he was raised on the third day' (1 Corinthians 15:3-4).

'Christ Jesus came into the world to save sinners' (1 Timothy 1:15).

'Christ also suffered for you... and while being reviled, he did not revile in return... he himself bore

our sins in his body on the cross...'
(1 Peter 2:21, 23-24).

Salvation

Man is not a sinner, so salvation from sin is unnecessary. But Mrs Eddy and her followers do speak of 'salvation', namely, salvation from false beliefs, so that a person is saved when he stops believing there is such a thing as sin. The death of Christ is entirely unrelated to salvation.

'God was in Christ reconciling the world to himself, not counting their trespasses against them' (2 Corinthians 5:19).

'For there is one God, and one mediator also between God and men, the man Christ Jesus, who gave himself as a ransom for all' (1 Timothy 2:5-6).

Death

Death is an illusion. There is an after-life when the mind continues in a conscious state of existence which is a time of probation for everyone. Here spiritual 'growth' is necessary for all because even after death some errors and sins remain in our consciousness.

'Thou dost turn men back into dust, and dost say, "Return, O children of men."... As for the days of our life, they contain seventy years... for soon it is gone and we fly away' (Psalm 90:3, 10).

'It is appointed for men to die once, and after this comes judgement' (Hebrews 9:27).

Holy Spirit

Christian Science is regarded as the Holy Spirit. To receive the Holy Spirit means to have a greater understanding of Christian Science.

'And the Spirit said to Philip, "Go up and join this chariot"' (Acts 8:29; cf. 16:7).

'But if the Spirit of him who raised Jesus from the dead dwells in you, he who raised Christ Jesus from the dead will also give life to your mortal bodies through his Spirit, who indwells you' (Romans 8:11).

Hell and heaven

Perfection is the goal for those who progress after death, but if people remain in error they will be 'self-annihilated'. Apart from the fire of a guilty conscience, there is no hell; heaven is not a place but a divine state of mind.

'But rather fear him who is able to destroy both soul and body in hell' (Matthew 10:28).

'And these will go away into eternal punishment, but the righteous into eternal life' (Matthew 25:46).

Devil

It is a great mistake to believe in good and evil spirits. There is no personal devil.

Second coming of Christ

The personal return of the Lord Jesus is interpreted by them as the birth and development of Christian Science. Mrs Eddy refers to a Bible expositor who, on the basis of prophecies in Daniel, fixed 1866-67 for the return of Christ, which 'happened' to be the years when she discovered Christian Science! Our Lord's personal and visible return in glory, the general physical resurrection of the body and final judgement are all denied by this cult.

'In my Father's house are many dwelling-places; if it were not so, I would have told you; for I go to prepare a place for you' (John 14:2).

'Satan then entered into him' (John 13:27).
'Your adversary, the devil, prowls about like a roaring lion, seeking someone to devour. But resist him, firm in your faith' (1 Peter 5:8-9).

'This Jesus, who has been taken up from you into heaven, will come in just the same way as you have watched him go into heaven' (Acts 1:11).
'Why is it considered incredible among you people if God does raise the dead?' (Acts 26:8).

11.
Mormons

In terms of membership and organization, Mormonism is the strongest cult in the Western world. Employing more than 1200 young men as missionaries in more than fifty-one countries, it is strongly missionary-orientated and spares no effort or expense in recruiting new members. Approximately 180,000 converts per year, it is claimed, are won by the work of its missionaries alone, who are clean and neatly dressed, polite in their approach and usually exemplary in morals. Compared with figures for 1950, the membership of the movement rose by 30% in 1960 to 1,650,000 and now the world-wide membership is estimated at over four million.

The work of missionaries is supported by extensive and attractive literature. In key areas expensive and elaborate temples are built as centres of recreation, culture and religion. The Mormon church takes tithing seriously, provides for its poorer members, thus rendering unemployment or social security payments by the government unnecessary, and encourages a responsible involvement in education, family and community life.

Their headquarters are in the state of Utah in the United States. It was Brigham Young, successor to their founder, who supervised the famous trek of Mormons to Utah in 1847, where they built Salt Lake City. They were not allowed recognition as a state within the U.S.A. until 1896 when they somewhat grudgingly agreed to ban polygamy among their members.

How it all began

The movement originally began with Joseph Smith (1805-1844) who, like other cult leaders, was psychic and the recipient of private 'revelations'. As a child he was confused by the numerous versions of the Christian church to be found in his home area of Sharon, Vermont. Although Wesleyan Methodism was the denomination he considered joining, he received a vision in 1820 in which, he claims, God the Father and the Son appeared, forbidding him to join any Christian denomination. The reason given him was God's displeasure with their beliefs. As a result of the vision the teenager felt God called him to be his special prophet to the world. Three years later he claimed an even more impressive vision in which he said an angel named Moroni disclosed to him the fact that details of the early history of America and a fuller revelation of the gospel had been written down in ancient Egyptian hieroglyphics on gold plates and hidden under the hill Cumorah. Although he wanted to see these plates immediately, he was told in another alleged appearance by Moroni that he would have to wait four years before retrieving them. Exactly four years later he returned to the place, obtained the plates and 'spectacles', or rather two crystals, by means of which he says he was able to translate the ancient hieroglyphics. Scholars deny the existence of this ancient language and the supposed translation includes several errors in historical detail. The whole story was a great fraud. A Presbyterian preacher, Solomon Spaulding, wrote an imaginary history of the primitive Americans called *The Manuscript Found*. No one wanted to publish it, so it was left at a printer's shop in Pittsburgh. The printer, by the name of Patterson, died within two years and a man called Rigdon,who was a frequent caller at the shop, found the manuscript and used it as a basis for writing *The Book of Mormon* with the help of Smith and Porley Pratt. Conveniently for the Mormons, the alleged gold plates disappeared and before the publication of the translation, called *The Book of Mormon*, Smith and another five friends had established the Church of Jesus Christ of Latter-Day Saints at Fayette in New York State.

Growth and dispersion

Although this movement grew, it was also exposed to considerable ridicule and persecution, and Smith was compelled to move to a number of different places, including Kirland in Ohio, Missouri and then Illinois, where in 1844 he was shot dead after being arrested and imprisoned for alleged immorality and dishonesty. Smith left the handsome sum of £400,000 and eight of his seventeen wives had died before him. He had as many as fifty-six children. Almost overnight he became a hero and under his successor, Brigham Young, who had even more wives than Smith (twenty-five to be precise!) the movement flourished. Young eventually took the Mormons to Utah, arriving there in 1847, but not all of Smith's followers were happy with Brigham Young's credentials. One group, the 'Josephites', insisted that Smith's successor should be his son, so they withdrew, renaming themselves the Re-organized Church of Jesus Christ of Latter-Day Saints, and established their headquarters in Missouri. At least five groups splintered off from the main stream of Mormons, and most of them are still active today. The most powerful, however, is the party of those who followed Young, and it is their teaching that we will consider.

The Book of Mormon

Early in October 1982, the First Presidency of the Mormon Church (its highest governing body, with a council of twelve apostles) unanimously voted to rename their *Book of Mormon* as the *Book of Mormon: Another Testament of Jesus Christ*. A spokesman explained the reason for the expanded title: 'We simply want to educate those who think the Mormon church is not Christian, to clarify that Jesus is a central figure in the *Book of Mormon*.'

Although the Mormon church was founded on the basis of the *Book of Mormon*, there exists a wide discrepancy between the book's teaching and that of contemporary Mormons; it seems that few Mormon leaders or scholars today believe in its teaching. Three examples can be given to verify this fact.

First of all, the *Book of Mormon* teaches that there is only one

God and he is an unchangeable spirit (Alma 11:26-31; II Nephi 31:21; Mormon 9:9-11, 19; Moroni 7:22; 8:18), but contemporary Mormons teach that three separate gods rule our planet and that all married Mormon males will themselves become gods! Secondly, their book insists upon the necessity of the new birth (Mosiah 27:24-28; Alma 5:14), but today the necessity of water baptism is stressed as a precondition of salvation and the new birth. Thirdly, the *Book of Mormon* teaches eternal glory or punishment, with no second chance of salvation beyond the grave (III Nephi 27:11-17; Mosiah 3:24-27; II Nephi 28:22,23; Alma 34:32-35), but we are now told by Mormons that almost everyone will enjoy some degree of glory and that proxy baptisms can release those people who go to the 'prison house' after death. Despite this inconsistency, Mormons try hard to commend their book as an authentic and final revelation from God.

However, two recent studies have again brought the *Book of Mormon* into disrepute. The family of the Mormon General Authority and apologist Brigham Roberts allowed scholars to examine two manuscripts which he wrote in 1922 and in which he argues cogently that Joseph Smith was probably the author of the *Book of Mormon*. In addition to this, there is a detailed study of the *Book of Mormon* by an ex-Mormon scholar, H. Michael Marquardt, in which he instances 200 quotations in the book from the Authorized Version of the Bible! Claims that their book is 'the most correct book on earth' and that 'An angel made fifteen trips from the throne of God to see that this *Book of Mormon* was properly translated and printed' are not confirmed by the real facts. Apart from the more compelling evidence it is true, for example, that nearly 4,000 changes have been made in their book since it was first published, that is, in the space of little more than 150 years! The Bible alone is the Word of God and as such it is trustworthy and powerful. Read the Bible and believe its teaching!

What Mormons teach	*What the Bible teaches*
God	
Mormons believe God is Adam. God was once a mortal like ourselves but progressed to become an exalted being. There are many gods	'The Lord, he is God; there is no other besides him' (Deuteronomy 4:35). 'God is spirit; and those who

and the Trinity for them comprises three separate individuals who are *physically* distinct from each other.

worship him must worship in spirit and truth' (John 4:24).

'There is one God, and one mediator also between God and men, the man Christ Jesus' (1 Timothy 2:5).

'I, the Lord do not change' (Malachi 3:6).

Bible

They believe that the *Book of Mormon* and the Bible have equal authority as the Word of God. They misuse Ezekiel 37:15-17, suggesting that 'the two sticks' referred to here are the Bible and the *Book of Mormon*. According to the Mormons, these become one stick, that is, God's Word. But verses 18-22 explain clearly that the sticks represent the tribes of Israel and Judah who together form one people.

Revelation for them is continuous and 'modern', for private revelations were given to Joseph Smith. In practice they neglect the Bible in preference for Smith's writings.

'All Scripture is inspired by God and profitable for teaching, for reproof, for correction, for training in righteousness; that the man of God may be adequate for every good work' (2 Timothy 3:16-17).

'But know this first of all, that no prophecy of Scripture is a matter of one's own interpretation, for no prophecy was ever made by an act of human will, but men moved by the Holy Spirit spoke from God' (2 Peter 1:20-21; cf. Revelation 22:18-19).

Person of Christ

Mormons claim that Christ was a god like the humans and a pre-existent spirit; in addition he was the brother of the devil and the son of Adam. He was not unique therefore in his nature or life, nor was his birth supernatural. They regard Christ as a polygamist who married both Mary and Martha at Cana of Galilee. Unmarried people and couples whose marriages are not 'sealed' in a Mormon temple can only become angels after death.

'In the beginning was the Word, and the Word was with God, and the Word was God' (John 1:1).

'No man has seen God at any time; the only begotten God, who is in the bosom of the Father, he has explained him' (John 1:18).

'And the Word became flesh, and dwelt among us, and we beheld his glory, glory as of the only begotten from the Father, full of grace and truth' (John 1:14).

'When his mother Mary had

Those 'sealed' for eternity become 'gods' — hence the importance for Mormons of Christ's being married.

been betrothed to Joseph, before they came together she was found to be with child by the Holy Spirit' (Matthew 1:18).

'Behold, a virgin will be with child and bear a son, and she will call his name Immanuel' (Isaiah 7:14).

Death of Christ

Since they regard man as being basically good and God as no more than an exalted man, there is no great problem in attaining salvation. There was no need for Christ to satisfy the justice of God on our behalf and his death dealt only with the sins of Adam and has no power to save us. Obedience to laws and Mormon ceremonies such as baptism is essential to salvation.

'Without shedding of blood there is no forgiveness' (Hebrews 9:22).

'Because by the works of the Law no flesh will be justified in his sight... But now apart from the Law the righteousness of God has been manifested... even the righteousness of God through faith in Jesus Christ for all those who believe... being justified as a gift by his grace through the redemption which is in Christ Jesus; whom God displayed publicly as a propitiation in his blood through faith' (Romans 3:20-25).

'Behold, the Lamb of God who takes away the sin of the world!' (John 1:29).

'He himself bore our sins in his body on the cross ' (1 Peter 2:24).

'But he, having offered one sacrifice for sins for all time, sat down at the right hand of God' (Hebrews 10:12).

Mormons claim to have both the Aaronic and Melchizedekan priesthood.

Hebrews 7:12 shows the Aaronic priesthood is fulfilled by Christ; see also verse 24 which states that the Melchizedekan priesthood belongs to Christ ('unchangeable' in the AV in Greek means 'untransferable').

Resurrection of Christ

Although it preceded others, his resurrection was in no way unique

'If Christ has not been raised, your faith is worthless; you are still in

and was completely unrelated to our justification. Every man who is eventually made perfect and raised from the dead will become like the Father and Son in *every respect*. Their claim that the risen Lord visited America in A.D. 34 has no historical support and is at variance with Acts 1:8-11 and other New Testament narratives.

Holy Spirit

Mormons regard the Holy Spirit in impersonal terms, frequently referring to him as 'it', and describe him as a substance composed of individual, material particles. They deny his indispensable work in applying redemption to sinners and reject the indwelling of the Holy Spirit in believers. Only the Mormon priesthood can confer the Holy Spirit on people through the laying on of hands.

your sins' (1 Corinthians 15:17).

'He who was delivered up because of our transgressions, and was raised because of our justification' (Romans 4:25).

'I am the resurrection and the life; he who believes in me shall live even if he dies, and everyone who lives and believes in me shall never die' (John 11:25-26).

'When the Helper comes, whom I will send to you from the Father, that is the Spirit of truth, who proceeds from the Father, he will bear witness of me' (John 15:26; cf. 14:26, 16:8, 13).

'...chosen according to the foreknowledge of God the Father, by the sanctifying work of the Spirit, that you may obey Jesus Christ and be sprinkled with his blood' (1 Peter 1:1-2).

'Do you not know that you are a temple of God, and that the Spirit of God dwells in you' (1 Corinthians 3:16).

'His Spirit who indwells you' (Romans 8:11).

'I will pour forth of my Spirit upon all mankind' (Acts 2:17).

'Having been exalted to the right hand of God, and having received from the Father the promise of the Holy Spirit, he has poured forth this which you both see and hear' (Acts 2:33).

Man and sin

Misusing the words of Satan to Eve, 'You will be like God', Mormons promise the faithful that

'The Lord God formed man of dust from the ground, and breathed into his nostrils the breath of life; and

they will be gods. Man is therefore a potential god and God was once a man like us (Adam). All humans and spirits (including Christ and Satan) existed as spirit beings from eternity but at their physical birth these spirit beings are given bodies and their life on earth is a time of probation which determines the status and destiny of the individual after the resurrection.

According to the Mormons, the sin of Adam proved to be a great blessing to mankind for, apart from it, he would not have known good and evil nor had a posterity. Man is not a sinner by nature.

Salvation

They reject the biblical doctrine of justification by faith and advocate faith *plus* works and baptism for salvation. A good life, the keeping of rules and baptism by immersion administered only by Mormons guarantee salvation.

From the age of eight upwards, baptism can wash away sins but without total immersion there is no pardon. On the basis of 1 Corinthians 15:29, they encourage people to be baptized by proxy on behalf of dead relatives and friends.

man became a living being' (Genesis 2:7; Romans 5:12-21).

'For all have sinned and fall short of the glory of God' (Romans 3:23).

'The heart is more deceitful than all else and is desperately sick' (Jeremiah 17:9; cf. 1 John 1:8, 10).

'For by grace you have been saved through faith; and that not of yourselves, it is the gift of God; not as a result of works, that no one should boast' (Ephesians 2:8-9).

'Justified as a gift by his grace through the redemption which is in Christ Jesus' (Romans 3:24).

'But to the one who does not work, but believes in him who justifies the ungodly, his faith is reckoned as righteousness' (Romans 4:5).

'He saved us, not on the basis of deeds which we have done in righteousness, but according to his mercy, by the washing of regeneration and renewing by the Holy Spirit' (Titus 3:5).

'This is the work of God, that you believe in him whom he has sent' (John 6:29; Acts 16:31).

Future state

People have a chance to be saved even after death; that is the teaching of Mormonism. Baptism by proxy for all the dead of past ages who have not had the opportunity of responding to the Mormon gospel is obligatory upon all members.

They have a materialistic view of the 'celestial' glory which awaits their people; non-Mormons will be damned.

'It is appointed for men to die once, and after this comes judgement' (Hebrews 9:27).

'Between us and you there is a great chasm fixed, in order that those who wish to come over from here to you may not be able, and that none may cross over from there to us' (Luke 16:26).

'If anyone's name was not found written in the book of life, he was thrown into the lake of fire' (Revelation 20:15).

'...when the Lord Jesus shall be revealed from heaven with his mighty angels in flaming fire, dealing out retribution to those who do not know God and to those who do not obey the gospel of our Lord Jesus. And these will pay the penalty of eternal destruction, away from the presence of the Lord and from the glory of his power...' (2 Thessalonians 1:7-9).

Mormons misuse 1 Corinthians 15:29 in support of their baptism by proxy for the dead. While there are as many as a hundred different interpretations of this verse, we should note the following points about the verse:

1. Paul is discussing in this chapter the resurrection of the dead and not baptism.

2. The verse does *not* say that baptism for the dead was practised by the Corinthian church nor acknowledged by them as a Christian rite.

3. Nevertheless it was practised in their area (although not in their church) so that Paul can appeal to this practice as something they had heard about.

4. I favour the following interpretation: Paul, intent on arguing and developing the doctrine of the general resurrection of the dead, is prepared here even to appeal to this pagan practice in the Corinth

area insomuch as it assumes the resurrection of the dead. In no way does Paul advocate baptism by proxy for the dead.

5. One important rule in interpreting the Bible is that we should interpret the obscure by the clear teaching of other passages. We must not build fanciful doctrines on obscure verses in the Bible.

12.
Jehovah's Witnesses

Who are the Jehovah's Witnesses? How did they originate? What do they believe? How should we respond to them? These are the questions we will answer as we consider one of the most active and zealous cults operating in Britain today.

Who are they?

It was 'Judge' Rutherford who recommended the adoption of the name 'Jehovah's Witnesses' at an international conference of his followers in Columbus, Ohio, in July 1931. Previously, they had used at least four different names by which to identify themselves. They were known, first of all, as 'Russellites' because of their original leader, Charles Taze Russell (1870-1916). After Russell's death the group was known as Millenial Dawn but this name was quickly changed to the International Bible Students' Association and then to the Watch Tower Bible and Tract Society. Their present name, 'Jehovah's Witnesses', alludes to the words of Scripture in Isaiah 43:10: 'You are my witnesses, declares Jehovah.'

Although they claim to teach the Bible, their views are not at all biblical, for they deny or alter all the major Bible doctrines, such as the Trinity, the deity of Christ, the personality of the Holy Spirit, the new birth, justification by faith, the sufficiency of the Saviour's atoning sacrifice, the bodily resurrection of the Lord and his visible, glorious return. Clearly, then, they are the devil's witnesses rather than Jehovah's witnesses.

How did they originate?

Despite the absurd claim that the cult originated with Abel in Genesis 4 and developed eventually from Jesus through Paul to the heretic Arius and then on from Luther to Russell, it really started with Charles Taze Russell, whose parents were Calvinists and members of a Congregational Church in Pittsburgh, Pennsylvania. Russell himself, born in 1852, accepted unquestioningly the beliefs of his parents until, at the age of sixteen, he tried to explain to a friend the doctrine of eternal punishment. On hearing about this truth, the friend proceeded to ridicule Russell for believing such an 'unreasonable' doctrine. This incident had disastrous consequences, for within weeks the young Russell had rejected the orthodox faith and begun to search for a more reasonable and acceptable creed.

Only two years later he received the stimulus and encouragement he wanted. Attending a Seventh-Day Adventist meeting, Russell was delighted to hear the speaker advocating the annihilation of unbelievers at death and scorning the doctrine of hell. Just as intriguing for him was to learn of attempts by the earlier Adventists or Millerites to fix the precise date of the Lord's return: 1844, for example, was the first date proposed by Miller. Russell was happy to join this new cult and he also invited his friends to meet with him regularly for Bible study.

Between 1870-1875 six people, including Russell and his father, met for regular Bible study in Pittsburgh but differences quickly emerged between this group and Adventists. Russell's influence over the local group increased, especially after he began to co-operate with another Adventist, N. H. Barlow of Rochester, New York, in the publishing of the defunct Adventist paper *Herald of the morning*. In 1877 these two men wrote their first book entitled, *Three worlds* or *Plan of redemption*. Within two years Russell had disagreed with his colleague and immediately launched his own magazine, *Zion's watch tower* and *Herald of Christ's presence*. This magazine was a major factor in the establishing of over thirty study groups in the following months and Russell

quickly registered the Zion's Watch Tower Tract Society as a
recognized legal society in 1884. Only in 1956 was this changed to
its present name, Watch Tower Bible and Tract Society. To publicize his views, Russell also wrote a series of books now known as
Studies in the Scriptures and published a weekly sermon which, it
is claimed, during the period 1909-1914 was sent weekly to about
3,000 newspapers in North America and Europe.

Scandals surrounding Russell

Despite his growing fame and the expansion of the work, Russell's
last years were marked by scandal and deceit. He was involved in
several court cases, the most famous being the 'Miracle Wheat'
case when he sued a local daily newspaper — *Brooklyn Daily Eagle*
— for $100,000 for denying that the wheat he sold was either
superior in quality or miraculous. Russell's magazine had claimed
that the wheat was of superior quality and would grow five times
faster than any other kind! Official government tests revealed the
quality of Russell's wheat actually to be inferior to the average type
of wheat sold by other merchants and the newspaper was vindicated. Russell also sued an Ontario Baptist pastor for a libellous
statement in his tract in 1912 denouncing Russell. This court case
is interesting for the fact that during it Russell was exposed more
than once as a liar. When, for example, a lawyer asked whether he
knew the Greek alphabet his positive answer was immediately
tested and he proved unable to read or even identify the letters of the
Greek alphabet. To add to the scandal of these later years, at least
two groups resigned from Russell's movement during his lifetime.
The first was in 1909, when some members criticized their leader
for regarding his own statements as having equal authority with the
Bible or even greater authority. Again, when Mrs Russell sued her
husband for divorce on the ground of 'improper conduct', a number
of people left the society in disgust.

  After his death in October 1916, 'Judge' Rutherford wrote of
him, 'When the history of the Church of Christ is fully written, it
will be found that the place next to St Paul in the gallery of fame as
expounders of the gospel of the great Master will be occupied by
Charles Taze Russell.' Quite obviously the facts disprove rather
than confirm Rutherford's biased view of Russell. More accurate

was the statement by a Baptist pastor in Hamilton, Ontario in 1912 when in a tract entitled *Some facts about the self-styled 'Pastor' Charles T. Russell,* he described Russell's *Studies in the Scriptures* as 'the destructive doctrines of one man, who is neither a scholar nor a theologian'. The Hamilton pastor, the Rev. J. J. Ross, went on to affirm that 'The whole system of Russellism is anti-rational, anti-scientific, anti-biblical, anti-Christian and a deplorable perversion of the Gospel of God's dear Son.' Furthermore, as Ross himself knew, Russell's character was far from exemplary. After eighteen years of marriage, his wife left him in 1897 and sued him for divorce in 1913 on the grounds of his 'conceit, egotism, domination and improper conduct in relation to other women'.

Russell's successors

The man chosen to succeed Russell was Joseph Franklin Rutherford (1917-1942) who had previously functioned as a legal adviser to the group. 'Judge' Rutherford reorganized the work, placed greater emphasis on witnessing and literature distribution, while at the same time amending some of Russell's views. He was a ruthless leader. Those who challenged his authority and disagreed with his interpretation of Scripture were expelled and, consequently, during the early years of his leadership several separatist groups were formed including the Dawn Bible Students' Association and the Laymen's Home Missionary Movement (altogether it is likely that as many as twenty groups have broken away from the Watchtower during its brief history). During his twenty-five-year presidency, Rutherford wrote twenty major books and many articles and pamphlets.

Nathan Homer Knorr was chosen as the third president after Rutherford's death in 1942. His administrative and intellectual gifts were quickly apparent as he remodelled the structure of the society and insisted on a more thorough training of its members. The most significant development during his leadership was the translation of the Bible completed in 1960 and known as the New World Translation of the Holy Scriptures. This translation is most unreliable and some examples of the wrong, deceitful translation of original words and the insertion of words not even found in the original Greek are provided in the following section on doctrine. Hoekema is justified in claiming that this 'is a biased translation in which many of the peculiar teachings of the Watchtower Society are smuggled into the text of the Bible itself'.[1]

The present leader is Frederick Franz, who is in his early nineties, and some of his possible successors are known to disagree with Franz concerning the ban on blood transfusion. These include Milton Henschel and A. D. Schroeder, who were both involved in translating the New World Translation of the Bible.

Disillusionment among former members

Frederick Franz's nephew, Raymond Franz, was excommunicated from the Watchtower Society in 1981 for disagreeing with certain decisions made by the Governing Body of the Watchtower. In 1983 Raymond Franz published his *Crisis of Conscience* in which he details some of the arbitrary, unbiblical decisions made by this Governing Body.[2] Raymond Franz speaks with authority on the matter for he spent nine years as a member of this élite, ruling body.

The problems, of course, confronting some Witnesses are of major importance. For example, should parents follow expert medical opinion and allow their child to have a life-saving organ transplant? Can Witnesses in Malawi comply with the government law that all citizens must have a 'party card'? On this latter question the Governing Body ruled it was wrong for Malawi Witnesses to comply with the law, but it approved the policy of Witnesses in Mexico who regularly bribe officials in order to obtain certification that they are members of the 'reserves' who have served a year of military service!

These and other problems are decided finally by the Governing Body. But Raymond Franz was disillusioned by what he saw and heard within this Governing Body. It raised for him a 'crisis of conscience' as this small group of men attached infallibility to their own human opinions and prejudices. The Lord's words in Matthew 15: 6, 9, insists Franz, are applicable today to the Watchtower's Governing Body: 'Thus you nullify the word of God for the sake of your tradition...their teachings are but rules made by man' (NIV).

At present there are about three million Witnesses throughout the world. There were 97,495 members in the United Kingdom at the end of 1985, 107,767 in 1987, compared with 83,521 members in 1980. In 1987 the cult had 10,400 ministers and 1213 congregations in Britain.

The Watchtower year-books reveal, however, that there are twice as many baptisms as there are active Witnesses, which means a high drop-out rate, and by now there are many more ex-Jehovah's Witnesses than active ones! To meet this situation, there now exists in America an annual National Convention of Ex-Jehovah's Witnesses, which is a useful means of providing members with encouragement and direction. What happens to them after leaving the Watchtower? Some are disillusioned and despair of ever finding the truth. A number have been converted to Christ and have joined Bible-teaching churches (see, for example, the personal testimonies of some in *We left Jehovah's Witnesses*)[3] while others have gone into Judaism or cults like the Mormons, the Worldwide Church of God or one of the Witnesses' breakaway groups like the Dawn Bible Students, etc.

In their National Convention in New Ringold, Pennsylvania, in October 1981 one ex-Jehovah's Witness referred to her previous experience in the cult. 'I hated every minute, every hour of being a Witness. But I thought it was the only way to survive Armageddon and live on paradise earth,' said Toni Jean Meneses of Washington. 'Many times over the years I would have left if someone had only presented the gospel to me.'

Witnessing to the Witnesses

You may feel convicted by this statement but at the same time be unsure as to how you should witness to Jehovah's Witnesses. Well, remember that even Witnesses are in great need of salvation so do not be fooled by their knowledge and use of the Bible. Give a brief, personal testimony as to the way you became a Christian and keep on quoting key verses such as John 3:16; Romans 3:23 and Ephesians 2:8-9. Monopolize the conversation for as long as possible, yet be courteous and loving, for the truth must always be spoken 'in love' (Ephesians 4:15). If your Jehovah's Witness visitors are at all interested or even if you cannot answer their questions, challenge them to have a Bible study with your pastor or other well-taught Christians in the church and suggest a theme or passage for study such as the deity of Christ or the Lord's sacrifice and resurrection. Whatever their response, start praying regularly for them and get down to a more thorough study of the Bible so that the next time you meet them you can use 'the sword of the Spirit' more effectively.

What Jehovah's Witnesses believe	*What the Bible teaches*

Person of Christ

Christ was the created archangel Michael and although he was 'a god' and a mighty one, yet he was not Jehovah.

Despite a virgin birth, Jesus was no more than a perfect, mortal man while on earth.

Two things happened at the baptism of Jesus — he was 'born again' and became 'the Christ' or Messiah.

'For to which of the angels did he ever say, "Thou art my Son..."?...But of the Son he says, "Thy throne, O God, is for ever and ever..."' (Hebrews 1:5, 8).

Also in Hebrews 1:10-12 the description of Jehovah in Psalm 102:25-27 is applied to Christ.

In his human nature, Jesus was filled with the Spirit (Matthew 3:16; Luke 4:1) *not* born again at his baptism. He was 'the Christ' at his birth according to Luke 2:11.

'In the beginning was the Word, and the Word was with God, and the Word was God' (John 1:1).

'I and the Father are one' (John 10:30; cf. vv. 31, 33).

'He who has seen me has seen the Father' (John 14:9).

'For in him all the fulness of Deity dwells in bodily form' (Colossians 2:9)

See also the section below on creation and chapter 35 on the Holy Trinity.

Death of Christ

Jesus atoned only for the sin of Adam and not for our personal sins. His death provided an exact payment for what Adam lost, namely, perfect human life in Eden. This

'Much more then, having now been justified by his blood, we shall be saved from the wrath of God through him. For if while we were enemies, we were reconciled to

'ransom sacrifice' was not a finished work, but rather the basis from which individuals work to provide their own salvation.

Resurrection of Christ

There was no bodily resurrection of Christ. He was raised only as a spirit-creature. No one knows what happened to his body. The post-resurrection appearances of Christ were materializations in different bodies; it was only because Thomas refused to believe that Jesus appeared in a body similar to that in which he died.

Second coming of Christ

Jesus was crowned as king on 1 October 1914 and returned secretly and invisibly; in 1918 he cleansed Jehovah's spiritual temple and raised certain believers to reign with him in heaven.

God through the death of his Son, much more, having been reconciled, we shall be saved by his life' (Romans 5:9-10).

'Their sins and their lawless deeds I will remember no more' (Hebrews 10:17).

'The blood of Jesus his Son cleanses us from all sin' (1 John 1:7).

'See my hands and my feet, that it is I myself; touch me and see, for a spirit does not have flesh and bones as you see that I have... He showed them his hands and his feet' (Luke 24:39-40).

'"Destroy this temple, and in three days I will raise it up"... But he was speaking of the temple of his body' (John 2:19-21).

1.   '...exalted to the right hand of God' (Acts 2:33).

'When he had made purification of sins, he sat down at the right hand of the Majesty on high' (Hebrews 1:3).

2.   It is wrong to set dates for the Second Coming: 'But of that day and hour no one knows, not even the angels of heaven, nor the Son, but the Father alone' (Matthew 24:36).

'Therefore be on the alert, for you do not know which day your Lord is coming' (Matthew 24:42).

'For this reason you be ready too; for the Son of Man is coming at an hour when you do not think he will' (Matthew 24:44).

'Be on the alert then, for you

Holy Spirit

The Holy Spirit is not a person but the invisible, impersonal force of God which moves people to do God's will.

Creation

All that exists was created by Jehovah; Jesus was the first to be created, then God used Jesus as his 'working partner' to create the rest of creation.

The universe was created at least four and a half billion years ago and each creative 'day' in Genesis 1 is 7,000 years in length.

do not know the day nor the hour' (Matthew 25:13).
3.   He will return visibly and gloriously: 'He is coming with the clouds, and every eye will see him' (Revelation 1:7; cf. Zechariah 12:10; Hebrews 9:28; 1 John 3:2).

'Why has Satan filled your heart to lie to the Holy Spirit?... You have not lied to men, but to God' (Acts 5:3-4).
'The Spirit said to Philip...' (Acts 8:29; cf. 13:2, 16:7).
'But one and the same Spirit works all these things, distributing to each one individually just as he wills' (1 Corinthians 12:11).

Several important verses are twisted by the Watchtower to prove that Jesus was created. Note especially the following:
1.   *Colossians 1:15* in their New World Translation is 'firstborn of all creation'. The Greek word translated 'firstborn' is *prototokos*, which does not mean 'created' but rather   sovereignty and priority over all. Even the NASV is misleading here and the NIV is more accurate: 'the firstborn over all creation'. *Prototokos* occurs eight times in the New Testament and nowhere means creation. If Paul had wanted to say Christ was created, he would have used a different Greek word, *protoktistos*. Sadly, the NWT introduces the word 'other' which is *not* in the Greek, in their translation of verses 15-17 in order to change the true meaning of the passage.

2. *Revelation 3:14:* their translation, 'the beginning of the
creation *by* God' is wrong because

1. The phrase 'by God' is not a
translation of the Greek which is
the genitive *tou theou*, meaning '*of
God*' not 'by God';

2. The Greek *arche* (beginning) means the origin or active
cause of what exists. Helpfully, the
NASV includes the footnote, 'origin or source'. Jesus is not, then, the
first of those created, but the originating source or agent of creation.
While he is the Creator (John 1:3),
he himself is uncreated.

Satan and angels

Through rebellion Lucifer became
Satan, who in turn corrupted other
angels. Satan and his host were cast
out of heaven in 1914 and their
influence and activity confined to
the earth. Complete annihilation
will be their doom after the
millennium.

'I was watching Satan fall from
heaven like lightning' (Luke 10:18
— long before 1914! cf. 2 Peter 2:4;
Jude 6).

'They *will* be tormented day
and night *for ever and ever*' (Revelation 20:10).

Man

Man was created perfect in the
image of God but, having no soul,
he is not immortal.

The distinction between soul and
body in man is seen in the following
verses:

Matthew 10:28: 'And do not
fear those who kill the body, but are
unable to kill the soul; but rather
fear him who is able to destroy both
soul and body in hell.'

Philippians 1:23-24: 'But I
am hard-pressed from both directions, having the desire to depart
and be with Christ, for that is very
much better; yet to remain in the
flesh is more necessary for your
sake.'

Hebrews 12:23, especially the

words 'the spirits of righteous men made perfect', refers to believers still awaiting a resurrection body but who continue to enjoy fellowship with God. Between death and the general resurrection there is a conscious, spiritual existence (cf. Isaiah 14:4-17; Ezekiel 32:21).

In *Revelation 6:9-11* it is not the blood of the martyrs (as Jehovah's Witnesses teach) but their souls that 'cried out in a loud voice', and the white robes given to them stress that those mentioned in verses 9-10 exist personally.

In *Revelation 20:4:* John saw the *souls* of the martyrs.

Hell

Hell is only a symbol of annihilation; there is no eternal punishment.

There are four different words translated 'hell' in the AV. The Hebrew word *'Sheol'* and the Greek word *'Hades'* usually refer to the place of the departed. *'Tartarus'* is used only in 2 Peter 2:4 to describe the place where the fallen angels are detained. *'Gehenna'* in the New Testament refers, *not* to annihilation, but to the eternal punishment of the wicked.

'And these will go away into eternal punishment...' (Matthew 25:46). The New World Translation's 'cutting-off' is incorrect. The Greek word *'Kolasin'* is used four times in the New Testament and in each case the idea is of punishment.

'They will be tormented day and night for ever and ever' (Revelation 20:10). The Greek *'Basanizo'*, translated 'tormented' in the NWT of Revelation 11:10, still means the same thing in Revelation 20:10! It is deceitful to give it the meaning of annihilation here.

For further study see Eryl Davies, *The Wrath of God* (Evangelical Movement of Wales) and *Condemned for Ever!* (Evangelical Press).

Blood transfusion

Receiving a blood transfusion violates the law of God and puts the guilty person's hope of eternal life in jeopardy. (Most of the groups, however, who seceded from the Watchtower disagree strongly with them on this point.)

Genesis 9:4: 'Only you shall not eat flesh with its life, that is, its blood.' This text does not forbid blood transfusions for the following reasons:

1. It is a divine command against eating or drinking the blood of *animals*, not humans.
2. Unlike the drinking of animal blood, blood transfusions do not involve the death of the donors; they actually preserve life.
3. There is no similarity between drinking blood through the digestive organs and transfusing a donor's blood directly into the patient's bloodstream.

Leviticus 17:10-11

1. The phrase 'any blood' does not include human blood for *no human* blood was offered on the altars by Jews.
2. The reason for the prohibition is given in verse 11, namely, in order to provide atonement for sin, God appointed the blood of animals; such blood was to be used *exclusively* for this purpose and not used as food.
3. The blood of animals was also important because it pointed to — and found fulfilment in — the shedding of Christ's blood on the cross.

Acts 15:20, 29

1. Gentile converts were advised not to eat animal blood to avoid unnecessary offence to Jewish

Christians who still preferred to
abstain from blood (see v. 21). To
maintain the closest possible fellowship between the two groups,
this decree was issued to the Gentile churches.

2.   There is no mention in the
passage of the possibility of losing
eternal life if the advice is ignored.
On the contrary, verses 9-11 show
that salvation is by grace through
faith and not through the keeping of
rules. It was not the subject of personal salvation that was under
consideration here but rather
church fellowship between Jews
and Gentiles.

Salvation

Through Jesus' ransom, which
removed our sin inherited from
Adam, we have a second chance to
start afresh from where our first
parents began. The perfect life
which Jesus lived gives us the
chance to *earn* our salvation, especially through visitation, the sale
of Watchtower literature and attending meetings and conventions.

Believers are divided into two
classes: the 'anointed class' — the
144,000 who must believe, be baptized by immersion, preach and live
'worthily' until death; and the
'other sheep' who must also believe, be baptized as a symbol of
dedication, do 'field work', like
selling literature, but do not need
justification, the new birth nor
sanctification.

Titles such as 'Study of Scriptures necessary for salvation' and
'Growth to salvation necessary' in
their book *Make sure of all things*
reveal their unbiblical doctrine of
salvation.

*1.   Christ's death is the only
ground of our salvation*
'On behalf of Christ, be reconciled
to God' (2 Corinthians 5:20).

'But now once at the consum-
mation he has been manifested to
put away sin by the sacrifice of
himself' (Hebrews 9:26; cf. vv. 13-
25; Romans 4:25, 8:3-4).

2.   Salvation cannot be earned
'The wages of sin is death, but the
free gift of God is eternal life in
Christ Jesus our Lord' (Romans
6:23).

'Who has saved us, and called
us with a holy calling, not according to our works, but according to
his own purpose and grace' (2
Timothy 1:9).

'He saved us, not on the basis
of deeds which we have done in
righteousness, but according to his
mercy' (Titus 3:5).

*3.   We receive salvation through
faith alone*

'For God so loved the world, that he gave his only begotten Son, that whoever believes in him should not perish, but have eternal life' (John 3:16).

'He who believes has eternal life' (John 6:47; cf. 20:31).

'For we maintain that a man is justified by faith *apart from* works of the Law' (Romans 3:28).

New birth

It is only Christ and his 144,000 'body-members' who are born again, that is, spirit-begotten with the hope of heaven. This number was completed in 1931 and there are only about 7,000 of them still alive.

Faithful men of God like Abraham, Isaac and Jacob and the prophets are not in the kingdom of God but they will be representatives of God on the earth.

There is no distinction in the Bible between 'born again' and unregenerate *believers* and up until 1935 the Jehovah's Witnesses themselves denied this distinction.

'But this he spoke of the Spirit, whom those who believed in him were to receive' (John 7:38-39).

'Repent, and let each of you be baptized in the name of Jesus Christ for the forgiveness of your sins; and you shall receive the gift of the Holy Spirit. For the promise is for you and your children, and for all who are far off, as many as the Lord our God shall call to himself' (Acts 2:38-39).

'If anyone does not have the Spirit of Christ, he does not belong to him' (Romans 8:9).

'Whoever believes that Jesus is the Christ is born of God' (1 John 5:1; cf. John 3:3, 5; Galatians 3:13-14).

'Many shall come from east and west, and recline at table with Abraham, and Isaac, and Jacob, in the kingdom of heaven' (Matthew 8:11-12).

'There will be weeping and gnashing of teeth there when you see Abraham and Isaac and Jacob and all the prophets in the kingdom of God, but yourselves being cast out' (Luke 13:28-29).

Second chance

They allege that John 5:29 and Hebrews 9:27 teach that some will have a second chance after death. For example, they claim that 'the resurrection of judgement' in John 5:29 is for people who, when on earth, wanted to do right but lacked the knowledge. Such people, they say, will be brought back into the paradise earth and, after being taught the truth, will be judged on the basis of their response to it and rewarded accordingly — either with life or annihilation.

According to Romans 1:18 and 3:23 *all* people are sinful, without excuse and guilty before God. Those who have not heard the Word will be judged according to the light of conscience (see Romans 2:12).

In John 5:29 note that their destinies are already decided. The past tense, 'did the good deeds' and 'committed the evil deeds', makes this clear.

John 3:18-21, and especially verse 18, shows that our destiny is settled before we die and is dependent on our acceptance or rejection of Christ.

13.
The Worldwide Church of God

The founder of this influential movement, Herbert W. Armstrong, was born in Iowa, U.S.A., in 1892. Although he worshipped in a Methodist Church in his earlier years, he quickly became disillusioned by religion and gradually immersed himself in his own business to the neglect of any church attendance. By the time his business collapsed in 1926, Armstrong's wife had already accepted some beliefs of a Seventh-Day Adventist neighbour, who had convinced her, among other things, that salvation was conditional upon obedience to the Ten Commandments and, particularly, the observance of the Jewish sabbath. Mrs Armstrong began to challenge her husband's more traditional beliefs and, somewhat irritated, Herbert Armstrong began to study the Bible. Sadly, however, within a short time he accepted his wife's heretical views and he subsequently scorned the orthodox, biblical faith.

An official publication of the WCG, *This is the Worldwide Church of God*, gives a biased and fanciful account of Armstrong's change of beliefs: 'His intensive almost night-and-day study, although frustrating at the time, swept his mind clean of teachings from his Sunday School and church upbringing! God caused him to now seriously and earnestly study the Bible afresh — as if he had never allowed previous teachings to have a place in his mind. No world religious leader, in all probability, has ever been brought to revealed truth in this unprejudiced manner.' Nonsense! The real truth is that Armstrong obtained most of his heretical views from his first wife, Loma, who died in 1967. Later, after worshipping for some months in the Church of God in Willamette Valley and Oregon City (a church which taught the errors the Armstrongs now believed), this small group of churches began to recognize Armstrong's speaking and administrative abilities and in 1931 ordained him as a minister.

Growth of the movement

'It was under his leadership', claims the WCG, 'that a new era of the Church of God was begun. The Church was revitalized and injected with new life and vigour...' Certainly Armstrong's enthusiasm, vision and strong personality helped him to develop the work quite dramatically and within two years he undertook a successful lecture tour in Oregon. During the early years of January 1934 his radio programme, *The World Tomorrow,* went on the air for the first time; it was gradually put on more and more local radio stations until by 1942 it had national coverage in America and in 1945 it became a daily programme. Since January 1981 the programme is being broadcast on 100 radio stations and 144 television stations in the United States and transmitted world-wide by a total of 168 radio and 192 television stations. It is beamed to Great Britain via Radio Luxembourg and the WCG claims that the programme relayed world-wide has at least one hundred million listeners.

The movement's glossy magazine *The Plain Truth* made its first appearance on 1 February 1934, when it had a circulation of only 250 copies. By 1982 the circulation had soared to almost four and a half million copies and to over eight million by 1986; details of new contacts are pouring in to their postal centre in Pasadena, California, at the rate of one hundred thousand per month. Besides this wide media coverage, Armstrong visited Europe in recent years, as well as the Far East, Australia, New Zealand and the Middle East. He tried to befriend world leaders and in Egypt, for example, he was received by President Hosni Mubarak. Armstrong also established two colleges which are both named 'Ambassador': one is located at Pasadena, (with 500 students) and the other, a junior college with 200 students, at Big Sandy, Texas.

Shock waves in the movement

More recently, the WCG has been shaken in two ways, both of which relate to Armstrong's family. First of all, the WCG leader divorced his second wife, Ramona Martin, who was forty-six years his junior, after only five years of marriage. In an article in the May 1982 issue of *The Plain Truth* entitled 'God hates divorce — yet he divorced his own wife! Why?', Armstrong likens his broken marriage to that of God with Israel: 'It's a case of an aged personage who loved a beautiful young woman and proposed marriage. He offered her a considerably increased lifestyle and many advantages — even to make her the "first lady" of all the earth — for this aged personage was God... But his wife was unfaithful and refused to live with him in peace,' so God judged and divorced his faithless bride. One reliable source insists that Armstong's wife did not want a divorce but was simply frustrated by her husband's refusal to support her and her son (by a previous marriage) or to continue payment on the mortgage of their Tucson home. The same informed source suggests that Armstrong divorced his wife out of fear lest she co-operated with other 'conspirators' to remove him from leadership of the church on grounds of senility or mental incompetence!

The other incident that also sent shock-waves through the WCG was the quarrel between the leader and his son Garner Ted Armstrong. In the late 1970s the differences were so deep that the son felt compelled to withdraw from the WCG and set up his own independent movement called the Church of God International. Membership of this breakaway group slumped from 3,000 to 1,800, but it seems that Garner Ted will only return to the fold if he is given complete freedom to reform the WCG from within.

'Passing on the baton'

Until his death at the age of ninety-three, on 16 January 1986, Herbert Armstrong was active in the daily administration and leadership of his movement. He was officially described as 'the Apostle and Pastor General' of the Worldwide Church of God. Armstrong had also appointed Joseph W. Tkach, the Director of

Church Administration, to succeed him as leader. At a board meeting shortly before his death, he spoke of 'passing the baton' to his successor.

Joseph Tkach, born in 1926, trained in basic engineering and industrial management. From 1950-1963 he worked for Hupp Aviation and then resigned to serve in the ministry of the WCG. He spent three years at Ambassador College from 1966, and then served congregations in Southern California. In 1979 Tkach was named Director of Church Administration, and he also became a personal assistant to Armstrong and an associate pastor with him of their Pasadena Auditorium Church.

Although the leadership has changed, WCG teaching remains unchanged. 'Readjusted,' writes the editor of their official monthly magazine *The Good News,* 'we're going to go on running with the baton that was given to Mr Armstrong before us...' In 1987 WCG claimed 2703 members in Britain and forty-one congregations.

What the Worldwide Church of God teaches	*What the Bible teaches*
God	
'God is a family — not a trinity. God's family will not be limited to an intractably closed circle of three. This is one group you don't have to be excluded from' (H. W. Armstrong).	'Before me there was no God formed, and there will be none after me' (Isaiah 43:10).
At the resurrection, believers will 'become God as God is God, God as Jesus Christ is God...' (D. J. Hill).	'I am the first and I am the last, and there is no God besides me' (Isaiah 44:6).
While God the Father and the Son are 'the two original Beings in the God family' yet all the followers of Armstrong will become God, too, in the same sense (this is similar to the Mormon teaching).	While believers will see God and enjoy his presence, they will never become God nor equal to Christ in terms of his deity and authority (see Job 19:25-27; Philippians 3:20-21; Ephesians 1:19-23; Revelation 5:9-10, 13; 20:6).

Christ

Christ is God and eternal but was no more than a perfect human being while on earth.

'Thou art the Christ, the Son of the living God' (Matthew 16:16).
'When the centurion, who was standing right in front of him, saw the way he breathed his last, he said, "Truly this man was the Son of God!"' (Mark 15:39; cf. John 4:25-26)

Death of Christ

The blood of Christ does not finally save any man. It only wipes the slate clean of past sins, it saves us merely from the death penalty and frees us to go on to merit salvation by obedience to the law.

Our Saviour's sacrifice accomplishes more than the forgiveness of our sins. According to Galatians 4:4-7, for example, believing sinners are freed from obedience to the divine law as the condition of life and made the sons of God as well as the heirs of eternal life on the sole ground of the Lord's sacrificial death.

Resurrection of Christ

'God the Father did not cause Jesus Christ to get back into the body which had died' (H. W. Armstrong).

'"Destroy this temple, and in three days I will raise it up." ...But he was speaking of the temple of his body. When therefore he was raised from the dead, his disciples remembered that he said this' (John 2:19-22; cf. Philippians 3:21).

Holy Spirit

The Holy Spirit is not a divine person like the Father and Son but merely the power and force of God.

The personality of the Holy Spirit is seen in the following verses: John 16:7-8, 13-14; 1 Corinthians 2:10-11; 12:11. He can be 'grieved' (Ephesians 4:30), 'quenched' (1 Thessalonians 5:19) and 'lied to' (Acts 5:3), all of which would be impossible if he was only an impersonal force. Notice how the attributes of God are applied equally to the Holy Spirit: he is omniscient (1

Corinthians 2:10-11), that is, he knows all things including the deep things pertaining to God; he is omnipresent (Psalm 139:7) and eternal (Hebrews 9:14). Also the Holy Spirit is mentioned in an inseparable and equal relationship with the Father and Son, as in Matthew 28:19 and 2 Corinthians 13:14. The names 'God' and 'Holy Spirit' are used interchangeably in, for example, Acts 5:3, 4; 1 Corinthians 3:16; 6:19.

Conversion

Armstrong likens conversion to conception and says that a believer is like a foetus in the womb waiting to be born, but it is impossible to be born again until the general resurrection of the dead at the end of the world.

Those converted to Christ are already born again; see John 1:12-13; 3:1-16; 1 John 5:1. Notice, too, how believers are described as 'babes' or 'infants' in 1 Corinthians 3:1 and 1 Peter 2:2; in other words, they are already born again and have become the children of God.

Salvation

Salvation is only for those who obey the laws of God summarized in the Ten Commandments and is particularly linked to observing the sabbath on the seventh day of the week.

'Nevertheless knowing that a man is not justified by the works of the Law but through faith in Christ Jesus, even we have believed in Christ Jesus, that we may be justified by faith in Christ, and not by the works of the Law; since by the works of the Law shall no flesh be justified' (Galatians 2:16, cf. Ephesians 2:8-9; Titus 3:4-7).

Church

Armstrong's church is the only true church of God in the world. All other churches are 'satanic counterfeits'.

'To the church of God which is at Corinth, to those who have been sanctified in Christ Jesus, saints by calling, with all who in every place call upon the name of our Lord Jesus Christ, their Lord and ours' (1 Corinthians 1:2).

Heaven

Heaven is pagan doctrine which is not taught in the Bible.

Heaven is where God is; our Lord describes it as the house of his Father where there are many mansions (John 14:1).

As a place, heaven is frequently mentioned both directly (e.g. 2 Kings 2:1, 11; Luke 15:7; Philippians 3:20) and indirectly (in passages like 2 Corinthians 5:6-8 and Philippians 1:21-23).

Israel

The Anglo-Saxons in Britain and the United States are the ten lost tribes of Israel and inherit as nations all the Old Testament covenant promises. While present-day Jews are identified with Judah and continue under the wrath of God, Britain is the tribe of Ephraim and the United States of America is the tribe of Manasseh. The throne of England is none other than the throne of David!

Armstrong wrongly bases the theory of the ten lost tribes of Israel on Deuteronomy 32:26 but if verse 27 is read also it is clear that God did not execute his threat to 'remove the memory of them from men'. Anna, the prophetess who rejoiced in the Saviour's birth, belonged to 'the tribe of Asher' (Luke 2:36) which was one of the tribes who, according to Armstrong, had already been 'lost' by that time. References like 1 Chronicles 28:6-7; Psalm 132:11-12 and Luke 1:32-33, 69 emphasize that the throne of David has been eternally established in Christ, the Son of David, and not in Buckingham Palace. The church of Jesus Christ is now the new Israel (Romans 4:11-12; Galatians 3:7-9, 27-29; 1 Peter 2:9-10).

Prophecy

Here are a few of the prophecies given by Armstrong over the years and printed in his *Plain Truth:*

'This year, 1935, is destined to witness an event foretold in the Bible 2,400 years ago: "The great

'"How shall we know the word which the Lord has not spoken?" When a prophet speaks in the name of the Lord, if the thing does not come about or come true, that is the thing which the Lord has not spoken. The prophet has spoken it

drought". The year 1935 is destined to see the final fulfilment of "God's great army of a nation of bugs" prophesied in Joel 1:4, 6-7. The "time of God's wrath — the last plague — is at hand"' (March 1935, pp. 1-2).

'Mussolini will capture Egypt, conquer one half of Jerusalem, and fight Christ at his second coming' (January 1939, p. 4).

'Britain will be invaded and conquered... Turkey will cause British defeat. But God will... cause Turkey utterly to be wiped out' (November-December 1940, pp. 2,7).

'Millions of lukewarm inactive professing Christians will suffer *martyrdom* — and that *before* the anticipated push-button leisure year of 1975 dawns upon us! You'll read of this martyrdom, the Great Tribulation, in Matthew 24:9-10, 21-22' ('1975 in Prophecy', 1952, p.10).

presumptuously...' (Deuteronomy 18:21-22).

'Herbert W. Armstrong... must be in the running for the most consistent false prophet of modern times' (*Awareness*, April 1984, no. 7, p.1).

14.
Rastafarians

There are now two million West Indians and over one and a half million Asians living in Great Britain. While most of the Asians are Muslims and present an enormous challenge to Christian churches, the West Indians have at least a nominal acquaintance with Christianity and an increasing number of them are responding to the gospel. During the last eighteen years about 250 West Indian churches have emerged in Britain and most of these new churches have strong links with America. The New Testament Church of God, for example, claims ninety-one congregations with some 20,000 people in regular attendance, while the Church of God of Prophecy has 100 congregations. Both groups are affiliated to American churches and are strongly charismatic but in the depressed, inner-city areas of England these churches are experiencing rapid growth.

One problem now facing the West Indian churches is the activity of Rastafarians, who pose a serious threat to the work of the gospel among West Indian young people. Rastafarians are easily recognizable in our cities, with their uncut hair combed into long braids, and they usually wear a multi-coloured hat of red, green, black and gold. The colours are significant for they are the colours of Ethiopia.

The historical background

Why Ethiopia? A prophecy given some sixty years ago by a Jamaican that a dark-coloured person would be made king in Africa was almost totally disregarded until 1930 when Ras Tafari succeeded to the throne of Ethiopia as Emperor Haile Selassie. His appointment gave new hope to many frustrated and economically poor Jamaicans who slowly recognized the Emperor as their messiah and 'King of kings'. While the emperor's death in 1975 stunned many Jamaicans, the Rastafarians believe in the continued life of Selassie in a different realm and worship him as a god. This movement continues to gain ground in Jamaica and overseas but particularly in America and England.

Rastafarian beliefs and practices

Despite their often untidy appearance, Rastafarians are told to live a respectable, moral life. Immorality, for example, as well as stealing, lying and the use of alcohol, are all forbidden but in order to meditate their followers are encouraged to smoke marijuana or 'ganja'. They do not have established churches or buildings.

This movement is built on, and fuelled by, hatred for white people. God's command is that we must love our neighbours, whoever they are (Matthew 5:44). It is only by the work of God in our hearts in the new birth that we are able to love people, for love is a fruit of the Spirit (Galatians 5:22; 2 Corinthians 5:17).

What Rastafarians teach	*What the Bible teaches*
Bible	
Black people wrote the Bible exclusively for blacks.	'No prophecy was ever made by an act of human will, but men moved by the Holy Spirit spoke from God' (2 Peter 1:21). 'All Scripture is inspired by God and profitable for teaching, for reproof, for correction, for training

in righteousness; that the man of God may be adequate, equipped for every good work' (2 Timothy 3:16-17).

God

Many Rastafarians believe that Haile Selassie is both God and Saviour.

'Before me there was no God formed, and there will be none after me. I, even I, am the Lord; and there is no saviour besides me' (Isaiah 43:10-11).

Incarnation

In the Emperor Haile Selassie, not Jesus, God became man. Jesus has been misrepresented by whites as a European. All the early Christians and Jesus were dark-skinned.

'When the fulness of the time came, God sent forth his Son, born of a woman, born under the Law, in order that he might redeem those who were under the Law, that we might receive the adoption as sons' (Galatians 4:4-5; Philippians 2:6-8).
    'Whoever believes that Jesus is the Christ is born of God...' (1 John 5:1).

Salvation

Salvation and freedom will be realized only when black people return to Africa, from where they were originally taken as slaves by white slave traders.

'There is salvation in no one else; for there is no other name under heaven that has been given among men, by which we must be saved' (Acts 4:12; cf. Galatians 1:4).

Devil

All white people are demons and belong to the devil.

By nature we are *all* slaves of sin (John 8:34) and belong to the devil (v.44) but we are transferred to the kingdom of God when we trust in Christ (1 Peter 2:9-10; Colossians 1:13-14).

Life after death

Reincarnation is a popular and common belief among Rasta-farians.

'It is appointed for men to die once, and after this comes judgement' (Hebrews 9:27).

Section 3
Some controversial and socially deviant cults

15. The Unification Church: Moonies

16. The Family of Love (previously called the Children of God)

17. The Way International

18. Scientology

Section 3
Some controversial and
socially deviant cults

15.
The Unification Church: Moonies

In 1954, at the age of thirty-four, the Rev. Sun Myung Moon founded the Unification Church in Korea. Moon's parents were Presbyterians and gave him a religious upbringing, but at an early age he manifested a deep interest in spiritism, and when only sixteen he claimed his first occult experience. While praying on Easter Sunday 1936 he claims to have seen Jesus Christ, who revealed that Moon 'was destined to accomplish a great mission in which Jesus Christ would work with him'.

He read the Bible regularly and then went to Japan to study electrical engineering. At the end of the Second World War, he joined an extreme Pentecostal movement in Pyong Yang which emphasized private mystical revelations and also the imminent appearance of a new messiah who would be a Korean. One of his key spiritistic experiences occurred in 1945. Describing this encounter in his *Divine Principle*, he claims to have 'fought alone against myriads of satanic forces, both in the spirit and physical world and finally triumphed over them all'. From this time, according to Moon, he became 'the absolute victor of heaven and earth... and the Lord of creation... the whole spirit world bowed down to him'.

For reasons which are somewhat obscure — varying from bigamy, adultery to social disorder and anti-communist activity — he was imprisoned in North Korea but was released when General MacArthur, at the head of the United Nations forces, occupied his area. Moving to the south, Moon established his church in Seoul in

1954, calling it the Holy Spirit Association for the Unification of World Christianity. That same year when his first wife left him, Moon remarked, 'She did not understand my religion.' A year later he was again imprisoned, but this time in South Korea, charged with avoiding military duties and later with adultery and immoral practices. The charges, however, were not proven.

It is likely that Moon has been married four times. He married his present wife, Hak Ja Han in 1960 and Moon describes this marriage as 'the marriage of the lamb', and regards their eight children as sinless because they are children of the messiah.

Success for Moon

1957 saw the publication of the *Divine Principle,* described as the 'key to the Scriptures', which records Moon's teachings in Korea to his followers. The Rev. Moon became a successful businessman in Korea, amassing considerable wealth from pharmaceutical products, tea and rifles, among other things. *The Times* of 30 April 1978 headlined their overseas report on Moon as 'Founder of Unification Church but better known in Korea as owner of weapons factories'. Their reporter in Seoul, Peter Hazelhurst, says, 'Moon owns one factory in the new Chang-won Industrial complex near Pusan which makes defence equipment classified as secret and another in Sutack Ri, twenty-one miles north-east of Seoul, which is an air-gun factory. His other businesses include Korea's largest exporter of ginseng products (White Fire Company), whose annual exports to Japan alone are worth five million pounds.'[1] Moon's personal fortune is estimated at eight million pounds.[2]

According to Moon, God 'appeared' to him in January 1972 telling him to prepare America for the Messiah's second coming. His subsequent activities in the States in the early mid-seventies were successful. In addition to winning many converts to his religion, he had meetings with Presidents Eisenhower and Nixon and supported Nixon during the Watergate scandal.

In 1975 the work of the movement was expanded as missionaries were sent out to ninety-five countries and it claims to have a total of three million members in at least 120 countries, but Professor Tak Myung Hwan of the Korea Theological Seminary believes this figure is grossly exaggerated. Possibly as part of their 'heavenly deception' (the belief that deception is justified in the propagating of Moon's teachings) they claim, for example, 360,000 supporters in Korea, but Professor Tak puts the figure at 10,000.[3] As a result of a poor public 'image' in recent years both in America and Europe, due to charges of 'brainwashing' and 'isolating' young people from parents, the movement appears to be on the wane, with a number of groups and individuals in the U.S.A. offering (for a fee) to 'kidnap' and 'deprogramme' Moonies in order to rehabilitate them to normal family and social life.

To quote Professor Tak again, 'Moon claims he is the new Messiah, superior to Buddha, Jesus and Confucius. The Unification Church has never been a Christian church. It is a cult. And it puts Korea to shame before the world.' A similar pronouncement was made by the National Council of Churches of Christ in the U.S.A. in 1977: 'It cannot be considered as a Christian church.' What is even more important, the religion of the Rev. Moon stands condemned as false by the Word of God.

The Daily Mail court case

Early in 1981 the Unification Church lost the longest and most expensive libel case in British legal history and was ordered to pay costs estimated at nearly one million pounds. Dennis Orme, leader of Sun Myung Moon's church in Britain, claimed damages against the *Daily Mail* for an article in 1978 that accused the church of brainwashing converts and breaking up families.

The allegations against them were as follows:

1. They establish control over recruits with 'sophisticated mind control techniques', developed from those used by the Chinese Communists in the Korean war, including extremely low-protein diets, sleep deprivation, 'love-bombing' and increasing blood sugar levels in order to muddle the brain — a technique called 'sugar-buzzing'.

2. The trademark of a recruit was a 'perpetual vapid smile' and a vacant glassy look.

3. Recruits were 'programmed as soldiers in a vast, fund-

raising army, with no goals or ideals except as followers of
the half-baked ravings of Moon, who lives in splendour
while his followers lived in forced penury'.

4.   Their motivation was just as strong, if not stronger, than
that of Communists.

5.   The church raised vast funds by deceiving the public.

The jury, who took five hours to reach their verdict and heard
evidence from more than 100 witnesses for over six months,
decided that the *Daily Mail* was justified in its accusations. They
made two recommendations:

1.   They urged that the charitable status of the Unification
Church should be examined by the Inland Revenue on the
grounds that it was really a political organization.

2.   They expressed their deep compassion for all the young
people still in the group.

The aftermath of the case

According to the *Daily Mail*, a review of the Moonies' activities
was to be undertaken by the Health Authorities, including an
examination of the effects of their psychiatric techniques on young
members. The government's investigation was also expected to
cover the effects of the Moonies' activities on the health of the
members and their families, the questions of charitable status and
money-raising methods, and whether there should be any restric-
tion on allowing the movement's overseas officials and followers
into Great Britain.

The *Daily Mail* also reported that 100 Members of Parliament
had signed a Commons motion deploring the activities of Moonies
and calling for the government to end the group's charitable status.

In May 1982 the Rev. Sun Myung Moon was found guilty in the
U.S.A. of failing to pay tax from 1973 to 1975 on $1,500,000
(£940,000) held in bank accounts in his name. He was sentenced to
eighteen months' imprisonment and fined $25,000 (£14,700).

In August 1987 the *Daily Mail*'s political editor, Gordon Greig, wrote a report for his paper under the heading, 'Moonies still escape.' 'Major new powers,' he wrote, 'over organizations running themselves as charities are called for in a Government report' — and this as much as six years after the famous *Daily Mail* court action in 1981. Despite possible new measures to be introduced and the large numbers of politicians and lawyers (including Lord Denning) who have called for specific legislation to strike their organizations off the Charity Commission's register, the Moonies continue to enjoy tax-free status.

A personal testimony

On a more personal note, a book was recently published in which the author, Jacqui Williams, describes her four years with the Moonies .[4] It is a sad and frightening story of a young Christian teacher from England who was drawn unknowingly into the web of the Unification Church while on holiday in San Francisco. Impressed by the friendliness and sincerity of her new Moonie friends, Jacqui was oblivious to the brainwashing techniques that were used to make her a follower of the Rev. Moon. She then spent much of her time fund-raising for the cult but after four years she had to return unexpectedly to England. Jacqui did not like what she saw of the Moonies in England and she left their headquarters to return to her family. Very slowly, Jacqui was helped by family and friends to renounce the teaching and life-style of the Moonies. Reflecting on her experience, she acknowledges that she was deceived, but in a subtle way, and she now wants to warn others of the dangers.

After the bad publicity of the *Daily Mail* court case in 1981, the Moonies have kept a low profile on the streets of Britain, but they are still active. 'They are desperate,' insists Jacqui, 'to gain recognition from the Christian church, and they are now more likely to join local churches and work from inside them.' Her message to us is loud and clear: if Christians are to weaken the influence of Moonies then people must be given information and teaching. But that is not all. Love and concern must be shown to those caught in the web of this evil cult. Their membership in Britain in 1980 was 570, which dipped to 347 in 1983, 350 in 1985 and increased to 500 in 1987.

What the Unification Church teaches

What the Bible teaches

God

God is an invisible essence manifesting the qualities of spirit and energy from which all that exists is generated.

'God is living in me and I am the incarnation of himself. The whole world is in my hand and I will conquer and subjugate the world' (Rev. Sun Myung Moon).

'The Lord reigns' (Psalm 97:1).

'And all the inhabitants of the earth are accounted as nothing, but he does according to his will in the host of heaven and among the inhabitants of earth' (Daniel 4:35; cf. Jeremiah 10:10).

'God is spirit' (John 4:24).

'To the King eternal, immortal, invisible, the only God, be honour and glory for ever and ever' (1 Timothy 1:17).

Bible

'Until our mission with the Christian church is over, we must quote the Bible and use it to explain the *Divine Principle*. After we receive the inheritance of the Christians, we will be free to teach without the Bible' (Rev. Sun Myung Moon in *Master Speaks*, March-April 1965).

'Heaven and earth will pass away, but my words will not pass away' (Luke 21:33).

'Thy word is truth' (John 17:17).

Person of Christ

The only difference between Jesus and other men was the fact that he had no original sin. The Rev. Moon stands above all previous saints, prophets and religious leaders and is greater than Jesus Christ himself.

'No heroes in the past, no saints or holy men in the past, like Jesus, or Confucius, have excelled us' (Rev. Sun Myung Moon).

'No man has seen God at any time; the only begotten God, who is in the bosom of the Father, he has explained him' (John 1:18).

'I am the way, and the truth, and the life; no one comes to the Father, but through me' (John 14:6).

Death of Christ

The mission of Jesus in the world was to take a bride in the place of Eve, marry and produce perfect children. By this example, other perfect families would be established and the world perfected.

But Jesus failed because he was crucified before he could marry. It was not God's purpose for him to die. John the Baptist's failure was a major cause of the crucifixion. God allowed Satan to invade the physical body of Jesus and crucify him.

'The Lord has caused the iniquity of us all to fall on him' (Isaiah 53:6).

'For the Son of Man has come to seek and to save that which was lost' (Luke 19:10).

'Christ Jesus came into the world to save sinners' (1 Timothy 1:15).

'But he, having offered one sacrifice for sins for all time, sat down at the right hand of God' (Hebrews 10:12; cf. Acts 2:23).

Resurrection of Christ

Jesus was raised as a spirit-man from the dead and in this way redeemed man spiritually.

'"Destroy this temple, and in three days I will raise it up"... He was speaking of the temple of his body' (John 2:19-22; cf. 1 John 3:2-3).

Holy Spirit

The Holy Spirit is female and has been one of the true parents of humanity with Jesus.

'If I go, I will send him to you' (John 16:7).

Second Coming

Jesus himself will not return. The Lord of the Second Advent will be born in Korea as the King of kings. The Rev. Moon is this Lord and has been confirmed as such throughout the spirit world. He now provides additional revelation.

1960 (the year that Rev. Moon married Hak-Ja-Han) saw the dawning of a new age when the marriage of the Lamb foretold in Revelation 19 took place. The Lord of the Second Advent and his bride became the true parents of

'If anyone says to you, "Behold, here is the Christ"; or, 'Behold, he is there"; do not believe him; for false Christs and false prophets will arise' (Mark 13:21-22).

'Take heed, keep on the alert; for you do not know when the appointed time is' (Mark 13:33).

'This Jesus, who has been taken up from you into heaven, will come in just the same way as you have watched him go into heaven' (Acts 1:11).

'...awaiting eagerly the

mankind. In the 1980s or from then onwards this new messiah will be revealed to the world.

Future state

Everyone will be saved eventually. When the Rev. Moon as messiah reveals himself to the world, the spirits of those who have died will join Moon's followers so they can develop into divine spirits. Reincarnation also applies to evil people. Through science the earth will be restored then all the religions of the world will be unified.

Creation

Creation is the body or outward form of God, so everything is ultimately part of the substance called God.

Man

From out of himself, God projected spirit beings. When a spirit is born into a body here it then becomes a form spirit. Each person has a physical man and a spiritual man. The first two persons, Adam and Eve, like every other person since, were a special part of God's infinite nature.

revelation of our Lord Jesus Christ' (1 Corinthians 1:7).

'...and to wait for his Son from heaven, whom he raised from the dead, that is Jesus, who delivers us from the wrath to come' (1 Thessalonians 1:10).

'So it will be at the end of the age; the angels shall come forth, and take out the wicked from among the righteous, and will cast them into the furnace of fire (Matthew 13:49-50).

'...for whom the black darkness has been reserved for ever' (Jude13).

'If anyone's name was not found written in the book of life, he was thrown into the lake of fire' (Revelation 20:15).

'By the word of the Lord the heavens were made' (Psalm 33:6).

'It is I who made the earth, and created man upon it. I stretched out the heavens with my hands, and I ordained all their host' (Isaiah 45:12).

'By faith we understand that the worlds were prepared by the word of God' (Hebrews 11:3).

Although created in the image of God (Genesis 1:26-27), man remains only a creature and is distinct from God the Creator.

'The God who made the world and all things in it, since he is Lord of heaven and earth' (Acts 17:24; cf. Isaiah 42:5; Psalms 102:25-27; 90:2).

Sin

Before Adam and Eve could achieve perfection (i.e. marriage and the forming of a trinity with God, thus producing children free of sin), Eve fornicated with Lucifer, with the result that mankind fell spiritually.

In a vain attempt to repair this damage, Eve persuaded Adam to live with her as husband, but he had not attained perfection either, so this union caused the physical fall of mankind. Eve and then Adam received the sinful features of Lucifer.

Sin is not fornication with Lucifer, but transgression of the law (1 John 3:4). This sin affected the whole subsequent history of mankind.

'Just as through one man sin entered into the world, and death through sin, and so death spread to all men, because all sinned' (Romans 5:12).

16.
The Family of Love (previously called the Children of God)

The formation in 1968 of the group now known as the Family of Love coincided, so its founder claims, with 'the end of the Gentiles', so that God is now gathering his Israel together rather exclusively through the ministry of this movement. David Berg was born in 1919 and was the son of an evangelist serving with the Christian and Missionary Alliance in the U.S.A. Claiming a call from God to preach the gospel, David Berg was ordained as pastor of an Alliance Church in Arizona but eventually resigned, because, he claimed, of the impossibility of supporting his large family on a low salary.

For a short time afterwards he assisted a Pentecostal pastor in radio work and then in 1968 he moved to Huntington Beach where he was responsible for a coffee-bar work amongst young people. At this time he was under the influence of the Jesus Movement, with its characteristic features of coffee-bar evangelism, community living, authoritarian leadership, exclusivism and the rejection both of conventional churches and the family unit. During this period Berg launched an organization called 'Teens for Christ'; converts were immediately encouraged to leave their homes, jobs and churches in order to settle into his communal group. An unfulfilled prophecy a year later that California would be the centre of an enormous earthquake brought Berg and his organization into disrepute.

The movement is established

It was in 1969 that Berg's followers began to use the title 'Children of God' and by 1977 they had established well over 850 communities in about seventy-five countries. They now claim to have two million members and 8,000 missionaries. This was the first group from within the more diverse Jesus Movement to reach Britain and to have an impact in London, the Midlands and South Wales and other areas. Thinking these people were sound and keen Christians, a Christian businessman in London, Kenneth Frampton, helped the group by allowing them to use one of his properties as their headquarters, but he later withdrew his support: 'Having backed this movement more than any since they arrived in Britain,' he writes, 'I repent for having encouraged the active propagation of what now proves to be false teaching, dishonouring to Christ.'[1] Frampton was horrified by their methods of isolating converts from their families and the exercise of rigid control over the actions and thinking of impressionable teenagers. When entering the group, for example, a member agreed to give all his money and possessions to the hierarchy and allow them to open all his correspondence. From what is normally called 'the babe's colony' the new member progresses to another colony of only twelve people and his time is spent chiefly in selling the group's literature as well as routine domestic work and fellowship.

More recently the movement was renamed as The Family of Love and David Berg (who changed his name to Moses David) stepped down as leader.

What the Family of Love teaches	What the Bible teaches
Bible	
1. The Bible is God's 'inspired word for yesterday', while the 'Moses letters' (MO letters are those written by David Berg, who later adopted the name Moses David) are the inspired word of God for today.	1. 'For ever, O Lord, thy word is settled in heaven' (Psalm 119:89). 'The sum of thy word is truth, and every one of thy righteous ordinances is everlasting' (Psalm 119:160).

2. The MO letters are more authoritative than the Bible and are the only valid interpretation of the Bible. Berg is regarded as God's 'mouthpiece', through whom alone the correct understanding of the Scripture has been given.

2. '...teaching as doctrines the precepts of men' (Mark 7:7).

'...invalidating the word of God by your tradition which you have handed down' (Mark 7:13).

Salvation

Conventional churches belong to the devil. Berg writes, 'We teach the kids to hate... the *false* church system... We hate the hypocrisy, self-righteousness, lies and deceitfulness of those who claim to be the Church, but are not and we hate the spiritual system of the Devil behind them.'

While many conventional churches have abandoned Bible doctrine and ethics yet the true church of God is visible in the world; it consists of all those who trust in Christ and have been born of the Holy Spirit (1 Corinthians 1:2; 1 Peter 1:1-2).

Discipleship

Misusing our Lord's words in Matthew 10:34-37, Berg taught that following Christ necessitates the forsaking of families, friends and employment, etc. and this wrong teaching has had tragic results for many families.

In Matthew 10:34-37 the Lord is stressing the believer's supreme loyalty to Christ. The gospel of Christ divides as well as unites families, for man's sinful nature frequently causes him to ridicule the gospel (1 Corinthians 1:23; 2:14) and oppose even relatives who become Christians. There are occasions, then, when Christ must come before parents and others but, wherever possible, the law of God insists that children should honour their parents (see Exodus 20:12; Ephesians 6:1-3). Berg's interpretation of Ephesians 6:1-2, namely, that obeying parents means obeying your spiritual, not human, parents is a perverse twisting of these verses. The word can only refer to human parents and children must honour them as far as is possible, for this is what the Lord demands.

The Family of Love also exploits members by taking all their money and worldly goods.

'We never came with flattering speech, as you know, nor with a pretext for greed — God is witness' (1 Thessalonians 2:5).

'They are upsetting whole families, teaching things they should not teach, for the sake of sordid gain' (Titus 1:11; cf. 1 Timothy 6:3-16).

Marriage and sex

1. Abraham, Solomon and David had concubines so Berg insists it is legitimate to have sex with others in the group.

1. The marriage of a man and a woman is an ordinance of God (Genesis 2:18-24); sex is God's gift to be used exclusively within the marriage relationship. The lapses of even godly men must *not* be taken as God's norm for mankind. These were departures from the original creation ordinance of marriage and were associated with backsliding (e.g. Solomon), unbelief, sin and trouble as in the cases of Abraham (Genesis 21), David (2 Samuel 11, 13) and Hannah (1 Samuel 1:1-6).

2. Husband and wife-swapping is justified by a wrong interpretation of Acts 2:44.

2. The sharing of 'everything in common' (Acts 2:44) is explained in verse 45 as being applicable only to possessions and material goods. This extensive sharing of goods was not a regular practice for the imperfect tenses are used by Luke, e.g. 'they used to sell' and 'they gave'.

3. Berg's writings are often pornographic and obsessed with sex. Women members are told to 'crucify the flesh' by giving themselves physically to other men in order to attract them to the group and to Christ. This is an expression of God's love which, Berg claims, is only properly experienced in sexual intercourse.

3. See 1 Corinthians 6:12-20; 7:1-40; 2 Corinthians 7:1; Ephesians 5:3-17; Colossians 3:5-8; 1 Thessalonians 4:3-8.

Occult

Occult practices such as astrology and witchcraft are encouraged in the MO letters. Berg himself claimed to be led by a spirit identified as a gypsy king who died over a thousand years ago; Berg also claims regular demonic intercourse.

Deuteronomy 18:10-12; Isaiah 8:19-22.

Second coming of Christ

Jesus will return to earth in 1993.

'Of that day and hour no one knows, not even the angels of heaven, nor the Son, but the Father alone' (Matthew 24:36, 42, 44).

17.
The Way International

Victor Paul Wierwille established 'The Way International' in 1958 and for well over twenty years led the work from his headquarters in New Knoxville, Ohio, U.S.A. After his retirement the leadership of the movement was entrusted to the Rev. Craig Martindale.

Having completed studies at Chicago University and Princeton Seminary, [1] Wierwille was ordained to the Christian ministry. For several years he pastored an evangelical, reformed church in Van Wert, Ohio, but his teaching soon became suspect. A denominational church committee was eventually appointed to assess the orthodoxy of Wierwille's views and to recommend appropriate disciplinary measures. However, in May 1958 Wierwille resigned from his pastorate before the committee's work was completed. Almost immediately, he formed The Way International and significant numbers of people joined the new cult. By 1987 there were an estimated 100,000 members in Europe and the United States.

How it began

For at least five or six years before his resignation, Wierwille had begun to develop and popularize his own unbiblical ideas. One important factor in this early period was the decision to burn his 3,000 theology books and commentaries. The reason he gave for this drastic action was that he had 'set out on an independent path for discovering the meaning of Scripture'. He added, 'I have read every commentary in existence; I consign every one of them to Gehenna.'

Another significant factor which contributed to Wierwille's unorthodoxy was his claim that God had spoken audibly to him one day as he prayed. God is supposed to have said to Wierwille, 'I will teach you the Word as it has not been known since the first century and you will teach it to others.' Wierwille consequently redefined an apostle as 'one who brings new light to his generation' and was convinced that he had a crucial apostolic role to fulfil. He had no hesitation in claiming that he was the only preacher who taught the original doctrine of the apostles!

In 1953, his study course entitled 'Power for Abundant Living' (PFAL) was published. This course became a popular and influential method of disseminating his teaching and still remains an integral part of The Way's initial teaching programme. However, many of Wierwille's ideas in this and other works can be traced to the writings of E. W. Bullinger. 'Even more serious,' affirms Joel A. MacCollam, 'Wierwille lifted numerous and substantial direct quotations from Bullinger's *The Giver and his Gifts* and *How to enjoy the Bible* without giving any credit to the original author. In much of Wierwille's work there is no 'new light' to this generation, only a reflection of another's efforts.'

How The Way works

Nearly all the recruits to this cult are contacted initially through the 'friendship' and personal witness of members. Recruits are mostly in their late teens or early twenties and have usually been impressed by the friendliness and concern of Way members. The work of personal friendship is then supplemented by fellowship in the home. Individuals are gradually pressurized and brainwashed into thinking that only Wierwille's statements and interpretation of the Bible are infallible.

Each Way member is called a 'leaf', while the local group is known as a 'twig' and the regional work as a 'branch'. The analogy is continued at all levels with the directors, for example, being known as the root and the headquarters in Ohio as the trunk. In the United States, Way members have infiltrated some evangelical churches and Bible Colleges with the specific aim of recruiting young believers. A person's 'faith' and commitment to The Way is evidenced when he enters upon and completes the expensive PFAL course of instruction.

Despite its emphasis on friendship and the Bible, The Way is a dangerous, heretical cult.

What The Way teaches	*What the Bible teaches*

Bible

The Old Testament and the four Gospels are unnecessary and not part of the Word of God. 'The Bible as a whole', asserts Wierwille, 'is not relevant to all people of all times.'

'Thy word is truth' (John 17:17).
'All Scripture is inspired by God and profitable for teaching, for reproof, for correction, for training in righteousness' (2 Timothy 3:16).

Trinity

A false doctrine not found in the Bible. 'Trinitarian dogma... degrades God from his elevated, unparalleled position...'

See other chapters, and especially chapter 35 on the Trinity for a detailed biblical answer.

Jesus Christ

'Jesus Christ's existence began when he was conceived by God's creating the soul-life of Jesus in Mary.'

Christ was a human being only and created specially by God.

Jesus had no direct fellowship or contact with God before his baptism.

'Truly, truly, I say to you, before Abraham was born, I am' (John 8:58).
'I came forth from the Father, and have come into the world' (John 16:28).
'Who, although he existed in the form of God, did not regard equality with God a thing to be grasped, but emptied himself, taking the form of a bond-servant, and being made in the likeness of men...' (Philippians 2:6-7).
No man has seen God at any time; the only begotten Son, which is in the bosom of the Father, he has

declared him' (John 1:18, AV).

'Did you not know that I must be about my Father's business?' (Luke 2:49 NKJV).

Death of Christ

Wierwille denies that Christ died sacrificially on behalf of other people.

'I lay down my life for the sheep' (John 10:15).

'...Christ... loved you, and gave himself up for us, an offering and a sacrifice to God as a fragrant aroma' (Ephesians 5:2).

Holy Spirit

The Spirit of God is regarded as an impersonal force or ability; his distinct personality and deity are denied.

'Do not grieve the Holy Spirit of God, by whom you were sealed for the day of redemption' (Ephesians 4:30).

'One and the same Spirit works all these things, distributing to each one individually just as he wills' (1 Corinthians 12:11).

Salvation

If we 'only believe' we will:
1. be saved;

'Believe in the Lord Jesus, and you shall be saved' (Acts 16:31).

'This is the will of my Father, that everyone who beholds the Son, and believes in him, may have eternal life' (John 6:40).

2. enjoy a legal right to victory over all sin;

'Sin shall not be master over you, for you are not under law, but under grace' (Romans 6:14).

'If we say that we have no sin, we are deceiving ourselves, and the truth is not in us' (1 John 1:8).

3. realize God's will for us, which 'is success in everything', including freedom from illness.
For example, if we have a headache we can say, 'Look here, headache you have no power over me. You were

'I entreated the Lord three times that it [thorn in the flesh] might depart from me. And he has said to me, "My grace is sufficient for you, for power is perfected in weakness." Most gladly, therefore, I will rather boast about my weaknesses, that the power of Christ

defeated over 1900 years ago. It says so in the Word and I believe the Word: therefore, be gone from me.'

Evidences of personal salvation

There are two infallible signs of the new birth:
1. Speaking with tongues. 'Open your mouth wide and breathe in,' exhorts Wierwille, 'You are now going to manifest the Spirit's presence... Move your lips, your throat, your tongue. Speak forth, the external manifestation is your proof in the sense world that you have Christ within.'

2. Willingness to pay a 'donation' (quite large) in order to receive Wierwille's twelve lessons entitled *Power for Abundant Living* (PFAL).

may dwell in me' (2 Corinthians 12:8-9).

'Not everyone who says to me, "Lord, Lord," will enter the kingdom of heaven; but he who does the will of my Father who is in heaven' (Matthew 7:21-23).

'But the fruit of the Spirit is love, joy, peace, patience, kindness, goodness, faithfulness, gentleness, self-control...' (Galatians 5:22-23).

Passages like Acts 8:14-17; 9:18-22 do not support the view that all believers spoke with tongues at their conversion.

Wierwille appears to teach for material gain and is condemned by biblical passages such as 2 Peter 2:3: 'In their greed they will exploit you with false words; their judgement from long ago is not idle, and their destruction is not asleep' (cf. 1 Timothy 6:3-5; Titus 1:10-11).

18.
Scientology

'Scientology is one of the oldest, wealthiest and most dangerous of the major "new religions" or cults operating today', wrote Eugene Methvia in the *Readers Digest*.[1]

Scientology is dangerous

It is dangerous certainly: some of its members have been involved in robbery, espionage, kidnapping, blackmail and conspiracy.

In October 1979, for example, nine Scientology workers, including the wife of the movement's leader, were found guilty by a United States court of conspiracy charges. The man who led this investigation and prosecution, Assistant U.S. Attorney Raymond Banoun, remarked, 'The evidence presented to the court shows brazen criminal campaigns against private and public organizations and individuals. The Scientology officials hid behind claims of religious liberty while inflicting injuries upon every element of society.'[2]

In August 1979 a jury in Portland, Oregon, agreed that the cult's behaviour was fraudulent and awarded considerable damages to seventeen-year-old Jülie Christofferson who had been recruited and abused by them.[3] In 1976 the FBI arrested two Scientology agents who were using forged credentials to search a government office at night. Later, in July 1977, the FBI seized 23,000 documents, including many U.S. government 'secret' papers, from the Scientology headquarters in Los Angeles plus burglars' tools and electronic surveillance equipment. There have been other cases as well as numerous law suits in Britain in the late 1960s and early '70s and '80s. A ban was imposed by the British government on all overseas members of Scientology seeking to study or work at their centres in Britain; the ban was in force for twelve years.

In August 1986, the *Daily Express* carried the front-page headline, 'Scientologists "adopt" daughter worth millions: Elvis heiress in cult shock.'[4] Lisa Marie, the daughter of Elvis Presley, inherited two million dollars from the superstar's estate on her eighteenth birthday; she is due to receive another two million dollars on her twenty-first birthday and up to thirty million dollars, as well as Elvis's palatial Gracelands estate, when she is twenty-five.

A waitress at the Scientology retreat said, 'She is being handled very carefully. They know she will come into a lot more money and they expect a large chunk of it.' The organization takes large donations from its rich adherents, with some donations running into six-figure sums. Lisa's mother, Dallas star Priscilla Presley, first introduced her to Scientology four years ago when they both attended a course of lectures.

Scientology is wealthy

The cult is wealthy, having purchased expensive properties in America and Britain, including a £3,500,000 American hotel. In 1976 the U. S. tax officials found £1,250,000 in cash on board Apollo, the ship used personally by the founder of Scientology, Lafayette Ron Hubbard. One of Hubbard's objectives was to make money and he charged between £1,700 and £6,300 for the privilege of following some of his more advanced courses. It is estimated that the Church of Scientology has an annual gross income of £45,000,000. On his fifty-seven acre estate at East Grinstead, West Sussex, Hubbard lived in the lap of luxury in his thirty-room mansion which he bought in the late 1950s as world headquarters for his movement. Young women, called 'messengers', lit his cigarettes, helped him out of bed, dressed him, cleaned his office, washed his clothes and recorded all that he said.

The historical background

Hubbard, the son of an American naval commander, was born in Nebraska, U. S. A., in 1911. As his father's work involved constant travel, Hubbard spent his early childhood years with his grandfather, but he was later allowed to join his parents in the Far East. Here the young Hubbard was fascinated by Asian religions and he became absorbed in the study of man himself. After extensive travel in the following years, he pursued and failed a college course in molecular and atomic physics before turning in the 1930s to writing for his livelihood.

During the Second World War he served in the United States navy but there are conflicting accounts of this period in his life. The 'official' Scientology story is that Hubbard was a nuclear physicist but was eventually wounded in action with the navy and taken 'crippled and blinded' to a naval hospital where within two years he claims to have achieved fitness again due to his discovery of 'Dianetics' and Scientology.

The real story, however, is somewhat different. There is no evidence of his being wounded or being involved in combat during the last war but he was discharged from the navy and given a 40% disability pension on the ground of his arthritis and ulcer complaints. He was also given psychiatric treatment because of his suicidal tendencies and depression.

In 1949 Hubbard attributed an improvement in health to his discovery of 'Dianetics' and a year later he published his first book entitled *Dianetics: The Modern Science of Mental Health*, which dealt psychologically with the 'reactive' or subconscious mind. From this inauspicious beginning, Scientology developed and now claims a world membership of fifteen million. Here in Great Britain the cult is recruiting effectively and boasts a membership of about half a million and it has several churches here. The full title of the group is the Church of Scientology and its aim is 'to establish a religious fellowship and association for the research into the spirit and human souls, and the use and dissemination of its findings'.

A 'con man'

Newsweek, the international news magazine, carried an article with the title, 'Is L. Ron Hubbard Dead?' Following many lawsuits and denunciations by former members, Hubbard's eldest son filed a petition in a Riverside, California, court for the trusteeship of his father's $100,000,000 estate. The petition claimed that Hubbard had not been seen since March 1980 and was either dead or mentally incompetent. The claimant, De Wolf, who changed his name from L. Ron Hubbard Jr in 1972, also accused his father of being 'one of the biggest con men of this century'. Approximately 30,000 documents were produced by De Wolf in court portraying Hubbard as 'a conniving fraud who was addicted to a variety of drugs, practised black magic, performing bizarre abortion rituals and suffered from severe mental illness'. De Wolf told a *Newsweek* reporter that on several occasions he saw his father tie his mother to a bed and inject her with amphetamines and barbiturates. Hubbard's son regards the Scientology church as a sham. 'My father', he says, 'claimed that his theories relating to Scientology were based on thirty years of case histories and research. In fact, they were written off the top of his head while he was under the influence of drugs.'[5]

Ronald E. de Wolf is the oldest of Hubbard's seven children and he helped his father establish the Church of Scientology in 1952. In 1959, however, he left the organization thoroughly disillusioned as his father had become 'further and further removed from reality', suffering from severe paranoia and delusion and also physical ill-health. 'In the process of trying to unravel Scientology out of my head,' he claimed, 'I read the Bible, and in the course of time became a Christian.'[6]

Speculation concerning Hubbard's whereabouts was ended when the Church of Scientology reported his death on 25 January 1986 at his ranch in California at the age of seventy-four. In the obituary notice, *The Times* concluded: 'Hubbard was the Henry Ford of occultism. He was not, by any standards, a nice man, but was a highly influential figure among the myriad inventors of magical and religious systems who have appeared in modern times.'[7]

Almost a month later, British friends and devotees of Hubbard paid for a full-page advertisement in *The Daily Telegraph* as a tribute to their leader. They described him as 'best-selling author...founder of Scientology...friend to millions'.[8]

Sadly, Hubbard's writings continue to deceive millions of people and 'The god of this world has blinded the minds of the unbelieving, so that they might not see the light of the gospel of the glory of Christ, who is the image of God' (2 Corinthians 4:4).

What Scientology teaches	*What the Bible teaches*

God

While Hubbard believes in the existence of God, there is no official or orthodox doctrine of God in his writings. God is assumed to be impersonal but divine holiness is ignored. Individual members are free to believe what they like about the character and purposes of God.

'God, after he spoke long ago to the fathers in the prophets in many portions and in many ways, in these last days has spoken to us in his Son...' (Hebrews 1:1-2).

'Holy, Holy, Holy, is the Lord of hosts, the whole earth is full of his glory' (Isaiah 6:3).

Bible

The Bible is only one of the numerous 'holy' books; its teaching, therefore, is not binding upon people. The Bible is viewed as one account of people's search after truth. Hubbard himself and his writings are the group's supreme authority.

'Thy word is truth' (John 17:17).

'For ever, O Lord, thy word is settled in heaven' (Psalm 119:89).

Christ

Christ is unimportant in this cult and there are very few references to Christ in their publications. Jesus Christ is respected as one of the great religious teachers.

'Thou art the Christ, the Son of the living God' (Matthew 16:16).

'This is my beloved Son, with whom I am well-pleased' (Matthew 17:5).

'He is the image of the invisible God...For in him all things were created...he is before all things, and in him all things hold together. He is also head of the body, the church...so that he himself might come to have first place in everything' (Colossians 1:15-20).

Man

Human beings willed themselves into existence trillions of years ago and then proceeded to will the material universe into being. In doing this, humans were trapped in physical bodies and they need to be 'untrapped' in order to return to their original god-like state. This requires the help of Scientology 'ministers', who can charge as much as $300 an hour. Human nature is basically good and evil is merely unreasonable or irrational behaviour caused by 'engrams'.

'There is none righteous, not even one' (Romans 3:10).

'I know that nothing good dwells in me, that is, in my flesh' (Romans 7:18).

Salvation

Psychological difficulties (what Hubbard calls 'engrams') spoil man's good nature. Salvation is obtained through the cult's philosophy and methods (i.e. sharing, counselling, confession, etc.) as individuals achieve for themselves fulfilment and release.

'By grace you have been saved through faith; and that not of yourselves, it is the gift of God; not as a result of works, that no one should boast' (Ephesians 2:8-9).

'There is salvation in no one else; for there is no other name under heaven that has been given among men, by which we must be saved' (Acts 4:12).

Section 4
Freemasonry

19.
Freemasonry

Estimates of the world-wide membership of Freemasonry vary from between three and six million, with about 25,000 lodges. Countries like Russia, China, Hungary, Spain and Portugal have outlawed the society but there are over one million members and 9,950 lodges in Great Britain alone. Only men are eligible for membership and they must be over the age of twenty-one, although the sons of Freemasons are allowed to join at the age of eighteen.

Freemasons are mostly professional and middle or upper-class people such as lawyers, solicitors, doctors, teachers, musicians, engineers, policemen, businessmen, tradesmen and ministers of religion.

While clergy from most denominations are involved in Freemasonry, Methodist ministers have their own Epworth Lodge.[1] 'The Church of England,' writes Stephen Knight, 'has been a stronghold of Freemasonry for more than 200 years. Traditionally, joining the Brotherhood and advancing within it has always been the key to preferment in the Church. This situation has altered in the past twenty years...even so, the Church is still rife with members of the Brotherhood.'[2] Dr Robert Runcie, the present Archbishop of Canterbury, is not a Freemason, but some of his predecessors were, including Dr Geoffrey Fisher. Some Anglican bishops also belong to the Brotherhood, as well as many of the lower clergy and laity. The Rev. Walter Hannah reports that the SPCK ordered their shops not to stock his book *Darkness Visible*, which was a scathing exposure of Freemasonry.[3] The Archbishop of Canterbury is the SPCK President and the archbishop in office at the time was Dr Geoffrey Fisher!

The Greek Orthodox Church and the Salvation Army, for example, still forbid their people to become Freemasons but the Roman Catholic Church has relaxed its papal edicts of 1738 and 1917 which condemned Freemasonry. Since November 1974 any Roman Catholic can join 'if he sincerely believes that membership of Freemasonry does not conflict with his deeper loyalty', but he will be excommunicated 'if the policy and actions of the Free-masons in his area are known to be hostile to the Church'. Stephen Knight claims to have evidence that the Vatican itself is infiltrated by Freemasons.[4] David Yallop also speaks of 'over 100 masons, ranging from cardinals to priests' inside the Vatican and argues convincingly that the last pope's plan to restrict their influence actually led to his death in 1978.[5]

Numerous members of the Royal Family, too, are Freemasons and the Duke of Kent is the Grand Master of the society. There are reliable reports that the Queen Mother dissuaded Prince Charles from becoming a Freemason and if the prince holds out in his refusal to join, he will be the first king for several generations not to be a mason. His father, Prince Philip, succumbed somewhat reluctantly under the pressure of King George VI, although the prince has not been actively involved in the society and regards much of its ritual as 'a silly joke'.[6]

Those working within industry, commerce and business are frequently involved in Freemasonry, particularly if they want promotion or improved sales. Freemasonry has infiltrated all levels of banking, from clerks to branch/regional/national managerial positions. The Bank of England, for example, has its own lodge and many of its employees are masons.

In most lodges you will find men who are accountants, commer-cial travellers, architects, shop managers and proprietors, builders, surveyors, estate agents, restaurant proprietors and travel agents, etc. A former master mason writes, 'Membership of Freemasonry is used considerably in the field of industry and commerce — because of the sign one can give which is unnoticeable by anyone else. You can make it known to the other person that you are what they call on the square, and if the other person is on the square he will recognize the sign, and that can influence either your being able to make a sale, or, if you are applying for a job, it can make the difference between whether you get the job or not.'[7]

Another area where Freemasonry is rife is in the legal profession — barristers, magistrates, judges and solicitors. The Law Society, for example, which is the governing body of over 40,000 solicitors in England and Wales, is 'one of the most masonic institutions in the world'.[8] One barrister, Rudy Narayan, claims that out of more than eighty High Court judges in Britain, thirty are Freemasons.[9]

'The insidious effect of Freemasonry among the police has to be experienced to be believed,' claimed the former head of Monmouthshire CID in 1969.[10] Since the Scotland Yard corruption in 1877, followed by the police cover-up of the Jack the Ripper murders in London in 1888 (perpetrated according to masonic ritual), claims of bias towards Freemasonry and its influence within the police force have been made regularly. These claims have been accompanied by some compelling evidence.

In 1984 the Police Federation gave financial support to a Chief Inspector who pressed for an independent enquiry into claims that his career had been unfairly influenced by Freemasonry.[11] Stephen Knight observes that 'Operation Countryman, the biggest investigation ever conducted into police corruption in Britain, would never have come about if the Commissioner of the City of London Police between 1971 and 1977 had not been corrupted and unduly influenced by Freemasonry.'[12] The same writer argues that 'an independent enquiry into Freemasonry in the police should be initiated' immediately. Furthermore, he insists that 'A compulsory register on which police officers have to list their affiliation to secret societies, and their status within such societies, is the minimum requirement if a grave situation is to be improved.'[13]

The historical background

As we have seen, the influence of Freemasonry in our society is extensive; today Freemasonry is the largest international secret society in the world But how did it begin and where?

Well, it began harmlessly enough. While some masons try to trace their history back to the building of Solomon's temple (in 1 Kings 5), the society really originated in the mediaeval lodge of the

English stonemasons. The main work of these masons was the building of churches and cathedrals, which often involved them in considerable travel. In order to obtain new work it was considered necessary for craft members to keep the skills secret, so various passwords were introduced in order to safeguard these secrets and ensure new work for themselves. The masons also built 'lodges' in close proximity to their work. These were recreational centres where they relaxed and talked together. With the decline of cathedral building, they augmented their numbers with honorary or unskilled members. During the seventeenth century lodges emerged which consisted wholly of unqualified masons. In 1717 all the different lodges united under the Grand Lodge of England and their *Book of Constitutions* was published in 1723.

The *Constitutions* of 1723, however, contained major changes which 'de-christianized' the society and authorized the introduction of pagan elements into its ritual. All references to Christ were eliminated and between 1723 and 1813 the invocation of Christ's name at the end of prayers gradually stopped. Even when Scriptures like 1 Peter 2:5 and 2 Thessalonians 3:2,13 were quoted in masonic ritual the name of Christ was removed from the text. Instead ancient Egyptian symbolism and ritual of a mystical nature were absorbed into the society in this period to give it a distinctly religious basis and expression. Various splits occurred throughout the eighteenth century, but in 1813 unity was re-established with the formation of the 'United Grand Lodge of Ancient Free and Accepted Masons of England'. While the society has been severely persecuted at times, it has become increasingly more popular and acceptable in Western Europe and North America since the end of World War II.

A great deal of humanitarian work is undertaken by this society, especially on behalf of its own members. A hospital and nursing home are maintained for sick masons, as well as two schools for the children of masons. There is also a Fund of Benevolence which is used to support needy masons and their dependents. Other charities are also supported by Freemasons but their benevolence falls far below the standard of the New Testament. For example, in the third degree obligation the new member must promise to relieve a brother mason only 'so far as may fairly be done without detriment to myself or my connections'.

Incompatibility with Christian teaching

There are many features of Freemasonry which are incompatible with the teaching of the Bible and the fact that it is a religion should prevent Christians from participating in its activities. One often hears the comment that masons do not take the religious aspect seriously, but why sing hymns, say prayers, swear oaths on their volume of Sacred Law, or have a temple and altar if this is so?

Another argument raised in defence of Freemasonry is that it is only an arm or extension of the church and not in any sense a rival. But this is unconvincing, for Freemasonry claims to possess secrets which help people to know how to worship and know God better, secrets which the Bible does not reveal and the church does not possess. One such secret is the sacred and mysterious name of God which is found, they claim, only in Freemasonry. The Christian, however, affirms that God has given a sufficient, perfect and final revelation of his character and purpose in the Bible alone. There is no need for additional revelation.

Some masonic writers suggest that initiation to Freemasonry is superior to Christian baptism in that it enriches man's spiritual experience. In this initiation ceremony, the candidate rolls his left trouser leg up to his knee, removes his jacket and tie, opens his shirt, replaces his right shoe with a slipper and empties his pocket of money as a symbol of his poverty. To symbolize 'his state of darkness', the candidate is then blindfolded; he acknowledges that while he is in darkness he is moving into the 'light' which is found supremely in Freemasonry. For the Christian this is offensive. Christ, not Freemasonry, is the light of the world (John 8:12) and only in Christ can we find true, spiritual light.

Preaching on the words of 1 Corinthians 3:11, ('For other foundation can no man lay than that is laid, which is Jesus Christ'), the Rev. A. W. Rainsbury detailed six Christian objections to Freemasonry.[14]

The first objection is that secret societies are unscriptural (see Matthew 10:26-7; John 18:20). Secondly, a candidate must make rash promises 'to secrecy and faithfulness in matters of which nothing is revealed to him previously...The man has got to sell his conscience to the Worshipful Master before he can proceed. But what right has any man to make another the custodian of his conscience?' (see Leviticus 5:4-6). A third objection to Freemasonry which the Rev. Rainsbury mentions is the use of monstrous masonic oaths which contradict our Lord's words in Matthew 5:33-37. Another is the exclusion of the Lord Jesus Christ from its precincts. 'The precious name of Jesus Christ is not allowed even to be uttered in a masonic lodge...How can any Christian mason offer such an insult to the One who hung upon the cross to save his precious soul?' The fifth objection to Freemasonry is that it rests upon a false doctrine of justification by works and, finally, it is an apostate religion, with its own universal theology which eliminates Jesus Christ. They also use a pagan, syncretistic name for God — JAH-BUL-ON!

'I am firmly convinced,' writes Walter Hannah, 'that for a Christian to pledge himself to a religious or even quasi-religious organization which offers prayers and worship to God which deliberately exclude the name of our Lord and Saviour Jesus Christ, in whose name only is salvation to be found, is apostatic...'[15] 'Masonry is not so much a religion as a parasite on religion and a rival to the church...'[16] Anyone who takes God and the Bible seriously cannot but agree with this conclusion.

What can we do about it?

What practical steps should Christians and churches take concerning Freemasonry?

Convinced of the incompatibility of Freemasonry with biblical Christianity, the Rev. Harry Woods recently urged the Free Church of Scotland to take the following steps:

'That the church issue a clear condemnation of Freemasonry...

'That those who are presently members of both the church and Freemasonry be asked to renounce their lodge membership, failure to do so being a disciplinary matter.

'That our people be warned against the errors of Freemasonry from pulpits...

'This is an important issue. We would not tolerate a man being a member both of our church and a Mormon temple. Why should we allow simultaneous membership of the church and a Freemason temple?...The Word of God teaches the exclusiveness of the Christian faith and the forsaking of the temples of idols (2 Corinthians 6:14-18).'[17]

There are encouraging signs that an increasing number of other churches in Britain are implementing the measures proposed by the Rev. Woods.

What Freemasonry teaches	*What the Bible teaches*

God

New members, in their initiation ceremony, are introduced to God as the 'GAOTU', that is, the Grand Architect of the Universe. They also learn another divine name, JHVH — a reference to Jehovah. At the top of the altar in the Royal Arch appears the 'sacred and mysterious name of the true and living God most High', namely, JAH-BUL-ON, which is composed of the Hebrew 'Jahweh', the Assyrian 'Baal' and 'On' used in ancient Egyptian mystery religion in offering prayer to the god Osiris. Other titles of God include 'Grand Geometrician' and the 'Great Overseer'. They claim to have the secrets concerning the 'lost name of God'.

'...nor does anyone know the Father, except the Son, and anyone to whom the Son wills to reveals him' (Matthew 11:27).

'No man has seen God at any time; the only begotten God, who is in the bosom of the Father, he has explained him' (John 1:18).

'God's mystery, that is, Christ himself, in whom are hidden all the treasures of wisdom and knowledge' (Colossians 2:2-3).

Bible

The Bible is not a unique nor sufficient revelation from God. The writings of other religions, e.g. the Koran and the Vedas, are equally authoritative although in 'Christian' lodges usually only the Bible is used.

'Thy word is truth' (John 17:17).

'Lord, to whom shall we go? You have words of eternal life' (John 6:68).

Christ

Christ is totally excluded from this movement and they deny that he is the world's only Saviour.

'He who does not honour the Son does not honour the Father who sent him' (John 5:23).

'For there is one God, and one mediator also between God and men, the man Christ Jesus, who gave himself as a ransom for all' (1 Timothy 2:5).

Sin

While Freemasonry encourages decency, good works and civil obedience, it hardly mentions sin or repentance.

'Jews and Greeks are all under sin; as it is written. "There is none righteous, not even one"' (Romans 3:9-10).

'God is now declaring to men that all everywhere should repent' (Acts 17:30).

Salvation

People are saved by their good deeds.

'Jesus answered and said to them, "This is the work of God, that you believe in him whom he has sent"' (John 6:29).

'But when the kindness of God our Saviour and his love for mankind appeared, he saved us, not on the basis of deeds which we have done in righteousness, but according to his mercy...' (Titus 3:4).

Section 5
Some self-improvement groups

20. EST: Erhard Seminars Training

21. Exegesis: a brief introduction

20.
EST: Erhard Seminars Training

The EST Training was established by Werner Erhard in 1971 and is described as 'a 60-hour educational experience' operating 'on the principle that there is only one thing powerful enough to transform the quality of your life in just four days — *you*'. More than 400,000 people have completed the training in countries as far afield as the United States, Australia, Canada, Germany, India, Israel and Britain. About 250 people attend each training course which takes place over two consecutive weekends and includes the presentation of data by trainers, 'processes' (an opportunity for people to look at detailed aspects of themselves and their lives), 'sharing' and questions. The purpose of EST Training is 'to transform your ability to experience living so that the situations you have been trying to change or have been putting up with clear up just in the process of life itself'.[1]

Who is Erhard?

Werner Erhard was born in 1935 and named by his parents Jack Rosenberg. It was in 1960, after leaving his wife and four children, that he changed his name. He was involved in a number of different businesses ranging from selling cars to selling encyclopaedias. While working in San Francisco, Erhard was introduced to Scientology and he also became closely involved with Alex Everett, the

founder of Mind Dynamics, a self-hypnosis mind control movement. During 1963, Erhard was driving his car on Highway 101 in
Marin County, California, when he claims to have had a radical
experience of enlightenment which transformed his life.

By this time, Erhard had also studied Zen Buddhism (later he
studied with Zen masters in the East), hypnosis, yoga, Silva Mind
Control, psychocybernetics, *Gestalt,* encounter therapy and
transpersonal psychology. John Weldon thus rightly describes EST
as 'the fruit of his "conversion" experience and personal research
into these and other disciplines'.[2]

What EST claims to do

Erhard teaches that our lives have two main aspects, namely *content*
and *context,* and whereas EST training does not change the content
of our lives it can deal with the context, that is, the way we hold the
content. 'People complete the training and return to the same
family, friends, jobs and other situations. What happens in the
training is a transformation — an essential shift in the context in
which the facts, circumstances and positions of one's life are held.'[3]
As an illustration of transformation, Erhard gives the example of a
person who believes it is better to be a man rather than a woman or
vice versa. This conviction may be so strongly held that it influences in a radical way the person's response to the whole of life.
Such a person is 'at the effect of that position...and is stuck with it.
It controls him and he behaves as if that is the way life really is and
that he is helpless to do anything about it.'[4] According to Erhard this
is an entirely negative response for a transformation of context is
possible, 'so that you become source of, author or creator of,
responsible for your position that being a man is better. You may
still retain that position, if you choose, but you would no longer need
to be run by it or be the victim of it. You realize it is *your* position.
You've created it and you can keep it or change it or give it up,
depending on which contributes most to your and other's aliveness.
You aren't stuck on a position. You can choose.'

EST disciple Marcia Seligson explains how this notion of
responsibility or divine control influences her life: 'I run my body,
it doesn't run me. I'm in charge here... Personal responsibility is a
potent force indeed, the sensation that one is the cause of one's life.

For me, it is the focal wisdom of training...to the degree that if I still hang on to my victim beliefs (i.e., that things outside my life control me), things don't work too well.'[5]

Is EST training akin to positive thinking? No, replies Erhard, positive thinking minimizes the 'downs' of life, while EST acknowledges the truth about life whether it's up or down. What happens after the training? Are people helped? As a result of their EST training over two weekends, for which they pay in excess of £200, some people claimed to have experienced 'expanded satisfaction', 'completeness in relationships', 'an enhanced willingness and ability to communicate with others', 'improved health', 'a renewed sense of the joy and the challenge of life', 'a clearer sense of meaning, direction and purpose' and 'a sense of competence and power', etc. However, success is not guaranteed and the reason given is that it all depends on the individual's 'commitment to transform the quality of his life'.[6]

A challenge to the gospel

Alongside Exegesis, EST is one of the most popular and influential self-improvement groups flourishing in the vacuum of Western society and it challenges the unique claims of the gospel. Erhard claims that EST 'is not a system of beliefs or techniques to be learned and practised' but his movement is built on assumptions and beliefs diametrically opposed to the Bible. He is careful not to criticize Christianity or any other religion but, unlike the Rajneesh Foundation, he requires no religious base in order to offer people fulfilment and transformation. EST then is completely humanistic in its attempt to resolve man's deepest problems and we will now look at five of its most basic beliefs in the light of the Bible.

What EST teaches	*What the Bible teaches*
Truth	
'Discovering truth in themselves is the greatest adventure people ever have...the truth fully recognized and acknowledged is an	Christianity is the truth. For example, Jesus is the truth personified and he mediates truth (John 14:6; 1:17).

enormously liberating and enlightening experience' (Werner Erhard).

God's transcendence, man's sin and spiritual blindness underline the need for God to take the initiative in unveiling his character and purposes to us and this he has done perfectly in the Bible (2 Timothy 3:16; 2 Peter 1:21).

The gospel is 'the word of truth' (Ephesians 1:13, AV) and Jesus identifies his word with 'the truth' in John 8:31-32.

Truth then is not primarily subjective, personal, relative or illusory but objective, divine and verbalized without error in the Bible.

God

Erhard writes, 'I believe that "belief" in God is the greatest barrier to God in the universe…I would prefer someone who is ignorant to someone who believes in God. Because the belief in God is a total barrier, almost a total barrier to God…To pay attention to personality is to pay attention to illusion or effects. That's all there is, there isn't anything but spirituality, which is just another word for God, because God is everything.'[7]

'In EST Training,' declares William Greene, 'you are God…Therefore you cannot look to any supreme being for special treatment, goodness or award.'[8]

EST, therefore, teaches pantheism, that is, the theory that God is the world.

God is not a part of humanity nor can he be identified with nature. By contrast, God is 'high and lifted up' (Isaiah 6:1), transcendent, independent, sovereign and uncontrolled by humans (Isaiah 40:12-26; 43:13; Daniel 4:35).

Man

Our lives have two main aspects: the *content*, or facts and circumstances of our lives, and the *context*,

1. *Man's nature*. EST thinking here is superficial and inadequate. Our lives do have two main aspects

that is, the way we hold these facts, circumstances and positions.

'You and I possess within ourselves at every moment of our lives, under all circumstances, the power to transform the quality of our lives' (Werner Erhard).

Law of God

Life has *no* rules at all.

'What you are doing is what God wants you to do. If you keep saying it the way it really is, eventually, your word is law in the universe.'[9]

Evil is denied.

'Life is always perfect just the way it is...this universe is perfect. Don't lie about it.'

A popular response by EST graduates to real-life situations of

but these are body and soul, not content and context. God gave humans both a body and soul (Genesis 2:7; Job 32:8; 33:4; Ecclesiastes 12:7). EST totally ignores this crucial and spiritual dimension of man. Although created in the image of God (Genesis 1:27; James 3:9), humans are nevertheless still finite, created beings. Our potential can only be realized when we come to know and enjoy God through the Lord Jesus Christ.

2. *Man's inability to do spiritual good.* Man, in common grace, can be a good neighbour, a responsible citizen, a kind parent and a respectable person, but sin has rendered him impotent in two main ways.

Firstly, he cannot meet the requirements of God's holy law. Because he is not motivated by God's glory, love and truth, man's best actions are all defective before God (Romans 3:10, 20, 23; 8:9; James 2:10).

Secondly, he cannot change his basic preference for sin and thus is incapable of spiritual good (John 1:13; 3:5; 6:44).

'Fear God and keep his commandments, because this applies to every person' (Ecclesiastes 12:13).

'Do not be wise in your own eyes; fear the Lord and turn away from evil' (Proverbs 3:7).

'Woe to those who call evil good, and good evil; who substitute darkness for light and light for darkness; who substitute bitter for sweet, and sweet for bitter! Woe to those who are wise in their own

greed, cruelty, suffering and corruption is 'So what?'

eyes, and clever in their own sight!' (Isaiah 5:20-21).

'Seek good and not evil...hate evil, love good and establish justice...' (Amos 5:14-15).

Conversion

EST talks of 'transformation' rather than conversion and it occurs as a 'recontextualization' from a context where you are 'at the effect of things' to a context where you are the source or 'at the cause of things'. The heart of transformation is going from being at effect to being at cause.

Erhard writes, 'We've been conditioned to look for answers outside ourselves. But that's not what people get from us. What they get is an experience of enlightenment, which is different from the belief system called salvation. If I get the idea that God is going to save me, therefore I'm all right, that's salvation; if I get the idea that nothing's going to save me, therefore I'm all right, that's enlightenment.'[10]

'Your willingness to be there (the EST training course) and your commitment to transform the quality of your life is all you need' (Werner Erhard).

True conversion to God is a radical, inward and permanent change grounded in the supernatural work of the Holy Spirit in regeneration (John 3:3-8) and involves repentance and faith.

Repentance involves a recognition of our sin against God, godly sorrow for it and a turning from sin to God (Romans 1:32; 3:20; Psalm 51:2, 10, 14; 2 Corinthians 7:9-10; Acts 2:38).

Faith includes some knowledge of, and full agreement with, the gospel, a deep interest in and thirst for salvation as well as personal trust in the Lord Jesus Christ (John 1:12; 3:14-16; 7:37-38).

You may like to read some of the conversions described in the Bible: 2 Chronicles 33:12-13; Luke 19:8-9; John 4:29, 39; 9:38; Acts 8:30-39; 9:1-18; 10:1-48; 16:14-15, 25-34.

Jesus said, 'Come to me, all who are weary and heavy-laden, and I will give you rest. Take my yoke upon you, and learn from me, for I am gentle and humble in heart; and you shall find rest for your souls. For my yoke is easy and my load is light' (Matthew 11:28-30; cf. 16:24).

21.
Exegesis

Another popular self-improvement movement is Exegesis, which has a distinctively British origin. Its founder, Robert D'Aubigny, whose previous name was Robert Fuller, lived in Essex and his father was a meat salesman in Wanstead.

A trained actor, D'Aubigny became fascinated with some of the cults and went to Scotland for a brief period to join a commune there. He then moved to the United States where he took a special interest in the subject of positive thinking. Returning to Britain, he began to propagate his views through an organization he established in 1977 called Infinity Training Seminars. His headquarters was a £70,000 house in Cobham, Surrey which his mother-in-law rented to him. One year later, in 1978, D'Aubigny changed the name of his organization to Exegesis, which is a transliteration of a Greek noun meaning to direct or expand. Exegesis is also known as the School of Economic Science.

Dangerous techniques

The seminars and training courses are expensive. According to a *Daily Mirror* investigative report, many of D'Aubigny's assistants have been happy to work for as little as £25 a month while D'Aubigny himself lives in luxury. 'Enlightenment' is promised to all who sign on for introductory, then refresher and graduate courses. The methods used, however, by this movement include threats, humiliation, force, starvation for as long as fifteen hours and stiff fines for trainees who forget to carry their Exegesis 'enlightenment' notebook, or fail to applaud when a leader stands up, etc. An expert in military interrogations warns: 'People who innocently go along to these seminars are like lambs going to the slaughter. The techniques that are used can cause incredible damage and destroy a person's whole life. They are methods guaranteed to break down willpower. No matter how strong minded you are, you can't win. You are worn down until you have no resistance left.'[1]

Belief in oneself

The basic philosophy of Exegesis is similar to EST and another group called Emin as well as to Scientology. These groups are all humanistic in their philosophy but are distinctive in that they are characterized by a belief in oneself, that is, in human potential and transformation.[2]

G. K. Chesterton's words are profoundly true: 'When a man ceases to believe in God, he does not believe in nothing. He believes in anything.'

Section 6
Some spiritistic groups and the occult

22. The occult — a general survey and warning

23. Spiritism

24. Theosophy

25. Eckankar

22.
The occult — a general survey and warning

There has been a resurgence of interest in the occult during the past twenty years. While only two per cent of the population in Great Britain attends church on a Sunday morning, an estimated fifty per cent of the population is involved in some form of occult activity. One English M.P. recently claimed in Parliament that seventy-eight per cent of secondary school pupils are, or have been, in contact with spirits. We are told that there are as many witches in Britain as there are clergymen and ministers. Ten years ago there were 10,000 witches in Britain but today, according to a recent newspaper report, there are an estimated 100,000. In addition there are well over 2,000 professional astrologers and fortune-tellers whose income is considerable. Over ten years ago, the magazine, *Man, Myth and Magic,* which investigates contemporary occult activity, reported: 'In Britain one person in twenty is actively concerned with the occult in one form or another,' but by 1989, sadly the ratio was much higher.

Eight years ago the first World Congress on witchcraft was held in Columbia and over 3,000 witches, sorcerers, spiritists and Satan-worshippers attended. Lady Sara Russell, the clever twenty-six-year-old granddaughter of the philosopher Bertrand Russell, intended participating in this convention; however, she never arrived. A few weeks earlier, after becoming demon-possessed through a Satanist ritual in a Cornish cemetery, she poured kerosene over her body and then, lighting a match, committed suicide.

While Anton La Vey formed a 'Satanist Church' in San Francisco in 1966 and gave new impetus to the movement, it is in Western Europe where the greatest revival of Satanism has taken place. In Germany, for example, there are reputed to be three million devoted devil worshippers and seven million sympathizers. Satanist Churches have been established in many of the main cities of Western Europe, including London, Paris, Basle, Berne and Rome. Outside their Paris building the Satanists have written, 'We worship and serve the Prince of this World.'

In the *Daily Post* of 13 May 1982 and on B.B.C. Welsh news programmes, the Presbyterian Church Youth Chaplain at Bala, the Rev. Dafydd Owen, reported that 'Devil worship by occult groups whose young members burn Bibles, cut their wrists and suck each other's blood is now happening on an increasing scale in rural Wales.' On 2 May 1982 the *News of the World* carried a feature article on 'The Rocker who is singing for Satan'. Rock singer Terry Jones was once the leader of thirty-six witchcraft covens throughout Britain. When the singer steps on to the stage with his band, Pagan Altar, he admits, 'The audience think they're listening to rock music but in fact they're participating in a Satanic rite. The stage is my altar and the audience are my congregation.' Jones, an admirer of the notorious Anton La Vey — self-styled Black Pope of the Church of Satan — was initiated into a coven in Peckham, London. 'I don't really believe there's good or evil,' he adds, 'it's all the same. Satanism interested me more and that's how I got into black witchcraft.' The same newspaper report gives detailed evidence of a verger, Alan Drew, who 'defiled the Exeter Cathedral he serves by joining a black mass which ended in an orgy beside the High Altar. The altar crucifix was turned upside down as an insult to Christianity and symbols hailing the devil were laid out.' Commenting on its investigation of the secret world of witchcraft and devil worship now flourishing in Britain, the newspaper declares, 'Our startling dossier reveals sinister new links between black magic and child abuse, racism and rock music.'

Doreen Irvine, former queen of the black witches, but now a devoted Christian engaged in warning people against the occult, confirms these reports: 'I've seen more people involved with the occult in the past two years than ever before. Satanism is spreading like a malignant cancer.'

The position is no better in America, where many millions of dollars are spent annually on computerized horoscopes and about ten million Americans refuse to leave for work before reading their horoscopes.

Every day, over fifty million Americans consult horoscopes in one or more of 1,200 newspapers and there are now supposed to be 10,000 full-time astrologers and 175,000 part-time ones in the U.S.A. During 1980, 208,302 people bought the *Handbook of Supernatural Powers,* while nearly 100,000 bought the book *Magic Power of Witchcraft.* According to one news agency, the 'available mailing lists of names of people [in the U.S.A.] involved in the occult now stands at 3.8 million'.[1]

But what is the occult?

The word 'occult' means 'hidden' and it is used to describe pagan practices in which magic, witchcraft and other means are used to explore and exploit the supernatural realm. Some of the activities include rhabdomancy (divining-rod phenomena), radiesthid (pendulum phenomena) and lycanthropy (changing of humans into wolves). There are well-known aspects of the occult such as astrology, spiritism, witchcraft, black and white magic, demonology, vampirism, etc. We will briefly refer to some of the most popular expressions of the occult in Britain today.

Spiritism

Spiritists believe it is possible to contact the dead, or the spirit-world, through the mind and particularly through clairvoyants or mediums, who, often while in a trance, allow their bodies to be used by spirits.

The Bible teaches that God forbids us to contact spirits or the dead. To do so is a great sin (see, e.g. Deuteronomy 18:10-12; Isaiah 8:19-22).

Refuse to attend séances and never dabble with tumblers or a ouija board, even though it is used as a party game.

Astrology

What astrologists believe

By observing the stars, sun, moon and planets, astrologers believe it is possible to predict the future; they assume that our character is determined by cosmic bodies at the time of our birth and the pattern of our life is then predictable. For this reason, astrologers stress the importance of the Zodiac signs under which we are born. Space exploration, coupled with man's insatiable curiosity, has given more credibility to astrology in recent years.

1. The Bible clearly condemns astrology.

'Let your astrologers come forward, those stargazers who make predictions month by month, let them save you from what is coming upon you. Surely they are like stubble; the fire will burn them up. They cannot even save themselves from the power of the flame... these you have laboured with and trafficked with since childhood. Each of them goes on in his error:' (Isaiah 47:13-15, NIV; cf. Deuteronomy 17:2-5).

2. Astrology ignores the first two commandments (Exodus 20:1-5).

3. God, not fate (as astrology implies), governs our lives and the universe (Psalms 96:10; 97:1; Daniel 4:34-5).

Christians can rejoice in the fact of God's providence (Romans 8:28-30).

4. Rather than prying into the future, our duty is to trust God, believe his Word and submit to his sovereign will in providence (see Proverbs 3:5-6; Romans 1:10; James 4:13-17).

Avoid reading horoscopes and do not allow anyone in any way to tell you your fortune. Read the Bible more!

Magic

Kurt Koch defines *magic* as 'the attempt to know and rule the spirit world, human, animal and plant world as well as dead matter in an extra-sensory way with help of secret means and ceremonies'.[2]

Black magic has been popularized in many recent novels and films; it is more obviously evil and is usually associated with immorality, sadism and drugs.

In *white magic* the devil transforms himself into an angel of light (2 Corinthians 11:14) for the purpose of healing or helping in other and more dramatic ways. Charms are used to bring the magic powers into action but the powers invoked belong to the devil, not God (see Leviticus 20:6, 27; Deuteronomy 18:10-12).

Witchcraft

Witchcraft is probably the oldest and most widespread of occult practices. Many of the witches have real powers and are dangerous: they can curse and injure people, perform supernatural feats and are involved with evil spirits.

Modern witchcraft was popularized in England by Gerald Gardner's *Witchcraft Today,* which was published in 1954. For the first time in many centuries, a witch — Gardner himself — openly acknowledged himself to be a worshipper of the Horned God and a member of a secret coven. Dennis Wheatley's novels have also helped to attract people to witchcraft. Witches meet either four or thirteen times a year and a coven has thirteen members including a high priest or priestess.

Avoid novels and films which describe and commend the practice of witchcraft. If anyone needs help through dabbling in occult practices, do not get involved but refer them to Christian pastors.

Satanism

Satanism involves devil-worship and the practice of black magic and/or witchcraft. One of the founders of contemporary Satanism is Alister Crowley, described as 'the great beast of Tottenham Court Road'. Although brought up in a Plymouth Brethren assembly, he hated Christianity from an early age. When he became a black magician, he baptized a frog as a symbol of Jesus Christ, arrested it, tried it for blasphemy and crucified it. His rituals, followed by most British Satanists, are degrading and wicked. Satanists meet secretly in small groups or cells.

What Satanists believe	*What the Bible teaches*
1. The devil is stronger than God.	'With God all things are possible' (Matthew 19:26). God 'does according to his will in the host of heaven and among the inhabitants of earth; and no one can ward off his hand or say to him, "What hast thou done?"' (Daniel 4:35).
2. The devil should be worshipped.	God declares, 'You shall have no other gods before me' (Exodus 20:3). 'Then Jesus said to him, "Begone, Satan! For it is written, You shall worship the Lord your God, and serve him only"' (Matthew 4:10).
3. Evil is beautiful and enjoyable.	'For thou art not a God who takes pleasure in wickedness; no evil dwells with thee... Thou doest hate all who do iniquity... the Lord abhors the man of bloodshed and deceit' (Psalm 54-6: cf. Proverbs 6:16-19; Habakkuk 1:13; Exekiel 8:1-18). 'Therefore what benefit were you then deriving from the things of which you are now ashamed? For the outcome of those things is death' (Romans 6:21).

'There are terrible consequences involved,' warns Kurt Koch, 'if we trespass into these areas, and God himself has forbidden us to touch these things.' Today's 'occult explosion' is a challenge to Christians. We must obey God's Word, and in the Lord's strength, use the armour of God (Ephesians 6:10-18) to withstand the devil. The Lord Jesus is Victor and, as believers, we share in his triumph and authority (Colossians 2:9-15; 1 John 3:8; Revelation 19:11-21; 20:1-10.

23.
Spiritism

Spiritism has a long and varied history but modern spiritism traces its origin to Margaret and Kate Fox, sisters who lived with their family in Hyderville, New York. In 1848, when the sisters were twelve and nine years of age, they claimed to have heard unusual and mysterious rapping noises in their home. When eventually the furniture in their room began to move without anyone touching it or any natural explanation and when a strange cold hand touched Kate's face, she decided to investigate the incidents further and contacted the spirits. Kate received answers which were allegedly conveyed by the number of raps given and the sisters claimed that a spirit revealed itself to them as Charles Rosma who had been murdered some years previously by someone living in their house. When at a later date, these claims were publicized in the press, they aroused considerable excitement and interest in the subject throughout America and many people began to organize séances. In 1863 the National Spiritual Association of the United States was established to co-ordinate and expand this work.

It has not been easy to test the claims of the Fox sisters, for they were young at the time, impressionable and prone to exaggeration and fabrication. In later years the sisters acknowledged that their childhood spiritistic experiences had all been a hoax, but this confession was withdrawn rather quickly. However, we are unable to respect their statements in subsequent years for they became alcoholics and unreliable as well as irresponsible in their behaviour.

Whether or not their earlier experiences were a hoax, we should not make the mistake of dismissing as absurd the phenomena of 'voices', strange 'manifestations' and the movement of furniture without human contact. Such things do occur today and are often related either directly or indirectly to spiritism.

The British Spiritualists Union now have more than 500 churches throughout Britain and their influence is considerable. In 1987 they had 52,000 members and 560 congregations in Britain. Many people have attended their séances, including those without any religious affiliation as well as some Protestants and Catholics. Unfortunately, spiritism is highly regarded by some Protestants and I can provide specific examples of involvement by Protestant church members in séances held by Spiritist churches. In his autobiography, *Chanctonbury Ring,* the former Anglican Bishop of Southwark, Mervyn Stockwood, claims to have spoken to his dead parents via a medium and he cites numerous examples of 'communication' in which he was personally involved.

Contact with the dead or with spirits is always forbidden in the Bible (e.g. Deuteronomy 18:10-11; Isaiah 8:19-20) and rather than consulting spirits our Lord and the apostles exorcised those who were possessed by them.

Saul and the witch of Endor

But someone may ask, did not King Saul ask the witch of Endor to contact the dead prophet Samuel on his behalf? Yes, and it is a tragic story that we find in 1 Samuel chapter 28. To appreciate this incident we must familiarize ourselves with the background. In chapter 15, when Saul failed to obey God's command to kill all the Amalekites and their animals, Samuel told him, 'Because you have rejected the word of the Lord, he has also rejected you from being king' (v. 23). Despite Saul's protests and acknowledgements of guilt (vv. 24-31), the Lord's rejection of Saul was final and his subsequent history was one of failure, jealousy, depression and violence. When the Philistines, assisted by David, the Lord's anointed, eventually came to fight Israel, Saul in desperation went to the witch of Endor.

There are two main ways of interpreting the incident. Matthew Henry, Matthew Poole and Bavinck all suggest that the séance was faked by the witch. Among the reasons put forward in support of this interpretation are the following. First of all, only God has power over the dead and since he refused to answer Saul earlier (1 Samuel 28:6) he would certainly not have answered Saul when he used a means clearly condemned in the Bible. Secondly, after revealing God's judgement and rejection of the king in chapter 15, Samuel never again met Saul nor did Saul bother again to seek Samuel's help. Thirdly, God would be unlikely to give another revelation, least of all in a way contrary to his law, after having already rejected the king for his disobedience and having withdrawn his blessing from him in the closing years of his life. Finally, it was Saul who told the witch to contact Samuel, so it was possible for the woman to fake it all and even by telepathic means to describe Samuel (v. 14) in the way that either Saul or she herself remembered the prophet in his lifetime. This seems possible especially as there is no mention of Saul himself seeing Samuel in this incident.

The second interpretation suggests that, even though the law of God had been violated, yet for the purpose of further judgement and confusion, God sovereignly permitted Samuel to return, but not in response to the witch. Before the medium was able to start the séance properly and begin her incantations, she saw Samuel and was obviously shocked (v. 12). In other words, God forestalled the séance by allowing the real Samuel to appear and six times (in verses 12, 13, 14, 15, 16, 20) we are told specifically that it was Samuel who spoke, and not an impostor. For this reason alone I find this interpretation more convincing, yet it is important to underline that Samuel did not return at the request of the medium, but at the command of God in order to pronounce a final message of doom upon Saul and at the same time to prevent the séance from getting under way. This is strictly an isolated incident of divine judgement and God's revealed will forbids and condemns any contact with spirits or the dead.

What Spiritism teaches	*What the Bible teaches*
God	
God is impersonal. He is the Infinite Intelligence expressed in the physical and spiritual worlds. This pantheistic teaching means there	'The Lord appeared to Abram and said to him, "I am God Almighty"' (Genesis 17:1). 'The Lord is our God, the Lord

are as many gods as there are people and that it is useless worshipping and serving only one God.

The Trinity has no adherents in the advanced realms of the spirit world. The devil, who is not recognized as evil, is thought of as being God the Father.

Bible

God did not reveal his character and purpose in the Bible. Their actual authority is the experiences of individual spirits. For example, the belief in life after death is accepted not on the authority of the Bible but on the basis of the claim that they talk to those who have died.

is one!' (Deuteronomy 6:4)

'The eternal God is a dwelling place, and underneath are the everlasting arms' (Deuteronomy 33:27; cf. Psalms 94:9-10; 147:7-11).

'But the Lord is the true God; he is the living God and the everlasting King' (Jeremiah 10:10).

'But men spoke from God as they were carried along by the Holy Spirit' (2 Peter 1:21, NIV).

'However, as it is written: "No eye has seen, no ear has heard, no mind has conceived what God has prepared for those who love him," — but God has revealed it to us by his Spirit. The Spirit searches all things, even the deep things of God. For who among men knows the thoughts of a man except the man's spirit within him? In the same way no one knows the thoughts of God except the Spirit of God. We have not received the spirit of the world but the Spirit who is from God, that we may understand what God has freely given us. This is what we speak, not in words taught us by human wisdom but in words taught by the Spirit, expressing spiritual truths in spiritual words. The man without the Spirit does not accept the things that come from the Spirit of God, for they are foolishness to him and he cannot understand them, because they are spiritually discerned' (1 Corinthians 2:9-14, NIV).

Person of Christ

Christ was only a good man, a medium and reformer. He is now an advanced spirit in the sixth sphere. He was one with the Father only in the oneness of mediumship.

'In the beginning was the Word, and the Word was with God, and the Word was God' (John 1:1).

'And the Word became flesh and dwelt among us, and we beheld his glory, glory as of the only begotten from the Father, full of grace and truth' (John 1:14; cf. Hebrews 1:3, 5, 8).

'Who is the liar but the one who denies that Jesus is the Christ?' (1 John 2:22).

'For many deceivers have gone out into the world, those who do not acknowledge Jesus Christ as coming in the flesh. This is the deceiver and the antichrist' (2 John 7).

Death of Christ

Our Lord's death as a substitutionary sacrifice for sin, appeasing the wrath of God, is described by them as 'unrighteous', 'immoral' and an 'outrageous lie'. His death was only an illustration of the martyr spirit and of unselfish and heroic devotion to humanity.

'In him we have redemption through his blood, the forgiveness of our trespasses, according to the riches of his grace' (Ephesians 1:7).

'Then Christ would have had to suffer many times since the creation of the world. But now he has appeared once for all at the end of the ages to do away with sin by the sacrifice of himself. Just as man is destined to die once, and after that to face judgement, so Christ was sacrificed once to take away the sins of many people' (Hebrews 9:26-28 NIV).

Man and sin

All people alike are the children of God and a spark of divinity dwells in each person. Genesis is a myth and man, who is basically good, is the product of a gradual moral evolution.

Because God sustains and rules over the whole of his creation, he may be described as the Father of all (see Acts 17:25-29; Malachi 2:10) but his fatherhood especially relates to those who have been redeemed and adopted in and through Christ.

'As many as received him, to them he gave the right to become children of God, even to those who believe in his name' (John 1:12).

'See how great a love the Father has bestowed upon us, that we should be called children of God' (1 John 3:1; cf. Galatians 4:6).

Holy Spirit

The personality and deity of the Holy Spirit are denied. Pentecost is regarded as 'the greatest séance in history' and they frequently alter the meaning of Bible words. For example, they like to substitute 'medium' for 'prophet', 'psychic phenomena' for 'miracles' and 'clairvoyant' for 'discernment of spirits'.

At Pentecost, not one voice from the dead was heard! Read Acts 2. It was God who (by the Holy Spirit) gave his revelation to the prophets (2 Peter 1:21; Jeremiah 1:7-9) and spirits were discerned by the Holy Spirit (1 Corinthians 12:10) and by the apostolic teaching concerning the person of Christ (1 John 4:1-3).

It is possible to use the Bible deceitfully (2 Corinthians 4:2) and twist its meaning (2 Peter 3:16).

Salvation

Man is his own saviour and makes his own happiness or unhappiness as he obeys or disobeys the physical and spiritual laws of nature. There is no mention at all of the name of Jesus in their hymn-book or prayers.

'For if Abraham was justified by works, he has something to boast about; but not before God. For what does the Scripture say? "And Abraham believed God, and it was reckoned to him as righteousness"' (Romans 4:2-3).

'I am the door; if anyone enters through me, he shall be saved' (John 10:9).

Hell

As a place of eternal punishment hell does not exist, although remorse and a purifying, chastising process may be experienced on earth and in the spirit world.

'And these will go away into eternal punishment' (Matthew 25:46).

'And besides all this, between us and you there is a great chasm fixed, in order that those who wish to come over from here to you may not be able' (Luke 16:26).

Resurrection of Christ

This is interpreted as confirming spiritistic phenomena. For example, the resurrection appearances are called 'manifestations' or 'materializations'. The removal of the body is regarded as apportism and the moving of the stone as levitation. All these phenomena were controlled by natural law.

'But they were startled and frightened and thought that they were seeing a spirit. And he said to them, "Why are you troubled, and why do doubts arise in your hearts? See my hands and my feet, that it is I myself; touch me and see, for a spirit does not have flesh and bones as you see that I have. And when he had said this, he showed them his hands and his feet' (Luke 24:37-40; cf. 1 Corinthians 15:1-9).

Second coming of Christ

Many believe that Jesus appeared in spirit in 1861 and referred to the inauguration of a new era called the coming of Christ about 1847. There is to be no other 'coming' of the Lord.

'For many will come in my name, saying, "I am the Christ," and will mislead many' (Matthew 24:5).

'They will see the Son of Man coming on the clouds of the sky with power and great glory' (Matthew 24:30).

'But of that day and hour no one knows, not even the angels of heaven, nor the Son, but the Father' (Matthew 24:36).

Spirits

There is no devil and there are no evil spirits. All the spirits in the other world are the souls of the dead.

'Then Jesus was led up by the Spirit into the wilderness to be tempted by the devil' (Matthew 4:1).

'When he arrived at the other side in the region of the Gadarenes, two demon-possessed men coming from the tombs met him. They were so violent that no one could pass that way. "What do you want with us, Son of God?" they shouted. "Have you come here to torture us before the appointed time?"' (Matthew 8:28-29, NIV).

'Beloved, do not believe every

spirit, but test the spirits to see whether they are from God; because many false prophets have gone out into the world. By this you know the Spirit of God: every spirit that confesses that Jesus Christ has come in the flesh is from God; and every spirit that does not confess Jesus is not from God...' (1 John 4:1-3).

24.
Theosophy

There is a close resemblance between Theosophy and several other cults. The founder of the Theosophical Society, Madame Blavatsky, was herself a Russian spiritist medium. When she founded the society in New York in 1875 with the help of a Colonel Olcott, she claimed, 'It is the same spiritualism but under another name!' To be more precise, it was the fact of extensive fraud and corruption among spiritists in America that led her to form this new group. Her successor in this society, Mrs Annie Besant, also had a history of spiritistic involvement.

Theosophy also has similarities with cults such as Rosicrucianism, Advanced Occultism and Anthroposophy, which are all similar expressions of a single semi-religious system, which, although it claims to respect Jesus, really traces its tradition back to ancient Egypt.

The leaders of the society

The founder of Theosophy and her successor both had difficult, unhappy lives. Born in Russia in 1831, Helena P. Blavatsky lost her mother when she was only twelve and at the age of seventeen she married General Blavatsky, who was considerably older than herself. Within three months she left her husband and during the years 1848-1873 she was unsettled, travelling as far as Paris,

London, Greece, Mexico, U.S.A. and India. Her life was far from exemplary. Living with different men, she lost a baby just after birth and this was followed by the drowning of her lover, Metrovitch. She used hashish, developed her abilities as a 'medium', and for some ten years came under the control of a spirit which she claimed identified itself as John King.

Her second marriage in April 1875 again ended within three months and she developed a 'platonic' relationship with Colonel Olcott, who left his wife and children to live with her in a New York apartment. She died in 1891.

Until 1914 William Judge led the American side of the work, whereas Mrs Annie Besant (1847-1933) assumed leadership of the group in England. The daughter of an English minister, Mrs Besant rejected orthodox Anglican beliefs and eventually left her clergyman husband, preferring to associate with radical, political and rationalist groups before embracing Theosophy. At this time she helped to publish immoral literature and, when convicted by the court, avoided imprisonment because of a technical legal wrangle.

Mrs Besant was an intellectual and soon became recognized as a capable speaker and writer. Mrs Blavatsky and Mrs Besant both visited India, where they were greatly impressed by Buddhist and Hindu teaching, and they incorporated much of this eastern philosophy into their system of Theosophy.

Arthur Pink and the Theosophical Society

It may have been the abilities of Mrs Besant or the eastern, spiritistic philosophy she so ably taught that attracted Arthur W. Pink, the now famous evangelical writer, to the ranks of the Theosophy movement. The young Pink rejected the biblical faith of his parents and to their distress became a Theosophist. Hearing of his gifted speaking on behalf of the cult, Mrs Besant wrote to Pink from Madras and later conferred on him a distinguished title which made him one of the movement's leaders.

But the continuing prayers and witness of his parents were not in vain. His father always waited for his son to return home from the meetings and, to the annoyance of Arthur, often added a verse of Scripture to his loving 'Goodnight'. When one evening in 1908 Pink returned home, the text he heard from his father was, 'There is a way which seemeth right unto a man, but the end thereof are the ways of death' (Proverbs 14:12, AV). Although he had intended to prepare an important speech that night he could not forget the text. Instead he took a bath, but still his mind was full of Proverbs 14:12 and, afterwards, under deep conviction, he prayed. He stayed in his room for almost three days and when he came out, his father exclaimed, 'Praise God, my son has been delivered!' When Arthur Pink went as promised to speak to the Theosophists, he preached the gospel and many thought he had 'gone mad'. When Mrs Besant eventually heard the news in Madras, Pink was described as 'insane'.[1]

Later developments

Pink's conversion left the cult leader still hardened and unrestrained. After adopting a son by the name of Krishnamurti, Mrs Besant later claimed that her adopted son was the messiah. However, in 1931, he himself renounced the title, saying, 'I am not an actor; I refuse to wear the robes of a messiah so I am again free of all possessions.' Mrs Besant died two years later and afterwards the Theosophical Society was divided for many years, with one faction organizing itself into the 'Anthroposophical Society' and another as the 'Society of the Friends of Madame Blavatsky'.

Theosophy has significant support throughout the world and claims to have more than 1500 branches. In Britain, their work is not well known and in 1987 they only had 4850 members and thirteen congregations.

What Theosophy teaches

God

When asked, 'Do you believe in God, the God of a Christian?' Madame Blavatsky replied in her *Key to Theosophy*, 'In such a God we do not believe.'

In Theosophy God is regarded as everything and everything is

What the Bible teaches

'The Lord appeared to Abram and said to him, "I am God Almighty..."' (Genesis 17:1).

'It is I who made the earth, and created man upon it. I stretched out the heavens with my hands, and I ordained all their host' (Isaiah

regarded as God; in this pantheistic teaching there is no difference between the world and God. God is all that exists and we are God, but we must delve deep into ourselves to find the God within us.

They also speak of a trinity which is only 'a threefold manifestation of Power, Wisdom and Activity'.

45:12; cf. Psalm 102:25-27).

'He who is the blessed and only sovereign, the King of kings and Lord of lords; who alone possesses immortality and dwells in unapproachable light...' (1 Timothy 6:15-16).

'Having been predestined according to his purpose who works all things after the counsel of his will' (Ephesians 1:11).

Bible

The Bible is just one of many revelations, the superior revelation being the Hindu scriptures.

'To the law and to the testimony! If they do not speak according to this word, it is because they have no dawn' (Isaiah 8:20; cf. Revelation 22:18-19).

Person of Christ

In Mrs Besant's view, Christ was born in 105 B.C. and became a monk; later some distinguished people from India and Egypt visited his monastery and introduced him to the mysteries of eastern religion.

Christ is only one of several divine teachers.

The 'Christ part' of his nature was given him at his baptism and withdrawn after the crucifixion. The name 'Christ' refers not simply to one person but also to the living presence in the human spirit of all people. Only through this presence is it possible for the human spirit to express its natural divinity. We can all become 'Christs' eventually.

'Today in the town of David a Saviour has been born to you; he is Christ the Lord' (Luke 2:11, NIV).

'No man has seen God at any time; the only begotten God, who is in the bosom of the Father, he has explained him' (John 1:18).

Death of Christ

The biblical doctrine of atonement 'is entirely repudiated'. The only significance in Christ's death was the identification of nature between

'The Son of Man did not come to be served, but to serve, and to give his life a ransom for many' (Matthew 20:28; cf. 2 Corinthians 5:21).

the divine man and men who are gradually becoming divine.

Man

Their view here is complex; man has a pre-existent spirit Atma which provides permanence and individuality, but which is reincarnated many times. Man also has three souls, Buddahi, Manas and Kamamepha, with a life principle called Prana. In addition to his physical being man also has an astral body.

'Then the Lord God formed man of dust from the ground, and breathed into his nostrils the breath of life; and man became a living being' (Genesis 2:7).

'Then God said, "Let us make man in our image, according to our likeness..." God created man in his own image' (Genesis 1:26-27).

Sin

There are no moral laws sanctioned by God.

'The conclusion, when all has been heard, is: fear God and keep his commandments, because this applies to every person' (Ecclesiastics 12:13; cf. 1 John 3:4, Romans 5:12).

Salvation

Through numerous incarnations, man must achieve his own salvation. Sin does not exist and forgiveness by any God is impossible.

'He saved us, not on the basis of deeds which we have done in righteousness, but according to his mercy, by the washing of regeneration and renewing by the Holy Spirit...' (Titus 3:5; cf. Ephesians 2:8-9).

Prayer

It is unimportant whether one prays to Buddha, to Christ, to Vishnu or the Father.

'I am the way, and the truth, and the life; no one comes to the Father, but through me' (John 14:6).

'And whatever you ask in my name that will I do, that the Father may be glorified in the Son. If you ask me anything in my name, I will do it' (John 14:13-14).

Devil

There is no personal devil.

'Resist the devil and he will flee from you' (James 4:7; cf. Matthew 4:1-4).

Death

The soul evolves and purges itself by regular incarnations, with the ultimate goal of communing with and being welcomed by the Mahatmas or Brotherhood of Teachers, who have evolved to the highest point of human attainment. After a suitable medium is found, the Great World Teacher, who is supreme over the Mahatmas, will provide the world with a fuller revelation.

'But now he has appeared once for all at the end of the ages to do away with sin by the sacrifice of himself. Just as man is destined to die once, and after that to face judgement, so Christ was sacrificed once to take away the sins of many people...' (Hebrews 9:26-28, NIV; cf. Matthew 24:24-26).

Eternal punishment

The eternal punishment of unbelievers in hell is regarded by them as an offensive doctrine.

'He who believes in the Son has eternal life; but he who does not obey the Son shall not see life, but the wrath of God abides on him' (John 3:36; cf. 2 Thessalonians 1:9).

25.
Eckankar: the ancient science of soul travel

Eckankar was founded in 1965 in the U.S.A. by Paul Twitchell. By now the movement is international and boasts a large membership, which is still growing. In addition to its religious aspect, Eckankar has developed an extremely wealthy business in jewellery, books and cassettes.

A journalist by occupation, Paul Twitchell was fascinated by the occult and expressed ideas about out-of-the-body soul travel in a series of articles and lectures during 1964-5. Within months, as growing numbers of people embraced his teaching, Twitchell formed his Eckankar movement.

False claims

At a very early stage in the history of this movement, Twitchell made three extreme and absurd claims. First of all, he announced himself to be the 'God-man', that is, God's unique incarnation in the world. Only through him, he claimed, could people discover the truth. His second claim was that Eckankar had always existed as an eternal system of truth; all that he had done in 1965, he insisted, was to publicize these ancient truths.

The third claim was even more deceitful. Twitchell fabricated his own life-story claiming, for example, to have been born as an illegitimate child on a Mississippi boat several years after his real

date of birth in 1908. Other details were invented too, but the true
story of his life is quite different.

The true story

Born in 1908 to Jacob and Effie Twitchell in Kentucky, he eventually studied at Western State Teachers' College, married a young
lady from his home town and then entered the American Navy for
a three-year period. Afterwards, he had a number of jobs in the New
York and Washington areas. During this period he also developed
a deep interest in Eastern religions and in 1950 joined a group
related to Paramahansa Yogananda's Self-Realization Fellowship.
After only five years, pressure was put on Twitchell to leave the
group and, almost immediately, he engrossed himself in the teaching of Kirpal Singh, the guru of *Ruhani Satsang* ('Divine Science
of the Soul').

In 1963 Twitchell wrote a book called *The Tiger's Fang*, in
which he claimed to describe journeys he had taken out of the body
and at 'soul' level, under the guidance of Singh. However, Singh
was unhappy with the contents and told Twitchell not to publish it.
This disagreement gave Twitchell the opportunity to abandon
Singh and deny having been influenced by his teaching in any way.
What cannot be denied is the fact that much of Twitchell's book had
been taken verbatim and without acknowledgement from an earlier
work by Julian Johnson entitled *The Path of the Masters*.

After his break with Kirpal Singh, Twitchell was ready to
present himself to the world as an incarnation of God. The
announcement was not long in coming. On 22 October 1965,
Twitchell claimed that the Rod of Power had been passed on to him,
thus making him the Mahanta and Living Eck Master. Through
lectures, articles and books, Twitchell publicized his claims and
teaching, describing himself as 'all-powerful, all-wise...and a law
unto himself'.

His authority as Mahanta should only have continued for five
years, but Twitchell used various tactics to extend the period of his
authority and anointing. But in 1971 he died and it was Twitchell's
second wife who announced Darwin Gross as the new Mahanta.
Gross functioned in this capacity for ten years and two other men
have since served as Living Eck Masters.

Spiritual mania

Eckankar 'is a perfect example of the spiritual mania characterizing the last two decades. It is a child of our times...a product created to fill a need in our bustling cosmic marketplace. Yet it has kept a low profile, has escaped critical media attention and thus has grown rapidly without impediment'.[1]

In the next section the theories of Eckankar are exposed as being no more than the fallible, false ideas of men.

What Eckankar teaches	*What the Bible teaches*
God	
God, whom they call Sugmad, is the totality of all that exists, but individual souls eventually fuse in the 'Absolute' yet retain some degree of individuality.	
God is without personality and 'We do not, and cannot, know God' (Twitchell).	God is personal; he loves people (John 3:16), reveals his character and purpose to them (2 Timothy 3:16) and God the Son became incarnate (John 1:1-18). God can be known.
	'"They shall all know me, from the least of them to the greatest of them," declares the Lord, "for I will forgive their iniquity, and their sin I will remember no more"' (Jeremiah 31:34).
	'This is eternal life, that they may know thee, the only true God, and Jesus Christ whom thou hast sent' (John 17:3).
'God of Itself is not interested in the individual and his cause, but only the continuation of life' (Twitchell).	'The Lord...is patient toward you, not wishing for any to perish but for all to come to repentance' (2 Peter 3:9).

'Casting all your anxiety upon him, because he cares for you' (1 Peter 5:7).

'To say God created the universe and then to say that he stands outside the universe is a contradiction' (Twitchell).

'In the beginning God created the heavens and the earth' (Genesis 1:1).

'Thus says the Lord, "Heaven is my throne, and the earth is my footstool...For my hand made all these things, thus all these things came into being," declares the Lord' (Isaiah 66:1-2).

'Is not God in the height of heaven? Look also at the distant stars, how high they are!...Clouds are a hiding place for him...' (Job 22:12-14).

All evil is traced back to God. The lower worlds are ruled by the wicked Kal, who deceives and ensnares souls in various illusions, but Kal is also a part of God.

'Thine eyes are too pure to approve evil, and thou canst not look on wickedness with favour...' (Habakkuk 1:13).

'Through one man [Adam] sin entered into the world...' (Romans 5:12: cf. Genesis 3; John 8:44; 1 John 3:8-10).

Sin

When people indulge in lust, anger, greed, excessive devotion to worldly possessions and vanity they incur Karmic debt; this debt can take hundreds and thousands of years, and almost endless reincarnations, to remove.

Contact with, and submission to, a Living Eck Master will shorten this process considerably, In fact, Eckankar claims to be 'the only direct path to God'.

As all people are born in sin (Psalm 51:5; Romans 5:19), specific sins originate in our sinful nature (Matthew 15:19). Sin is a cruel tyrant enslaving unbelievers (Romans 6:17-22).

We are all responsible for our sins and guilty before God (Ezekiel 18:20; Romans 3:19-20) but, after death there is no reincarnation nor 'second chance' for unbelievers (Hebrews 9:27).

Only the Lord Jesus Christ, through his substitutionary death, can save us from the guilt, power, corruption and penalty of sin

Christk

Christ

'We really see [Jesus] as a son of
Kal Niranjan, king of the lower
worlds' (Twitchell).

Salvation and enlightenment

Through 'soul-travel', it is possible
to ascend through the eleven different realms of the cosmos to God.
Earth is the first realm or plane and
the second is the 'astral' realm in
which occult activity dominates
together with out-of-the-body projection. God is in the eleventh
realm.

How can one participate in
'soul travel' and find God and enlightenment?

First of all, there must be complete surrender to the Living Eck
Master or Mahanta.

Secondly, followers must 'not
depend on books, nor waste time on
discussions of what truth is, or God
Itself' (Twitchell). Rather, they
must 'enter into the centre of Supreme Reality and learn' for themselves.

(Galatians 3:13-14; 1 Peter 2:24:
Romans 5:19-21). No one can
know God except through Jesus
Christ (John 14:6).

See Matthew 16:16; 17:5; John
9:36-37; Hebrews 1:1-3.

'You shall worship the Lord your
God, and serve him only' (Matthew
4:10).

'Do not trust in princes, in
mortal man, in whom there is no
salvation. His spirit departs, he returns to the earth; in that very day
his thoughts perish. How blessed is
he whose help is the God of Jacob,
whose hope is in the Lord his God'
(Psalm 146:3-5).

'Beloved, do not believe every
spirit, but test the spirits to see
whether they are from God; because many false prophets have
gone out into the world...' (1 John
4:1-3).

'They received the word with
great eagerness, examining the

scriptures daily, to see whether these things were so' (Acts 17:11).

Thirdly, there must be a willingness to use telepathy, trances, dream-states, meditation, imagination and direct projection, in order to travel out of the body. Spiritism is also encouraged.

'But the Spirit explicitly says that in later times some will fall away from the faith, paying attention to deceitful spirits and doctrines of demons...'(1 Timothy 4:1).

'If any one advocates a different doctrine, and does not agree with sound words, those of our Lord Jesus Christ, and with the doctrine conforming to godliness, he is conceited and understands nothing...' (1 Timothy 6:3-4; cf. Isaiah 8:19-20).

Section 7
Some Near- and
Far-Eastern movements

26.   The New Age Movement

27.   Baha'i

28.   Hare Krishna: International Society for Krishna Consciousness

29.   Yoga

30.   Transcendental Meditation

31.   Divine Light Mission

32.   Rajneesh Foundation

26.
The New Age Movement

Although the New Age Movement emerged in the 1970s, it has developed significantly in America and Europe during the 1980s. The roots of this movement, however, go back at least to the early 1960s, when Western society was exposed increasingly to Eastern mystical teachings with their occult bias. The New Age Movement also has links with, among others, Transcendentalism, Spiritism, Theosophy, New Thought and Christian Science.

Regarding the Christian church as both irrelevant and lacking in spiritual vitality, many young people in the 1960s, including the Beatles, were fascinated by the teachings of individual gurus from the East and consequently joined groups such as Transcendental Meditation, the Rajneesh Foundation, Zen Buddhism and the Divine Light Mission. However, some people refused to restrict themselves to one particular guru or group. While committed to the basic ideas of these groups, they were especially attracted to the prospect of a new age in which they believed that differences of culture, religion and politics would be replaced by universal love and unity.

Eastern influences

In his valuable *Encyclopedic handbook of Cults in America*, J. Gordon Melton claims that the New Age Movement can best be dated from 1971. With the relaxing of immigration laws both in the United States and Britain in the preceding decade, Asian religious teachers moved to these countries along with many other immigrants. The result was 'a major missionary thrust by the Eastern religions towards the West'.[1] Various ashrams and centres were established in key areas and in 1971 the *East-West Journal* was launched by a Boston group. This may have been the 'first national periodical to focus the issues of the New Age Movement'.[2] The same year saw the publication of *Be Here Now,* by Baba Ram Dass, which was the earliest book popularizing the ideas of the New Age. Dass's real name is Richard Alpert, a Jew who had been a professor of psychology at Harvard before going to India in search of a guru. By 1972 New Age directories had been issued and groups had been linked together through national networks and periodicals such as *New Age, New Realities* and the *Yoga Journal.*

Among the early leaders of the movement were Baba Ram Dass, Marilyn Ferguson, David Spangler, Judith Skutch, Patricia Sun, Sam Keen, Shirley MacLaine and Paul Solomon. The latter was a Baptist pastor in the United States but is now a committed and leading teacher in the New Age Movement. He offers seminars/workshops on subjects such as guided meditation, dream analysis and master-victim consciousness. Solomon established a group called Inner Light Consciousness with a community in Virginia Beach. To the question, 'Should Jesus be my Lord of life, or should I seek my higher self?', Paul Solomon answers, 'Both paths are valid since the historical Jesus is supposed to be one with the Consciousness of God, and if you seek your Higher Mind, you seek the expression of God that is the source of your being.'[3]

Another important leader is David Spangle. He served as a leader of the Findhorn community in Scotland for three years before returning to the United States, where he established a New Age community called the Lorian Association near Madison in Wisconsin. In 1976 he published *Revelation, the birth of a new age,* in which he expressed New Age ideas in popular style. Perhaps even more influential than Spangler is Marilyn Ferguson, who is the editor of two bulletins, *Brain mind bulletin* and the *Leading edge bulletin.* What gave her greater prominence was her book, published in 1980, entitled *The Aquarian conspiracy,* which is regarded as one of the best statements of the beliefs and aims of the movement. Similarly, it was the publication of *A course in miracles* in 1975 by the new Foundation for Inner Peace which gave prominence to Judith Skutch. This became a popular and well-used study book among New Age groups and between 1975-1985 several hundred groups were established in North America alone.

Basic to the New Age philosophy are two convictions. The first is that all religions and secular systems of thought lead eventually to God. Secondly, they believe that New Age philosophy is superior to all other faiths, including Christianity. This can be illustrated in many ways, but I want to use the example of the New Age community based in Findhorn.

The Findhorn community

The small village of Findhorn is situated forty miles east of Inverness in Scotland. In 1963, a community called the Findhorn Foundation was established there and at times there have been as many as 200 living in this community. Members are accommodated on a caravan site in the village and also in a nearby hotel in Farres which is owned by the Foundation.

Findhorn is an important centre for the movement in Britain. One workshop available there deals with 'Christianity in the New Age'. It offers 'an experimental exploration of the Cosmic Christ in the light of the Western mystery tradition and the Ancient Wisdom. It will include a suggestive reading of Gospel narratives both as an allegorical presentation of stages of subconsciousness in the unfoldment of the soul and as a practical path to "enlightenment" given us by the Master Jesus.'[4] Peter and Eileen Caddy founded the Findhorn community in 1963. They claimed that 'The work of this centre is to usher in the New Age, to raise the vibrations by the awareness of the Christ consciousness within each one, to find contact with me; to create light and more light and radiate it; to bring down my King on earth and see it start right here and go out to the four corners of the earth.'[5]

In order to understand this quotation, we need to be aware of the New Age belief that mankind is in the process of moving from the age of Pisces, into the age of Aquarius. They claim that each age continues for about 2,000 years and that the different ages are influenced by the earth's movement. They regard the Pisces age as the age of Christianity, but they believe this age is now ending as mankind moves into a transitional period between the ages of Pisces and Aquarius. The adjustment from one age to another is supposed to mean that we are affected by different and higher energies from the cosmos. These energies are believed to enter the planet by means of 'lay-lines' (that is, lines which criss-cross the globe) and the 'power-points' are precise places where these lines cross. Stonehenge is thought to have been built on such a 'power point', but for the New Age the three main power-points in Britain are Glastonbury, Iona and Findhorn.

While Findhorn is an important centre for Britain, there are other and more important communes in the United States. These include the Lama Foundation and the Stelle Community, while some Eastern teachers have established their own organizational communes such as the Ananda Co-operative Community of Swami Kriyananda and also the New Vrindvan, which belongs to the International Society for Krishna Consciousness in West Virginia.

High regard for nature

New Age devotees attach great importance to occasions such as the full moon, equinoxes and solstices, for they believe that the cosmos energies are at their strongest at these times. Meditation is an indispensable means of adapting to these energies but it is also deemed important to develop a high regard for nature generally. Even man-made objects tend to be personalized in the New Age philosophy and one practical result of their reverence for nature is the claim to be able to grow exceptionally large vegetables/flowers even in poor soil and without the use of chemicals. Their view of nature amounts to pantheism, for they identify the world with deity and see divinity within everything.

Eventually, they believe the New Age will be characterized by one universal religion and a perfectly harmonized mankind committed to caring for the planet. This allegiance to the planet already finds expression in concerns such as ecology, peace, natural/wholesome foods, co-operation in community living and the desire to effect social, political changes of a radical nature but by peaceful means.

What the New Age Movement teaches

What the Bible teaches

God

They believe that God is a power rather than a person and that this power resides in each human person. People should realize that they are also gods. Shirley MacLaine once stood on the shores of the Pacific Ocean chanting, 'I am God, I am God, I am God.'

God is a living, personal, loving Being who as Creator is distinct from the universe (Isaiah 43:10-13; 44:6-9; 1 John 4:8; cf. Isaiah 45:18, 22) yet sovereign over it and active in it.

Jesus Christ

Although they call Jesus a Master, yet his unique person as God the Son is denied. Their claim is that Jesus was the first one to realize and express the Christ-energy/consciousness. For them, Jesus was only a man, while the Christ is the God-essence that indwelt him and all other humans. Influenced to some extent by Teilhard de Chardin, they prefer to talk about 'the Christ' or the 'cosmic Christ' rather than the Jesus of history.

Christ is unique in his nature as the Son of God (Hebrews 1:1-13; John 1:1-16); in his incarnation he became the God-man and Saviour of the world (Philippians 2:5-8; 1 John 2:2).

Man

Humans are all 'gods in the making' and can become God! Because man has a 'higher' nature, there is no mention of the Fall or of personal sin. In fact, no real distinction is made between right and wrong. Sin is thought of only as ignorance of one's own divinity.

Man is unique for he was made in the image and likeness of God (Genesis 1:27; 5:1), but man is not, and cannot become as, God: 'I am God and there is no other; I am God, and there is no one like me' (Isaiah 46:9).

Salvation

The word 'salvation' is rarely used in their writings but the concept is understood as the recognition and appreciation of one's own divinity. Man needs to develop his psychic powers and reach his higher consciousness in order to become aware of his personal divinity. Meditation, yoga, drugs, martial arts, hypnosis and various occult activities are all legitimate means of realizing one's own divinity.

Because man is not a sinner nor under the wrath of God, there is no need of a Saviour or of atonement.

In his sin, man is guilty and condemned before the holy God (e.g. Romans 3) and he can only be reconciled to God through the substitutionary sacrifice of Jesus Christ on the cross (John 1:29; 2 Corinthians 5:18-21; 1 Timothy 2:5-6). The salvation procured by the Lord Jesus can only be received through faith in the person of the Lord Jesus Christ (Acts 16:31; Ephesians 2:8-9).

Knowledge

The New Age belief is similar to Gnosticism, where man is born without the essential knowledge of his own soul and identity. Man needs to know about himself and the universe through meditation and other means.

Knowledge and wisdom come from God alone (Proverbs 2:5-10; 1 Corinthians 1:20-31); more particularly, such knowledge comes from the Bible, which is the Word of God (2 Timothy 3:16-17), and by the ministry of the Holy Spirit who illumines our minds concerning God's Word (1 Corinthians 2:10-14).

Heaven and hell

Their belief is that these places are only good or bad conditions of consciousness in this life with no real counterpart beyond death.

Heaven is where God is and is a place where only believers go after death, whereas hell is the place where unbelievers are punished consciously and eternally (Matthew 25:31-46; Luke 16:19-31; Philippians 1:21-23).

Reincarnation

There are repeated reincarnations; but these are not a curse or punishment but a spiritual path or

'It is appointed for men to die *once* and after this comes judgement...' (Hebrews 9:27).

sadhana. Such a *sadhana* is rarely completed in the span of one life on earth. Through several lifetimes in a physical body spiritual development can occur, culminating in a mystical consciousness or awareness of one's own higher nature and divinity.

Future age

According to the New Age teachers, the personal and individual awareness of one's own divinity leading to mystical transformation will eventually extend to the whole of society. Opinions vary as to the precise description of this new age, but all agree there will only be one universal religion with all people at harmony with each other and with nature as well.

At the personal return of the Lord Jesus Christ, believers and unbelievers will be separated, the dead raised, all opposition to Christ will finally be put down and the devil also will be punished. The Lord will establish 'new heavens and a new earth in which righteousness dwells' (2 Peter 3:13; Matthew 25:31-32; 1 Corinthians 15:25-28).

27.
Baha'i

The Baha'i faith has its roots in Islam, especially in Shi'ite Islam. After the death of Muhammad in A.D. 632, Muslims were soon divided concerning a leader. Muhammad himself had no sons and had not chosen a successor, so the majority of his followers (the Sunnites) chose Abu Bakr as 'Caliph' (successor). A minority, however, called the Shi'ites, argued that God, not men, should appoint their leader, and ruled that any successor to Muhammad must be a descendant of his and be called 'Imam' (leader). Accordingly, they accepted Muhammad's cousin and son-in-law Ali as the first Imam. This basic division between the Shi'ites and the Sunnites has been perpetuated ever since. Iran has been strongly influenced by the Shi'ites and today, while about ninety-eight per cent of Iranians are Muslims, the majority belong to the Shi'ite group. Several sects have splintered off from the Shi'ite group and when the leader of one such sect (the Shaykhis) died in 1826, its adherents were confused as to which of two rival claimants should be recognized as the new leader. Baha'ism stems from the stronger faction, which followed Sayyid Ali Muhammad of Shiraz who chose the title 'Bab' for himself.

The 'Bab'

The 'Bab', a descendant of the original Muhammad, was born in Southern Iran in 1819 or 1820. Brought up from an early age by an uncle because of his father's death, he eventually left his uncle's business on the Persian Gulf, visiting the shrines of the Shi'ite Imams in Iraq and attending lectures by Kazim, the leader of the Shaykhi movement. Returning to his birthplace in Shiraz, he married in 1842 and two years later, after a considerable amount of time spent in prayer and meditation, he declared that he had a special divine work to fulfil. The Bab's claims were propagated by his followers and in 1848 the Babi chiefs severed their links with Islam and declared the Bab to be a new prophet in the place of Muhammad. His message, however, had a mixed reception in Iran and he himself was later imprisoned then executed on 8 July 1850 at the command of the Shah.

Before his execution, the Bab had named his successor as Mirza Yahya, who received the title 'Subh-i-Azal' (Morning of Eternity) and for two years all went well for the new leader. But in 1852 an unsuccessful plot by some Babis to kill the Shah caused the latter to determine to punish and kill all the movement's leaders and adherents. However, Subh-i-Azal and his brother Baha managed to escape to Baghdad.

Baha's leadership

Now began a long period of opposition and intrigue, in which the older brother, Baha, coveted the position of leader and worked subtly to oust his younger brother by putting him into virtual seclusion. Within a brief space of time, Baha became the most popular leader of the movement and, although others made claims to leadership, it was Baha who in 1866 declared himself to be 'He-whom-God-will-manifest', that is, the one whom the Bab had predicted would eventually come to the world. Most followers accepted this new claim although the Bab's nominee, Subh-i-Azal, refused to recognize it, arguing that the Bab's teachings were still relevant and adequate, for the Bab had taught that at least 1511 years would elapse before this manifestation appeared. To resolve the crisis, Baha managed to 'remove' the leading supporters of his younger brother (Babis) and then he rewrote many Babi writings and much of its history in order to justify his own claim to be the Major Manifestation. Sadly, about twenty Babis who rejected the new leader were murdered by Baha's supporters and Baha even tried to poison his own brother. However, along with a small group of followers, Subh-i-Azal lived in Cyprus with his family under sentence of life imprisonment until his death in 1912 at the age of eighty-one. Today in Iran there are several thousand people who still recognize Subh-i-Azal as the Bab's true successor and call themselves Babis.

Meanwhile Baha chose a new title for himself, namely, Baha'u'llah, which means 'the glory of God' and this is the name by which he is known today. In 1880 he moved into the Bahji Palace in Akka, Turkey, and many pilgrims journeyed to the palace in order to gaze for a few seconds on a man whom they regarded as the 'Blessed Perfection'. Baha'u'llah was a prolific writer, the author of over 100 books and numerous letters. While the Baha'is regard all these writings as the Word of God, Baha'u'llah himself singled out one book, the *Al-Kitab Al-Aqdas*, written in Arabic in 1872, as the most holy book. By the time Baha'u'llah died in 1892 the Baha'i faith had grown considerably and it had an estimated 500,000 followers in Iran alone.

Into the twentieth century

The subsequent history of the Baha'i movement can be mentioned briefly. Baha'u'llah nominated one of his four sons, Abbas Effendi, to succeed him and he also chose Effendi's successor, another son by the name of Mirza Muhammad Ali, but there followed a sad, bitter story of disagreement and opposition between the two brothers and their rival factions. Eventually on the death of Shogli Effendi in 1957 a more democratic form of leadership was devised in the form of a nine-man Council of Hands at Haifa. They in turn appointed the Universal House of Justice to govern the Baha'i faith.

Since the first Baha'i missionary arrived in the U.S.A. in 1892, the movement has achieved considerable success there, and after missionary work in many other countries it now purports to be world-wide in its activity and support. Its claim, however, to be the universal authentic religion is rejected as false and unbiblical by Christians.

What Baha'i faith teaches

God

Baha'u'llah is God; he is infallible, possessing knowledge no one else has.

Bible

The inspiration of the Bible is acknowledged alongside that of other religious books such as the Koran, but all these writings have been superseded by the writings of Baha'u'llah, which are regarded as unique, more complete and reliable.

Traditional dogmas that are unreasonable and unintelligible must be rejected as superstition and false religion.

Person of Christ

Jesus is one of the great divine revealers, like Krishna, Zoroaster and Muhammad, who stand out among the prophets of the world. Baha'u'llah is the great world-teacher who appeared in the 'fulness of time'; he was also the channel of a marvellous grace that transcends all previous manifestations of God in all previous forms of religion. Baha'u'llah alone is the hope and foundation of world unity.

What the Bible teaches

'"Before me there was no God formed, and there will be none after me, I, even I, am the Lord; and there is no saviour besides me... you are my witnesses," declares the Lord, "and I am God"' (Isaiah 43:10-12).

'I am the Lord, and there is no other; besides me there is no God...I am the Lord and there is no other' (Isaiah 45:5-6).

'Thy word is truth' (John 17:17).

'Heaven and earth will pass away, but my words will not pass away' (Luke 21:33).

'According to the revelation of the mystery which has been kept secret for long ages past, but now is manifested, and by the Scriptures of the prophets, according to the commandment of the eternal God, has been made known to all nations, leading to obedience of faith' (Romans 16:25-26).

'False Christs and false prophets will arise and will show great signs and wonders, so as to mislead, if possible, even the elect' (Matthew 24:24; cf. Colossians 1:15-18).

Death of Christ

Jesus did not die for our sin, nor are his sufferings and death unique. He suffered to prove the everlasting life of the Spirit.

Resurrection of Christ

The physical resurrection of Jesus Christ from the dead is denied and reinterpreted to describe merely the subjective change in the feelings and attitudes of the disciples after the martyrdom of Jesus.

Holy Spirit

Baha'is believe there was a great outpouring of the Spirit through the prophet Baha'u'llah, who was born in Persia in 1817 and died in the Holy Land in 1892, causing a sudden awakening throughout the world.

Man and sin

The universe is without a beginning

'It was the Father's good pleasure for all the fulness to dwell in him, and through him to reconcile all things to himself, having made peace through the blood of his cross; through him...whether things on earth or things in heaven' (Colossians 1:19-20).

'[Thomas] said to them, "Unless I shall see in his hands the imprint of the nails, and put my finger into the place of the nails, and put my hand into his side, I will not believe." And after eight days again his disciples were inside, and Thomas with them...Jesus came...Then he said to Thomas, "Reach here your finger, and see my hands; and reach here your hand, and put it into my side; and be not unbelieving, but believing." Thomas answered and said to him, "My Lord and my God!"' (John 20:25-29).

"He shall glorify *me*; for he shall take of mine, and shall disclose it to you" (John 16:14).

'God has sent forth the Spirit of *his Son* into our hearts' (Galatians 4:6).

'Having been exalted to the right hand of God, and having received from the Father the promise of the Holy Spirit, he has poured forth this which you both see and hear' (Acts 2:33).

'In the beginning God created the

in time and is a perpetual emanation from the great first cause, consistent with evolution over billions of years. Genesis 1 and 2 provide a crude and false account of the creation. Man's nature is basically good.

Salvation

Through education we can free ourselves from imperfections such as injustice, tyranny, hatred and strife.

Death and the future state

At death the soul is set free from the body and man continues to live in his soul and mind, sustained by the spirit of faith, and enters into one of 'the many mansions', that is, into that degree of spiritual awareness which he attained before death. Terms like 'the last day', 'the day of judgement', 'the resurrection', 'the Second Coming', 'heaven and hell' are all interpreted symbolically and are related to this world and especially the appearance of Baha'u'llah. His appearance was the resurrection and the raising of the dead means the spiritual awakening of those who are asleep in the graves of ignorance and lust. The coming of the supreme manifestation of Baha'u'llah is the great day of judgement. The trumpet blast of which Christ, Muhammad and others speak is the call of the manifestation which is sounded for all, whether dead or alive. Meeting with God through his manifestation

heavens and the earth' (Genesis 1:1).

'All things came into being by him' (John 1:3).

'There is not a righteous man on earth who continually does good and who never sins' (Ecclesiastes 7:20).

'The hearts of the sons of men are full of evil' (Ecclesiastes 9:3).

'By lovingkindness and truth iniquity is atoned for, and by the fear of the Lord one keeps away from evil' (Proverbs 16:6; Ephesians 2:8-9).

'I am stirring up your sincere mind by way of reminder, that you should remember the words spoken beforehand by the holy prophets and the commandment of the Lord and Saviour spoken by your apostles. Know this first of all, that in the last days mockers will come...saying, 'Where is the promise of his coming?'...But the present heavens and earth by his word are being reserved for fire, kept for the day of judgement and destruction of ungodly men...But the day of the Lord will come like a thief' (2 Peter 3:1-10).

is the gateway to the paradise of knowing and loving him, but those who prefer their own way thereby consign themselves to the hell of selfishness, error and enmity.

Prayers for the dead

Contact with the dead is legitimate provided the motive is not prompted by curiosity or selfishness. This 'contact' can be made in a condition of love and prayer.

Baha'is are instructed to pray for the dead. They believe progress can be made in the next world, so they pray for forgiveness, enlightenment, happiness and progress for the departed. Creatures, however, cannot become the Creator.

While it is impossible to contact the dead, it is nevertheless possible to contact evil spirits/demons. These demons are not the spirits of the dead, but sinful angels who along with the devil rebelled against God and continually oppose the Lord and his people (2 Peter 2:4; Ephesians 6:12). When people try to communicate with the dead they are in danger of contacting demons, thus the significance of warnings such as, 'Do not turn to mediums or spiritists; do not seek them out to be defiled by them. I am the Lord your God' (Leviticus 19:31; see also Isaiah 8:19-20; 20:6, 27).

Man's spiritual condition and destiny cannot be altered after death (Hebrews 9:27; Luke 16:26), so prayers for the dead are forbidden.

28.
Hare Krishna: International Society for Krishna Consciousness

Over fifty years ago in India a guru told a middle-aged factory manager to go and spread the message of the Hindu god Krishna in the U.S.A., but it was not until 1965 that A.C. Bhaktivedanta Swami Prabhupade obeyed his guru's directive. Born in Calcutta in 1896, Prabhupade eventually graduated in the local university and in 1933 became a disciple of the Hindu guru Siddartha Goswami, whose speciality was the teaching of Krishna Consciousness. As Goswami's devotee, Prabhupade studied hard and wrote a commentary of the Indian holy book, the *Bhagavad-Gita*. In 1950 he decided to resign his managerial post, abandon his wife and five children and withdraw from society in order to devote himself entirely to his religious work. Fifteen years later, encouraged by the provision of a free passage and a sum of money, the seventy-year-old Prabhupade left for America. Wearing the distinctive saffron robe of an Indian holy man, he quickly began to instruct groups of Americans on the virtues and superiority of Krishna. Large numbers of people, including disillusioned and drug-addicted youngsters, embraced his teaching and within weeks the International Society for Krishna Consciousness (ISKCON) was founded in New York. The movement spread quickly across America and Europe. In 1968 a farming community was established in West Virginia and four years later a school was founded in Texas.

The daily routine

Hare Krishna followers lead austere lives, rising no later than 3.00 a.m. Before their breakfast at 7.30 a.m. they spend four hours in personal chanting, corporate worship and the study of the *Bhagavad Gita*. They live in temples which also house numerous statues of Hindu gods believed to be reincarnations of Krishna. Each day these deities must be found and cleaned; they are washed in a mixture of cow's urine, milk and rose water, and afterwards, followers have the dubious privilege of drinking the mixture themselves! Devotees are compelled to accept a vegetarian diet and, in addition, tea, coffee, alcohol and tobacco are banned. Approximately eight hours are spent in the daytime soliciting donations from the public, while the evenings are again devoted to study, worship and housework. In addition to wearing saffron robes, Krishna followers mark their faces, shave their heads except for a small pigtail, and carry small cloth bags containing their prayer beads used for chanting.

The current scene

After Prabhupade's death in 1977 the leadership was assumed by an international group of twelve men. Numerically this movement remains relatively small world-wide but a significant growth is being recorded in several countries. In the United Kingdom, for example, the number of active members has increased remarkably from 5,000 in 1970, 35,000 in 1980 to an estimated 50,000 in 1987, with the projected figure of 55,000 for 1990.[1] Members work extremely hard to promote the knowledge of Krishna and the society is now international.

What Hare Krishna teaches	*What the Bible teaches*
God	
Vishnu or Krishna is the personal God, the highest of all deities, living on a heavenly planet and is to some extent remote and	'I am the Lord, and there is no other; besides me there is no God... I am the Lord, and there is no other' (Isaiah 45:5-6).

inaccessible. Being fully divine, he cannot understand man and, despite appearances to the contrary, he does not hate or like anyone. He is beyond good and evil and one title he claims for himself is 'master of demons'.

Krishna cries in the skies as he beholds the behaviour of earth's inhabitants.

'God so loved the world...' (John 3:16).

'Thou art not a God who takes pleasure in wickedness; no evil dwells with thee... thou dost hate all who do iniquity' (Psalm 5:4-5; cf. Hebrew 2:17-18; 4:15).

Bible

'Abandon all varieties of religions and just surrender to me' (Krishna).[2]

The Bible, including the teaching of Christ, is relative and incomplete, needing to be supplemented by the *Bhagavad-Gita* which is the gospel of the Hindu scriptures, containing a conversation between the warrior Arjuna and the god Krishna.

'Thy word is truth' (John 17:17).

' To the law and to the testimony: if they speak not according to this word, it is because there is no light in them' (Isaiah 8:20, AV).

'Lord, to whom shall we go? You have words of eternal life. And we have believed and have come to know that you are the Holy One of God' (John 6:68-69).

Person of Christ

Christ is not God, but rather a pure devotee sent from another planet by the inhabitants who had compassion on the earth people.

'Who, although he existed in the form of God, did not regard equality with God a thing to be grasped' (Philippians 2:6).

'In order that all may honour the Son, even as they honour the Father. He who does not honour the Son does not honour the Father who sent him' (John 5:23).

'I and the Father are one' (John 10:30).

Creation

The world is *Maya* or illusion, a product of man's wrong thinking. In previous ages Krishna expanded so considerably that he became the 'Great Vishna', with the direct

'And God saw all that he had made, and behold, it was very good' (Genesis 1:31).

'Thou didst create all things, and because of thy will they

result that the universe was created. As this expansion was untypical of the Hindu deities, the creation was only illusory.

Man

Man's body is unreal and, while his soul is individual it is also part of the divine soul.

existed, and were created' (Revelation 4:11).

'The Lord God formed man of dust from the ground, and breathed into his nostrils the breath of life; and man became a living being' (Genesis 2:7).

'What is man, that thou dost take thought of him? And the son of man, that thou dost care for him? Yet thou hast made him a little lower than God, and dost crown him with glory and majesty' (Psalm 8:4-5).

'It is I who made the earth, and created man upon it. I stretched out the heavens with my hands' (Isaiah 45:12).

Sin

Good and evil are also illusions. The inhabitants of the material universe rebelled against Krishna and pursued the satisfaction of physical lusts and other illusory pleasures. Man's basic problem is that he has forgotten Krishna and absorbed himself with the temporal.

'Far be it from God to do wickedness, and from the Almighty to do wrong' (Job 34:10).

'Sin is lawlessness' (1 John 3:4).

'Your iniquities have made a separation between you and your God, and your sins have hid his face from you, so that he does not hear' (Isaiah 59:2).

Salvation

Each follower carries a beaded string, and the 108 beads represent the 108 cowherdess lovers of Krishna. With each bead there is a sixteen word chant called *'Mahamantra'* which is:

'When you are praying, do not use meaningless repetition, as the Gentiles do, for they suppose that they will be heard for their many words. Therefore do not be like them' (Matthew 6:7-8).

Hare Krishna, Hare Krishna,
Krishna, Krishna, Hare, Hare,
Hare Rama, Hare Rama,
Rama, Rama, Hare, Hare.

When a person chants the divine name in this way he or she is released from pain, and then experiences ecstasy or 'transcendental love' without any sexual contact. People save themselves by chanting the *Mahamantra*, keeping the Four Rules, and by constant efforts to keep their minds and bodies free.

To help towards Krishna Consciousness, a 'Spiritual Master' is provided whose ancestry is related to spiritual leaders like Chaitanya. They regard Prabhupade as having this kind of ancestry and he is worshipped as a manifestation of God.

'For by grace you have been saved through faith; and that not of yourselves, it is the gift of God; not as a result of works, that no one should boast' (Ephesians 2:8-9).

'A man is justified by faith apart from works of the Law' (Romans 3:28).

'For there is one God, and one mediator also between God and men, the man Christ Jesus, who gave himself as a ransom for all' (1 Timothy 2:5-6).

Future state

A person's response to important illusions like passion, ignorance and goodness determines where he spends his next existence. Hell is the destruction of those controlled by ignorance; future reincarnations on earth await those who allow passion to rule them. The pursuers of goodness — that is, a complete repudiation of the material world and total obedience to Krishna — will live in higher spirit planets.

'It is appointed for men to die once, and after this comes judgement' (Hebrews 9:27).

'He who believes in him [Jesus] is not judged; he who does not believe has been judged already, because he has not believed in the name of the only begotten Son of God' (John 3:18).

'The Lord Jesus shall be revealed from heaven with his mighty angels in flaming fire, dealing out retribution to those who do not know God and to those who do not obey the gospel of our Lord Jesus. And these will pay the penalty of eternal destruction, away from the presence of the Lord and from the glory of his power, when he comes to be glorified in his saints on that day...' (2 Thessalonians 1:7-10).

29.
Yoga

To most Westerners the word 'Yoga' is associated with a set of complex physical exercises enabling people to relax and maintain peak physical fitness, but for millions of people in the East it is a complete way of life undergirded by philosophical and religious ideas expressed mainly through Buddhism and Hinduism. The word 'Yoga' is derived from the verbal root '*yuj*', meaning 'to bind together', 'to yoke', and it has many meanings such as 'union, the conjunction of stars... team, aggregate, sum...', but specifically the word refers to a set of spiritual ideas and techniques which developed in India over many thousands of years. Yoga is the generic name for various Indian paths of 'union' with the absolute and the name is sometimes also used to refer to other movements which, directly or indirectly, have been inspired by Indian sources, such as Tibetan Yoga (Vajrayana Buddhism) and Chinese Yoga (Taoism). The popular definition of Yoga as 'union with the absolute' stems from *Vedanta,* one of the major philosophical movements of India, which views Yoga as 'union of the living self with the supreme self', but it is important to note that this definition does not cover all forms of Yoga, particularly Classical Yoga, which is also sometimes known as Raja Yoga.

There are numerous Yoga paths which lead to the ultimate union with the divine consciousness *(samadhi)*. These include:

Jnana Yoga	— union by knowledge;
Bhakti Yoga	— union by love;
Karma Yoga	— union by service;
Mantra Yoga	— union by speech;
Hatha Yoga	— union by bodily control;
Raja Yoga	— union by mental control.

Hatha Yoga and Raja Yoga are the paths most commonly followed, but the various paths are not at all mutually exclusive and many devotees or Yogins follow all of them in order to achieve the perfect Yoga life. Common to all forms of Yoga are eight indispensable practices.

1. Yama

This means abstention from evil or restraint.
There are five ethical rules included in Yama:
  a. 'non-hurting', which is the absence of violence in thought and deed;
  b. 'truthfulness';
  c. 'non-stealing';
  d. 'chastity', which involves abstaining from all sexual activity, in deed, thought or word, for sex deflects the yogin's mind from the absolute and feeds his appetite for physical satisfaction;
  e. 'greedlessness' is the non-acceptance of gifts because of the disadvantages arising from the possession of material things, as, for example, excessive attachment to them, or unwillingness to lose or share them.
When these rules are kept, the yogin develops certain powers such as insight, vigour and peace.

2. Niyama

Self-discipline and the five norms of 'purity', 'contentment', 'austerity', 'self-study' and 'devotion to the Lord' are intended to guide one's personal relationship to the Transcendent Reality.

3. Asana

'Posture' keeps the body steady and relaxed.

4. Pranayama

This is breath-control, which has a powerful effect on the mind.

5. Pratyahara

This involves 'sense-withdrawal', for both posture and breath-control lead to a progressive insensitivity to external stimuli.

6. Dharana

This results from the process of withdrawing from external reality when the mind is held in a motionless state.

7. Dhyana

This means meditative absorption and is the next stage in which the object held in the mind fills the entire consciousness 'space'.

8. Samadhi

This means self-realization and is the climax of a long and tedious process of mental discipline which has been likened to hypnosis.

In the East the decision to follow Yoga as a complete way of life is usually taken in childhood and while still young the person becomes a pupil of a teacher or guru. More often than not, the pupil lives with his teacher and serves him in return for regular and detailed instruction. After several years the pupil will leave his guru in order to become a teacher himself and will continue towards the attainment of the ideal, which is 'the silencing of the mind's activities which leads to the complete realization of the intrinsic nature of the Supreme Being called Yoga'. Once a yogin has defeated pain he is capable of lying on a bed of sharp nails, drinking acid, suspending breathing for the forty days during which he is buried alive and holding one arm above his head until it withers. Many yogins have extra-sensory perception and are involved in occult activities. We will now compare the teaching of Yoga with that of the Bible to see how unbiblical and dangerous it actually is.

What Yoga teaches	*What the Bible teaches*

God

God is all-pervasive and universal; he is viewed as being identical with the world (pantheism) and is 'the ultimate substratum of all there is'.

As Creator, God is apart from, and independent of his creation although he governs and directs it according to his will (Psalm 102:25-27; Isaiah 42:5; Acts 17:28; Colossians 1:16-17).

Christ

The life of Christ is a valuable example to us, but Christ is not unique: he is one of many religious teachers who were all divinely inspired.

Read 1 Peter 2:21-25.
  'I am the first and the last, and the living one; and I was dead, and behold, I am alive for evermore, and I have the keys of death and of Hades' (Revelation 1:17; cf. John 14:6; Hebrews 1:1-3).

Salvation

There is no need of a personal Saviour to save us from sin. Yoga prefers to speak of emancipation — from the physical body at death, and in the present life through enlightenment and the transcending of 'conditional existence'.

'Without shedding of blood there is no forgiveness' (Hebrews 9:22).
  'But now having been freed from sin and enslaved to God, you derive your benefit, resulting in sanctification, and the outcome, eternal life. For the wages of sin is death, but the free gift of God is eternal life in Christ Jesus our Lord' (Romans 6:22-23).
  'If you abide in my word, then

Suffering

Suffering is not the result of a sin for which man was punished by God; its roots are rather in man's lack of self-knowledge.

Suffering is a positive evil, the exact opposite of the blissful self or being.

you are truly disciples of mine; and you shall know the truth, and the truth shall make you free' (John 8:31-32).

Genesis 3:17-19; cf. Romans 8:22.

'We exult in hope of the glory of God. And not only this, but we also exult in our tribulations, knowing that tribulation brings about perseverance, and perseverance, proven character, and proven character, hope...' (Romans 5:2-4; cf. 2 Corinthians 12:7-10).

Death and the future state

Besides having their immediate visible effects, man's actions also decide the quality of his life after death and the nature of his eventual reincarnation or rebirth. Some actions cannot be paid for after death so that a person who is guilty of many bad deeds will be compelled to re-enter the world in new human or animal bodies for as long as is necessary.

There is no reincarnation for 'It is appointed for men to die once, and after this comes judgement' (Hebrews 9:27).

God eternally punishes sinners after death in hell (see Matthew 25:46; Luke 16:23; 2 Thessalonians 1:8-9).

For those who die believing upon the Lord Jesus, there is eternal bliss in heaven (Romans 6:23; 2 Corinthians 5:6-8; Philippians 1:21-23; Revelation 14:13).

30.
Transcendental Meditation

It was in 1978 that Transcendental Meditation bought Mentmore Towers in Buckinghamshire and its eighty-three acres of land for £240,000 to become the movement's British headquarters. Previously the home of the Rothschilds and the Earls of Roseberry, Mentmore Towers now houses eighty disciples of His Holiness Maharishi Mahesh Yogi and helps towards fulfilling the Maharishi's ambition of establishing a 'world government' to administer the 'age of enlightenment'. *The Times* describes a visit to Mentmore: 'One can not only gawp at the artistic treasures sold with Mentmore to the new owners but also discover something of the mysteries of TM. The tour provides some interesting incongruities. A portrait of the Maharishi sits over the Rubens marble fireplace in the great hall, the old billiard room is filled with foam mattresses for levitation and 'flying', and the room where the servants used to clean the Rothschild silver is now a bio-chemistry laboratory where samples of meditators' blood are analysed. Using impressively complex scientific equipment, the new occupants of Mentmore claim to have proved that meditation reduces stress, increases hearing power and even reverses the ageing process.'[1]

The man behind the movement

TM is also known as the International Meditation Society, World

Plan Executive Council and Age of Enlightenment. Transcendental Meditation is practised by more than two and a half million people throughout the world, including some Christians. The man responsible for this astonishing success is Maharishi Mahesh Yogi, who was born in the north of India in 1918. At about the age of thirty-one he obtained a degree in physics at Allahabad University and then for five years he worked in a factory. During this period he studied Yoga and then went to the Himalayas in 1947 to study and meditate with his guru, Swami Brahmananda Saraswati (Guru Dev). Mahesh Yogi stayed with the guru for thirteen years but before the latter died, he told Mahesh Yogi to develop a form of meditation which everyone could use. When Mahesh Yogi eventually publicized his new meditation techniques in Madras there was hardly any response from the people. He then moved to London, where his movement was initially known as the Spiritual Regeneration Movement and then as the Science of Creative Intelligence. Once again there was no immediate response to his teachings but in 1967 he achieved success and fame when the Beatles became his most celebrated disciples. The group made exaggerated claims about their newly found guru and the help his teaching had given them; this publicity attracted other entertainers to the guru, including the Rolling Stones, and many other people began to practise TM. The Maharishi also attracted people by his claim that TM would provide permanent, inward peace for individuals and the world, provided that a sufficient number practised his teaching. However, it was not long before the Beatles and others were disillusioned with the Maharishi's message and, bitterly disappointed, the guru flew back to India, conceding, 'I know I have failed. My mission is over,' and promising never to return to the West.

In India he conceived a new world plan and he then moved his headquarters from India first to Italy, then to Spain and now it is located near Lake Lucerne in Switzerland. The world plan involved the establishing of 350 TM teacher-training or university centres throughout the world and in the last decade or so TM has gained respectability, acceptance and many recruits. In Britain, for example, about 900 people per month join the movement while the monthly figure in the United States is as high as 300,000.

Unfulfilled promises

Since 1980 TM in Britain has tried to convince the National Health
Service that its practice reduces stress and therefore ought to be
available on prescription. The British Association for the Medical
Application of Transcendental Meditation wants the NHS to pay
for further research. Some national and religious newspapers,
however, are becoming more aware of the dangers implicit in the
Maharishi's teaching and methods. Early in 1980 five people told
the *Guardian* that between them they paid a total of more than
£30,000 after TM tutors had promised they would learn to fly, walk
through walls, become invisible and acquire superhuman strength,
but none of these promises was realized. One person who had
practised TM alleged, 'I sometimes sank into a vortex of depression
and insanity. Twice I tried to kill myself with pills. On other
occasions I kept threatening to throw myself out of a fifth-floor
window.' Another meditator said, 'I got nothing out of TM except
heartache and financial loss.' A former TM teacher, Hesta Fisch-
berg, has called for an official enquiry into the aims and methods of
TM and claims that Britain is the only country in which the
movement is not the subject of a government investigation. 'Britain
has always been proud of her heritage of freedom and justice,' she
said, and 'the last thing we should allow on our soil is this horrible
falsehood. It is about time someone started to do something. The
Maharishi has got one hundred thousand of our people under his
control...'

Hindu elements

Pat Means, in his helpful study, *The Mystical Maze*, describes TM
as 'Hinduism in a Scientist's Smock' [2] and this is confirmed by
Maurice Burrell when he claims that TM 'operates within a Hindu
philosophical framework, uses Hindu mantras and addresses itself
to Hindu deities'.[3] Such claims can easily be verified. For example,
the Maharishi explains the significance of the *mantra* used by each
disciple in a religious way: 'We do something here according to
Vedic rites, particularly, specific chanting to produce an effect in
some other world, draw the attention of those higher beings or gods
living there. The entire knowledge of the *mantras* or hymns of the

Vedas [Hindu scriptures] is devoted to man's connection, to man's communication with the higher beings in different strata of creation.'[4] Again, the Maharishi describes Transcendental Meditation as 'a path to God'[5] and 'the only way to salvation and success in life'. The initiation ceremony involves the following: 'To Lord Narayana, to lotus-born Brahma, the Creator... to Shankorachorya the redeemer, hailed as Krishna... I bow down...' Thus, in addition to psychological problems, TM poses spiritual dangers, including exposure to demonic activity and a false, substitute experience of God. The Maharishi writes, 'He who practises Transcendental Meditation becomes acquainted with the inner divine consciousness. Although we are all one hundred per cent divine, consciously we do not know that we are divine so there is no connection, there is no bridge and we suffer on the conscious level.'[6] For these reasons alone, TM should be avoided as a dangerous and subtle denial of the gospel of Christ.

What Transcendental Meditation teaches	What the Bible teaches

God

There is no personal God; instead God and creation are one (pantheism). The purpose of TM, that of delving into a deeper level of consciousness, is to experience oneness with the world and God, sometimes described as the Absolute or the All, etc. In this way a condition is reached where people feel themselves to be God.

'Before the mountains were born, or thou didst give birth to the earth and the world, even from everlasting to everlasting, thou art God' (Psalm 90:2).

'He is the God who formed the earth and made it, he established it and did not create it a waste place, but formed it to be inhabited' (Isaiah 45:18).

Bible

TM is anchored in Hinduism and its most popular proponent and founder is Maharishi Mahesh Yogi. The Hindu scripture — *Bhagarad Gita*, an alleged divine revelation to the world — is the basis for TM. Maharishi Yogi was taught the

'Thy word is truth' (John 17:17).

'The sum of thy word is truth, and every one of thy righteous ordinances is everlasting' (Psalm 119:160).

principle of TM by Guru Dev (Divine Teacher) who is worshipped by TM followers.

Person of Christ

He was only one of a number of great religious teachers in the history of the world.

'I am the way, and the truth, and the life; no one comes to the Father, but through me' (John 14:6; Matthew 16:16).

Work of Christ

There was no need for our Lord's sacrifice at all. Maharishi Yogi, for example, does not think that Christ ever suffered or could suffer.

'For all have sinned and fall short of the glory of God, being justified as a gift by his grace through the redemption which is in Christ Jesus; whom God displayed publicly as a propitiation in his blood through faith. This was to demonstrate his righteousness, because in the forbearance of God he passed over the sins previously committed; for the demonstration, I say, of his righteousness at the present time, that he might be just and the justifier of the one who has faith in Jesus' (Romans 3:23-26; cf. 1 Peter 2:21, 23-24).

Salvation

An equivalent term to salvation in TM language is 'self-realization', which is the awareness of one's essential deity and unity with the all-pervasive being of God. TM 'is the only way to make a success in life; there is no other way' (Maharishi Mahesh Yogi).

'There is salvation in no one else; for there is no other name under heaven that has been given among men, by which we must be saved' (Acts 4:12).

'Having overlooked the times of ignorance, God is now declaring to men that all everywhere should repent, because he has fixed a day in which he will judge the world in righteousness through a man whom he has appointed, having furnished proof to all men by raising him from the dead' (Acts 17:30-31).

Holy Spirit

There is no belief in the Holy Spirit but TM involvement can lead to contact with evil spirits. Although the Maharishi discourages people from seeking spirit-contact, TM opens the door wide to spiritism. Levitation, for example, is actively encouraged.

'"God anointed him [Jesus of Nazareth] with the Holy Spirit and with power"... While Peter was still speaking these words, the Holy Spirit fell upon all those who were listening to the message' (Acts 10:38, 44).

Spiritism is condemned: 'When they say to you, "Consult the mediums and the wizards who whisper and mutter," should not a people consult their God? Should they consult the dead on behalf of the living? To the law and to the testimony! If they do not speak according to this word, it is because they have no dawn' (Isaiah 8:19-20).

'Do not turn to mediums or spiritists; do not seek them out to be defiled by them. I am the Lord your God' (Leviticus 19:31).

Man and sin

Man is basically good and an emanation from God. The world is simply the absolute spilling over its being. Ignorance of his own deity is man's basic problem. There is no absolute right or wrong and no need of forgiveness. The purpose of all life is happiness.

'There is not a righteous man on earth who continually does good and who never sins' (Ecclesiastes 7:20).

'Out of the heart come evil thoughts, murders, adulteries, fornications, thefts, false witness, slanders' (Matthew 15:19).

'...in that they show the work of the Law written in their hearts, their conscience bearing witness, and their thoughts alternately accusing or else defending them' (Romans 2:15).

Future state

Man's purpose in the world is to enjoy 'bliss-consciousness' and

Reincarnation is denied in the Bible (Hebrews 9:27) as is also Karma,

then enter a condition of eternal liberation which is called *Nirvana* or *Moksha*. Reincarnation and Karma can only be avoided by experiencing the loss of all individuality and becoming absorbed in the Brahman, the Hindu god. This is what is meant by eternal liberation.

that is, the belief that results of our actions in this life will affect our future lives (cf. John 9:1-3). At death the believer goes to heaven to be with his Saviour and the unbeliever to hell (Matthew 25:46).

Our bodies will also be resurrected at the second coming of Christ (1 Corinthians 15:35-54).

Meditation

Each TM adherent is given a secret Sanskrit word to use in his meditation. This is called a *mantra* and both morning and evening the meditator has to repeat quietly this *mantra*, which has a deep religious significance. The Maharishi explains it as something related to ancient Vedic rites which has the purpose of gaining the attention of 'gods' or 'spirits' in the spirit world.

Christian meditation is radically different from TM.
1. It is meditation upon the Word of God, the Bible (Psalms 1:2; 119:11; Colossians 3:16).
2. It is meditation upon the triune God revealed in the Bible (Psalms 63:6; 77:12).
3. It is meditation arising from a personal knowledge of God himself in Christ (1 John 4:10-19).
4. It is meditation which is orientated towards obeying God's revealed will (cf. John 8:29; 14:15; 2 Corinthians 5:9; Ephesians 5:8-10).

31.
Divine Light Mission

The founder of the Divine Light Mission, Shri Hans Ji Mahoraj, died in India in 1966. After claiming to have received 'knowledge' (a technical Hindu term describing the highest possible spiritual experience) from an Indian guru, Shri Sarupanand Ji, in the early 1920s, Mahoraj Ji began to teach his new ideas to others and quickly gained a large following until at his death his disciples were estimated to number millions. In order to communicate his ideas more widely and co-ordinate the work of his disciples, the Divine Light Mission was established in 1960.

Promises of peace

The Mission's present leader is Guru Mahoraj Ji who was born in India on 10 December 1957. At the age of six he received 'knowledge' from his father and when only eight years old he announced to the mourners on the day of his father's funeral, 'Dear children of God, why are you weeping? Haven't you learned the lesson that your Master taught you? The Perfect Master never dies. Mahoraj Ji is here, amongst you now. Recognize him, obey him and adore him!' The response was almost unanimous and immediate and this youngest son was recognized as the Perfect Master. His ashram (shelter) on the side of the Ganges river quickly attracted many thousands of followers and in 1969, only three years after his father's death, he sent his first recruiting agents to Britain. He drove through New Delhi in 1970 in a golden chariot followed by elephants, camels and many thousands of disciples and, addressing a crowd of almost two million he declared, 'I will establish peace in this world.' He then moved his home and headquarters to the United States and in late 1973 a huge festival called 'Millennium 73' was held in the U.S.A. under the auspices of the Divine Light Mission. The main purpose of the festival was to announce to the world the beginning of the millennium of Revelation 20 in which the guru promised to abolish all suffering and introduce 1,000 years of uninterrupted peace on the earth.

The mission today

In 1974 the guru married a former American airline stewardess, Marolyn Johnson, but far from establishing a millennium, his marriage and indulgent life-style provoked opposition and trouble from his family and in 1975 his mother declared his older brother, Bal Bhagwan Ji, to be the legitimate Perfect Master and a rival group was formed. Despite this setback and continuing family tension, the Divine Light Mission is regaining some lost ground at present and recruiting many teenagers. During the summer of 1980, for example, Guru Mahoraj Ji met with about 10,000 of his followers in Olympia, London, and there are alleged to be between five and six million devotees throughout the world. Some of these live in ashrams where they are expected to abstain from meat, alcohol, tobacco and sex, while others live in a *premie* house and a lower standard is required of them. Meanwhile, the guru himself lives in the lap of luxury, with Rolls-Royce cars, cabin cruisers, expensive food and night-life, which are paid for by his disciples and by the mission's business enterprises, which include the *Divine Times* newspaper, 'Divine Sales' (a chain of second-hand shops), electronics, filming and recording companies, garage repair servicing and a large food co-operative, as well as a New York restaurant for vegetarians. Despite its glaring inconsistencies and denial of Bible teaching, the Divine Light Mission remains a force to be reckoned with in the current confused religious scene.

What the Divine Light Mission teaches	What the Bible teaches

Bible

The scriptures of Hinduism, Buddhism, Islam and Christianity are all respected, but truth has now been revealed exclusively through the Guru Mahoraj Ji and his statements are honoured above all other sacred writings. They accuse Christians of changing the true meaning of the Bible!

'Lord, to whom shall we go? You [Christ] have words of eternal life. And we have believed and have come to know that you are the Holy One of God' (John 6:68-69).

'To the law and to the testimony: if they speak not according to this word, it is because there is no light in them' (Isaiah 8:20, AV).

God

God is infinite but impersonal and is described as 'Cosmic Energy', 'Universal Mind' and 'Ultimate Reality'. This is akin to pantheism, that is, the identification of the world and God.

1. God and his creation are distinct but creation is dependent upon God for its existence and preservation (Isaiah 42:5; Psalm 102:25-27; Acts 17:28; Colossians 1:16-17).
2. God is also holy (Isaiah 6:3), righteous (Psalm 145:17), almighty (Matthew 19:26), and manifests wrath (Romans 1:18) and love (1 John 4:7-12).
3. God is personal and enters into a personal relationship with his people (Matthew 6:25-34; John 17:3, etc).

Sin

Sin exists only as an illusion in the mind, and it is illusion, not sin, which prevents us from enjoying harmony with God.

'If we say that we have no sin, we are deceiving ourselves, and the truth is not in us' (1 John 1:8).

'But your iniquities have made a separation between you and your God, and your sins have hid his face from you, so that he does not hear' (Isaiah 59:2).

Christ

Consistently with his Hindu background, the guru teaches that 'God' has manifested himself at different periods through avatars such as Jesus, Buddha, Krishna, Muhammad, etc. Each manifestation is called 'Christ'. What Christ was to the world 2,000 years ago, Guru Ji is to the world today — Saviour, Lord and Master. Guru Ji is 'the treasure house of unlimited happiness and peace' and 'the ocean of kindness' and he will soon relieve the world of all its suffering.

Salvation

'I will give you salvation', claims Guru Mahoraj Ji, 'if you surrender your lives to me.' Salvation involves deliverance from the world's illusions, not from sin or hell, and it occurs when the human mind is in perfect harmony with the Universal Mind.

How are we saved? By receiving 'knowledge', i.e. feeling God directly through his manifestation in our age, which is Guru Mahoraj Ji.

Second Coming

All the prophecies relating to the second coming of Christ are applied to the leader of the mission. For example, when he flew into London, the guru believed he was the Christ 'coming in the clouds of heaven'!

'God, after he spoke long ago to the fathers in the prophets in many portions and in many ways, in these last days has spoken to us in his Son, whom he appointed heir of all things, through whom also he made the world' (Hebrews 1:1-2).

'Jesus Christ is the same yesterday and today, yes and for ever' (Hebrews 13:8).

'In him all the fulness of the Deity dwells in bodily form, and in him you have been made complete, and he is the head over all rule and authority' (Colossians 2:9-10).

'There is salvation in no one else [Jesus Christ]; for there is no other name under heaven that has been given among men, by which we must be saved' (Acts 4:12).

'Having now been justified by his blood, we shall be saved from the wrath of God through him' (Romans 5:9; cf. Titus 2:11-14; 3:4-7).

'Believe on the Lord Jesus Christ and thou shalt be saved' (Acts 16:31, AV).

'Jesus answered…"See to it that no one misleads you. For many will come in my name, saying, 'I am the Christ,' and will mislead many…And many false prophets will arise, and will mislead many"' (Matthew 24:5-11).

32.
Rajneesh Foundation

'He is one of the most remarkable orators I have ever heard,' wrote the *Times* columnist Bernard Levin after visiting Indian guru Bhagwan Shree Rajneesh in Poona, India, in 1980. Levin was not alone in this estimate of Rajneesh's oratory. From 1973-1981 many thousands of people, mostly from the West, had begun to attend Rajneesh's daily lecture. By 1987, the guru had centres operating in many major cities and towns throughout the world.

How it all began

Rajneesh was born in central India in December 1931 and was the eldest of twelve children. He spent most of his childhood and teenage years with his grandparents and after his grandfather died he developed a morbid interest in death. Philosophy and psychology were the subjects he later studied in college and in 1957 he obtained his M.A. degree in philosophy from the University of Sangur. For the next nine years he was a philosophy lecturer at two different colleges in India, but he also travelled extensively during this period speaking on sex, religion and politics. As an eloquent and controversial speaker, Rajneesh became increasingly more popular and his influence began to spread beyond India.

In 1969, Rajneesh decided to concentrate exclusively on teaching a small group of his devotees in Bombay. He later moved with this group to the industrialized area of Poona where Rajneesh assumed the name Bhagwan (which means 'God').[1] In 1974 he established a religious community (an ashram) of about 300 people who were carefully chosen from a large group of eager candidates. Those accepted into the ashram had to give complete submission to Rajneesh and accept all his teaching and directions without reservation. In addition to the 300 ashram residents, as many as 7,000 people, mostly Westerners, lived in the area in order to attend the ashram for daily instruction.

Silence

His devotees were stunned in March 1981 when, as he had predicted years earlier, Rajneesh began his period of 'silence' and thereby ended his work of public teaching. Rajneesh claimed that by means of silence he would succeed in communicating the highest form of enlightenment to people. Within three months he flew to the United States in order to extend his work.

Almost immediately, Rajneesh paid $6,000,000 for a 64,229 acre site some 200 miles from Portland in Oregon. The guru wanted the State of Oregon to incorporate the site, which was renamed Rajneeshpunam, as a city and many professional people joined Rajneesh in the work of establishing a 'world centre of enlightenment' which was intended to include a self-sufficient farming co-operative. The state authorities, however, refused to sanction Rajneesh's plans for the site.

Disillusioned with materialism, politics and churches, an increasing number of people have turned to the guru for enlightenment and for a sense of purpose in life.

Claims made by followers

Some claim that in meeting Rajneesh they have experienced God. A Roman Catholic charismatic, Ma Prem Samadhi, for example, affirms, 'Jesus was my first master, but Bhagwan is a living master. My master is inside myself. Bhagwan is an outer expression of it...'[2] Similarly, an 'American Methodist minister claims that his bishop encouraged him to become a disciple (or *sannyasin*) of the guru. 'He saw it as adding to my spirituality... I see no conflict between where I am now [Rajneeshpuram] and what the church has promulgated. This is an extension of my ministry. We are focused in our love for Bhagwan. I had a longing inside that was not being fulfilled. Bhagwan is an extension of Christ.'[3]

Ma Anand Poonam, director of Medina Rajneesh, which is the cult's British headquarters in Heringswell, Bury St Edmunds, first entered the strange world of group therapy and mysticism with her husband Swami Anand Teertha as far back as 1967 in San Francisco. In the group they were expected to express their feelings and gaze into each other's eyes. 'Teertha and I were terribly English,' she remarked, 'very uptight amongst those liberal, easy-going, relaxed Americans. We sat on the edges of our cushions just terrified.' They decided to complete the six-week course and by the end they were both hooked. The next step was to train as group leaders before eventually establishing a Quasitor group in England.

When Teertha was holidaying in India in 1972 he rang his wife from Bombay and rather excitedly announced, 'Everything we've been doing, everything we've been experiencing in the past three years has been leading to this. This is what we've been looking for. Come right now!' Teertha had heard Rajneesh and, like many other people, believed that the latter could provide the strong mystical and inspirational base needed to fulfil his quest for self-realization.

What does Rajneesh promise and offer to people? Using meditation, Sufi dancing, *Gestalt,* rebirthing, Rolfing, hypnosis, psycho-drama, Samadhi tanks, sex and at times, violence, Rajneesh seeks to impart enlightenment and also the transformation of the inner selves of his followers. Rajneesh's teaching resembles Buddhism and Julia Duin describes it as 'a mixture of Eastern mysticism, American if-it-feels-good-do-it philosophy and holistic medicine'.[4] One disillusioned follower who later became a Christian believes the cult is 'a perfect model of mind control. Rajneesh is a spiritual Hitler, a highly developed demonic figure. His ultimate goal is to create the mindless man, because the mindless man can reach enlightenment.'[5]

Surprisingly, very few people actually see Rajneesh. Having conveniently taken a vow of silence, he stays in his own private house except for a regular drive in his Rolls Royce. However, Rajneesh has been one of the most influential and dangerous of the gurus in the contemporary religious world.

What Rajneesh teaches

Truth

Rajneesh insists that truth is relative and subjective; it is seen and experienced rather than understood. There is no higher authority than the words of Rajneesh.

His therapy is a synthesis of Western growth practices and Eastern methods of meditation, including those from within Hinduism, Buddhism and Zen, etc.

God

'There is no God sitting somewhere, presiding over the world. The very world, the very being is God. God is not a person, but a process' (Rajneesh).

The term 'God' is only one of several terms which are used to describe the whole of reality; other equally suitable terms are Void, Silence, Brahman or Beingness.

Christ

Followers of Rajneesh believe their guru has reached the same level as Jesus Christ.

'Jesus is an art of inner transformation, of rebirth' (A Rajneesh Foundation advertisement alongside a picture of Rajneesh himself).[6]

What the Bible teaches

Truth is what God has revealed infallibly in the Bible, the Word of God; it always remains objective, valid truth, irrespective of human feelings or views or reactions (see Hebrews 1:1-3; John 8:31-32; 2 Timothy 3:16; 2 Peter 1:21).

'Do you not know? Have you not heard?... It is *he* who sits above the vault of the earth... He it is who reduces rulers to nothing, who makes the judges of the earth meaningless...' (Isaiah 40:21-23).

'Thus says the Lord, your Redeemer, and the one who formed you from the womb, I, the Lord, am the maker of all things...' (Isaiah 44:24).

'It is I who made the earth, and created man upon it. I stretched out the heavens with *my* hands, and I ordained all their host' (Isaiah 45:12).

'Know for certain that God has made him both Lord and Christ — this Jesus whom you crucified' (Acts 2:36).

'Jesus answered and said to them, "See to it that no one misleads you. For many will come in my name, saying, 'I am the Christ',

'I will be revealing a totally different Christ that you are not acquainted with...' (Rajneesh).

and will mislead many'" (Matthew 24:4-5).

Sin

'I declare that you are not sinners, that no one is a sinner...'

'There is no such thing as sin or right and wrong.'

Regarding sex, it's left to the individual to do what he wants. 'There are no rules against anything.'

'If we say that we have no sin, we are deceiving ourselves, and the truth is not in us' (1 John 1:8; see also Romans 3:23).

'Sin is the transgression of the law' (1 John 3:4, AV).

'For this is the will of God, your sanctification; that is, that you abstain from sexual immorality...' (1 Thessalonians 4:3-6; cf. Exodus 20:3-17).

Message

'My beloved ones, I love you. Love is my messge. Let it be your message, too. Love is my colour and climate. To me, love is the only religion... Here the whole message is "Hallelujah"; the whole message is of ecstasy, love, joy, celebration is the keyword here.'

'This is the message we have heard from him and announce to you, that God is light, and in him there is no darkness at all' (1 John 1:5).

'We know love by this, that he laid down his life for us; and we ought to lay down our lives for the brethren' (1 John 3:16).

'In this is love, not that we loved God, but that he loved us and sent his Son to be the propitiation for our sins' (1 John 4:10).

Heaven and hell

'We are not going to divide existence into this world and that world, we are going to live existence in its totality. We are going to live as scientists, as poets, as mystics, all together.'

'If we have only hoped in Christ in this life, we are of all men most to be pitied' (1 Corinthians 15:19; cf. Luke 12:19-20; Matthew 7:13-14).

Occult

Occult involvement is legitimate and helpful. The Rajneesh Midsummer Ball at Medina, Suffolk on

'There shall not be found among you anyone... who uses divination, one who practises witchcraft, or

21 June 1982 included, by popular demand, aura readings, tarot booths, crystal ball gazing, astrological charts, phrenology, palmistry, magicians, wizards, etc.

one who interprets omens, or a sorcerer, or one who casts a spell, or a medium, or a spiritist, or one who calls up the dead. For whoever does these things is detestable to the Lord...' (Deuteronomy 18:10-12; cf. Isaiah 8:19-20).

Section 8
An outline of major Bible doctrines

This section provides a positive outline of the biblical teaching on thirteen major doctrines. Readers who are unsure or confused about what the Bible actually teaches can use this section to clarify further and check their understanding of the biblical revelation.

33. The Bible

34. What God is like

35. The Holy Trinity

36. The works of God

37. Man: his creation and fall

38. Man in sin

39. The person of Christ

40. The sacrifice of Christ

41. The exaltation of Christ

42. The Holy Spirit

43. Becoming a Christian

44. The church

45. Death and the after-life

Section 8
An outline of major Bible doctrines

33.
The Bible

Who is right? Which teaching should I accept? How can I know what is true or false? These are important questions which people are continually asking in our contemporary, confused situation. Where should we turn for reliable answers to these questions? The claim made in this book is that *the Bible alone* provides truthful and, therefore, dependable answers to our questions concerning God, salvation and life after death, etc.

Can we trust the Bible? Why is the Bible so special? Here are some reasons why you should turn to the Bible and accept its teaching.

1. *The Bible is divine*

One major reason why the Bible is unique is that it is God's book; it comes from God and is God's self-revelation of himself and his purposes. Writing to Timothy, the apostle Paul declares, 'All Scripture is inspired by God...' (2 Timothy 3:16). 'Inspired' here means 'breathed out' from God: the Scripture is not a record of man's search for God and his ideas, but rather truth which originates with God and which he communicates through the Bible. Peter tells us, 'No prophecy was ever made by an act of human will, but men moved by the Holy Spirit spoke from God' (2 Peter 1:21). The Bible is no ordinary book; in fact, it is described as 'the Word of God' (1

Thessalonians 2:13) or 'thy Word' (John 17:17). This is the only book which we can safely trust and use.

2. The Bible is dominant

Because the Bible is divine, it should dominate both our thinking and behaviour. Our Lord Jesus is an example to us in this respect. When resisting the devil in the wilderness, he appealed to the authority of God's Word by telling his enemy three times, 'It is written' (Matthew 4:4,7,10). Altogether, the Lord used the phrase, 'It is written' on another fifteen occasions, particularly when answering people's questions. For the Lord Jesus Christ, the words and teaching of Scripture settled all these questions. Similarly, God's Word alone should determine what we believe and how we live.

3. The Bible is dependable

Despite the cynical claims of the critics, there is compelling evidence for the dependability and trustworthiness of Scripture. For example, consider its origin: 'All Scripture is inspired [i.e. breathed-out] by God' (2 Timothy 3:16). Can you really believe that 'the God who cannot lie' (Titus 1:2; Hebrews 6:18) breathed out mistakes and discrepancies in this self-revelation through the prophets and apostles? Remember also that the Old Testament prophets recognized that they were under the authority and leading of the Holy Spirit (Micah 3:8; 2 Samuel 23:2; Zechariah 7:12, etc). They were unable to change, or detract from, or add to the words God had given them (Numbers 24:13; Amos 3:8). In addition, the New Testament apostles and writers were also led by the Holy Spirit in their preaching and writing (2 Peter 1:21; 1 Thessalonians 4:2; 1 Corinthians 14:37; Galatians 1:6-12). What is important to notice here is that the inspiration of the apostles was a fulfilment of Christ's promise to them that he would send the Holy Spirit to them, to 'teach you all things, and bring to your remembrance all that I said to you' (John 14:26); 'He will guide you into all the truth... and he will disclose to you what is to come' (John 16:13). One of the most convincing arguments for the trustworthiness of Scripture is the attitude of the Lord Jesus Christ himself. He believed in the historicity of creation, including Adam and Eve (Matthew 19:4-5) and the universal flood in the days of Noah (Matthew 24:37-39), as well as Jonah's experience of being in the belly of a large fish for three days (Matthew 12:40). Christ saw the Old Testament as pointing to, and finding fulfilment in, himself (Luke 4:16-21; 24:25-27, 44-47; John 5:39-47). Like our Saviour, we can safely depend upon the Bible as being completely trustworthy.

4. The Bible is diverse

Because the Bible is such a remarkable book, it is rich and diverse. For example, in the writing of the Bible, God used about forty human authors over a period of approximately 1,500 years to write sixty-six books. The style and content varies, too: Hebrew is the dominant language of the Old Testament and Greek of the New Testament. There is a progressive revelation by God of himself and his purposes, until the climax is reached with the ministry of the Son of God (Hebrews 1:1-2). But we must be careful how we interpret the Bible. We need to ask questions such as, 'Is the chapter or book historical, poetical or prophetical? What is the background and the meaning intended by the writer? Do I understand the meaning of the words and am I able to study the passage in the light of the whole of Scripture?' In this way, we can avoid the errors and absurd interpretations of those who have twisted the meaning of the biblical text (2 Peter 3:16).

5. The Bible is durable

Yes, the Bible is 'the living and abiding Word of God' (1 Peter 1:23). Quoting Isaiah 40:7-8, Peter tells us, 'All flesh is like grass, and all its glory like the flower of grass. The grass withers, and the flower falls off, *but the word of the Lord abides for ever.*' The Bible never changes and will always remain the only true and relevant Word of God.

6. *The Bible is directing*

Like a signpost, the Bible points to, and unveils, the glories of the triune God and his salvation in Christ. In particular, the Bible points to Christ as the only mediator between God and man (1 Timothy 2:5), and Christ himself affirmed, 'It is these [i.e. the Scriptures] that bear witness of *me*' (John 5:39).

7. *The Bible is dynamite*

God uses the Bible, in preaching, personal reading and witness, in powerful ways to save sinners and edify and sanctify saints (Romans 1:16; 1 Thessalonians 2:13; Romans 10:17; John 17:17).

34.
What God is like

What is God really like? The same question can be expressed differently: how does the Bible describe the nature and character of God? The following paragraphs give some of the answers the Bible gives to these questions.

God is spirit

This truth was emphasized by the Lord Jesus Christ in John 4:24; it means that God does not have a physical body, nor can we identify him with anything material. God's nature is spiritual and, therefore, he is invisible (1 Timothy 1:17; 6:15-16). This was why the Lord Jesus told the woman of Samaria to be more concerned about how, rather than where, she worshipped God. True worship does not depend upon external things like a beautiful building, music or colourful vestments. Because 'God is spirit', he wants us to worship him 'in spirit and truth'. In other words, we must worship God in a spiritual, inward and believing manner.

Although God is spirit, yet he has all the characteristics of personality, that is, understanding, will and affection (Ephesians 1:3-6, 9, 11), which enable us to know and have fellowship with him.

God is independent

No human being can live independently of other people. We depend on other people to provide food and work or prepare medicines and houses for us. Nor is it possible for us to live independently of God: God sends the sunshine and the rain and enables the seeds to grow (Psalm 104:13-15; Matthew 5:45); indeed, our breath is in his hands and he decides what we do with our lives (Daniel 5:23). If God did not support and preserve us, we should die quickly.

By contrast, God is completely independent. No one brought God into existence or contributes to his welfare. No, for God is completely self-sufficient. He has no need of anything from outside either to support or to enrich himself. While God creates and preserves all his creation, he himself is complete and independent (Isaiah 40:12-28).

God is unlimited

As humans, we have many limitations. No human being, no matter how clever, can know everything. There is also a limit to our strength. For example, there are some weights which are too heavy for us to carry and there are bacteria and germs which our bodies cannot resist. Nor can we be in more than one place at a time and this is a real limitation upon us. There is also a limit to our physical lives on earth. God does not have any of these limitations.

God has unlimited knowledge (Psalm 139:1-6; Romans 11:33-36; 1 Samuel 2:3) and power (Genesis 18:14; Exodus 15:3-18; Luke 1:37; Ephesians 3:20-21). He is also omnipresent (Psalm 139:7-10) and cannot be confined to one place. Unlike us, God has no beginning or end: 'Even from everlasting to everlasting, thou art God' (Psalm 90:2; 102:11-12; Isaiah 57:15). He is the eternal 'I am' (Exodus 3:14).

God is unchanging

Our lives and circumstances are continually changing, either for better or worse, but God himself never changes. 'I, the Lord, do not change' (Malachi 3:6). He does not change in his being, for he is eternal and has 'no variation' (James 1:17). Neither does God change his purposes (Isaiah 46:11; Numbers 23:19; Ephesians 1:11).

God is sovereign

'The Lord reigns' (Psalm 97:1) is the consistent message of the Bible. He reigns over the entire universe. The winds, seas, rain, sun, moon and all living creatures are ruled over by God. Even unbelievers are under his control and 'He does according to his will in the host of heaven and among the inhabitants of earth' (Daniel 4:35; 1 Chronicles 29:11; Psalm 115:3; Ephesians 1:11). Despite the rage and malice of men, the evil and ceaseless attacks by Satan and even the weaknesses of God's own people, the Lord will carry out his plans. He is the supreme being. That is why the Lord Jesus could say with certainty, 'I will build my church; and the gates of Hades will not overpower it' (Matthew 16:18). Each person chosen to salvation by God will come to him; his purposes will not fail.

God is holy

'Holy, Holy, Holy is the Lord of hosts...' is the anthem of praise the seraphim sing in heaven as they gaze upon the holy nature of God (Isaiah 6:3). Day and night, the choirs of heaven 'do not cease to say, Holy, Holy, Holy, is the Lord God, the Almighty, who was and who is and who is to come' (Revelation 4:8). God is 'majestic in holiness...' (Exodus 15:11) and 'There is no one holy like the Lord' (1 Samuel 2:2).

The holiness of God means that he is free from all sin (1 John 1:5) and that he hates all sin with an intense hatred (Psalm 5:4-6). Closely related is the *righteousness* of God which means that God always speaks and works consistently with his own holy nature and law (Ezra 9:15; Psalm 119:137; 145:17; John 17:25; 1 John 2:29; Revelation 16:5).

The controlled, permanent opposition of God's holy nature to all sin is described as *wrath*. This wrath of God is not temper nor a bad mood, nor is it capriciousness, but the necessary reaction of his glorious and holy nature to sin (Romans 1:18; 2:5; Revelation 19:15). For this reason, wrath is as basic to the divine nature as is love; and without wrath God would cease to be God.

God is love

This is a truth which is underlined, expounded and illustrated extensively in the Bible, both in the Old and New Testaments. John declares, 'God is love' (1 John 4:8) and 'Love is from God' (1 John 4:7).

In his love, God is good towards all his creatures (Psalm 145:9, 15-16; Matthew 5:45; 6:26; Acts 14:17), but he loves believers with a special love in Christ. Christians love God only 'because he first loved us' (1 John 4:19; John 3:16). 'In this is love', adds the apostle John, 'not that we loved God, but that he loved us and sent his Son to be the propitiation for our sins' (1 John 4:10; cf. Romans 5:8).

Such divine love towards sinners is described as *grace,* for it is undeserved and completely unmerited (Ephesians 2:7-9; Titus 3:4-7). *Mercy* refers to the expression of the love of God in pitying sinners who desperately need the help and salvation of God (1 Timothy 1:12-16).

35.
The Holy Trinity

Jehovah's Witnesses and several other cults claim that the orthodox doctrine of the Trinity is a false, unbiblical doctrine originating with the devil in pagan Babylon and they frequently misrepresent the doctrine. For example, they accuse Christians of believing in three gods, or in a 'three-headed God', or of accepting the mathematical absurdity that one equals three. Here, then, is some of the Bible evidence for the doctrine of the Trinity.

1. There is only one God, not three

This truth is clearly stated in, for example, Deuteronomy 6:4; Isaiah 44:6; James 2:19. Besides this one, living God, there is no other. E. C. Gruss in his helpful book, *Apostles of Denial*[1] draws attention to the significance of the Hebrew word *echad* translated 'one' in Deuteronomy 6:4: 'The Lord is our God, the Lord is one!'

Far from denying the Trinity, this word and text actually support the doctrine! *Echad* expresses a compound unity, that is, a plurality within one. The same word, for example, is used in Genesis 1:5, where day and night are united into 'day one', and in Genesis 2:24 Adam and Eve were united as husband and wife to 'become one flesh'. Here two individuals constitute a real oneness. Again in Ezra 2:64 the New World Translation (NWT), which Jehovah's Witnesses regard as the most accurate translation, correctly gives the sense of this Hebrew word, 'the entire congregation as *one* group'. What is still more interesting is that the Hebrew word *yachid*, denoting absolute oneness, is never used in relation to the unity of God, although it occurs twelve times in the Old Testament in other contexts.

2. *Within the one Godhead, there are three distinguishable but equal persons*

Not only is the plural title *Elohim* used of God (Genesis 20:13; 35:7) but God also speaks of himself in the plural, for example, 'Let *us* make man in *our* image, according to *our* likeness' (Genesis 1:26, NWT); 'The man has become like one of *us*' (Genesis 3:22, NWT); 'Let *us* go down and there confuse their language...' (Genesis 11:7-8, NWT). These references indicate a plurality within the Godhead. Again, in Zechariah 2:8-11 we find there are two persons called Jehovah, while in Zechariah 3:1-2 one person of Jehovah refers to another.

Some passages in the Old Testament (e.g. Isaiah 48:16; 63:8-10) bring together all the three persons and in the New Testament the apostles are commanded to baptize converts 'in the name' (that is, only one, single name) of the Father, the Son and the Holy Spirit (Matthew 28:19; cf. 2 Corinthians 13:14; 1 Peter 1:2).

The Lord Jesus Christ

The crucial question, of course, concerns the deity of the Lord Jesus. Is he God, or, as Jehovah's Witnesses teach, a created angel and therefore only *a* God? Consider the evidence set out below for our Lord's deity.

1. The 'angel of Jehovah' in the Old Testament is also identified as Jehovah

Jehovah's Witnesses agree that 'the angel of Jehovah' is Jesus Christ in his pre-incarnation appearances. But, using their own NWT Bible, we can show that 'the angel of Jehovah' is also Jehovah himself. Consider Genesis 16:7-14. In verses 10-12, 'Jehovah's angel' speaks, but in verse 13 we read, 'She began to call the name of Jehovah who was speaking to her...' In Genesis 21:17-19 the angel of God is identified with God, then in 22:11-18 the angel of Jehovah speaks as Jehovah and Abraham knows he has seen a theophany, that is, an appearance of Jehovah himself (v. 14).

Jacob is told by the angel of God that 'I am the God of Bethel...' (Genesis 31:11, 13). Hosea 12:4-5 reveals that the man who wrestled with Jacob in Genesis 32:24-30 was the angel of Jehovah but Jacob says, 'I have seen *God* face to face.' Other passages could be cited, such as Exodus 3:2,4; 14:19,21,24; Judges 6:11-24; 13:2-23.

2. In the New Testament the Lord Jesus is identified as Jehovah

Old Testament verses referring to Jehovah are applied without hesitation to Christ in the New Testament.

Psalm 102:25-27 (the psalm is a prayer to Jehovah, see verse 1) is applied to Christ in Hebrews 1:8-12. 'Taste and see that Jehovah is good' (Psalm 34:8) is quoted by Peter then applied to Christ in 1 Peter 2:3. The prophet's vision of the glory of God in Isaiah 6 is explained in John 12:37-41 as a vision of Christ's glory. See also Matthew 3:3 and Mark 1:2-3 which quote Isaiah 40:3. Philippians 2:10-11 applies Isaiah 45:23 to Christ. Romans 10:13 quotes from Joel 2:32 and Romans 14:11 from Isaiah 45:23. In these and other references the Lord Jesus is identified as Jehovah.

3. The titles of Jehovah are also applied to Christ

'I am' (John 8:58; cf. Exodus 3:14); 'Shepherd' (John 10:11; Hebrews 13:20; cf. Psalm 23:1); 'Saviour' (2 Peter 1:1,11; cf. Isaiah 43:3); 'First and the Last' (Revelation 2:8, 13, 17; cf. Isaiah 41:4; 44:6; 48:12).

The name Jesus, which is Jeshua in the Hebrew, means 'Jehovah the Saviour'.

4. While worship must only be given to God, the Lord Jesus himself received worship

Consider the evidence in Matthew 8:2; 9:18; 14:33; 15:25; 28:9; John 9:35-38. In each of these references the same word — *proskuneo* — is used and this is the word used to describe the worship of God. In Matthew 4:10 the Lord told Satan, 'You shall worship *[proskuneo]* the Lord your God, and serve him only.' The worship of angels and men is clearly forbidden, so the worship of Jesus indicates his deity. Like Thomas we can rightly worship him, saying, 'My Lord and my God' (John 20:28). When being stoned to death, Stephen prayed to the Lord Jesus (Acts 7:59), but if Jesus was only a spirit-creature, as the Witnesses claim, this would have been idolatry.

5. Some claims of Christ and the apostles

John 1:1: 'In the beginning was the Word, and the Word was with God, and the Word was God.' This verse has been translated by Witnesses to prove their belief that Jesus was not *the* God but only *a* God, inferior to Jehovah-God. The main reason given by them for this translation ('The Word was a God') is that when the word *Theos* (God) occurs first of all in the verse, the definite article ('the' — Greek: *pros ton theon*) also occurs, whereas the next time the word God occurs, there is no definite article at all. They take this to mean that the Word is an inferior God.

That this is a wrong and deceitful translation can easily be shown. For example, in this same chapter the word *Theos* (God) occurs in four other places *without* the definite article, as it does at the end of verse 1, and yet each time in these other verses they correctly translate the word as 'God', not as 'a God' (see verses 6, 12, 13, 18). To be consistent, they should also translate the end of verse 1 in the same way but, unfortunately for them, it does not support their heresy!

John 10:30: 'I and the Father are one.' That this means more than a oneness in purpose, as the Witnesses teach, is clear from the verses 30-31 which follow and also from John 5:18. The Jews understood this claim as implying deity and the Lord did not contradict them.

John 14:9: 'He who has seen me has seen the Father.' Despite Jehovah's Witnesses' insistence that they only saw the Son, our Lord clearly says they did see the Father.

John 14:28: 'The Father is greater than I.' As John Calvin observed in his commentary on this verse, the Lord is not comparing the Father's deity with his own deity, nor his own human nature with the Father's divine essence. What he is actually doing is comparing his present condition with the glory which he would soon receive in his exaltation.

Furthermore, if we compare these words with Hebrews 1:4 we find confirmation of the Lord's deity here. The Greek word *meizon* translated 'greater' in John 14:28 is not the word used in Hebrews *(kreitton)* to show that the angels were inferior to Christ. If the Jehovah's Witnesses' teaching was correct, the other word, *(kreitton)* should have been used by the Lord in John 14:28. But, of course, our Lord was not saying he was an inferior God; he was referring to his position as a servant, a subordinate position which he had voluntarily assumed in order to redeem sinners.

Remember, too, that our Lord's aim here is to comfort his disciples in the light of his approaching death, but there is no suggestion here that he was a created being.

Colossians 1:15-17. In the NWT the word 'other', which is *not* in the original Greek, has been included in their translation of these verses to twist the true meaning. Also the NWT, 'first born of all creation' is wrong because the Greek word *prototokos* does not mean 'created' but expresses priority and sovereignty. Another Greek word, *protokistos*, would have been used if Paul had wanted to say that Jesus was created.

Colossians 2:9. All that constitutes God resides in Jesus Christ bodily (cf. Philippians 2:6; Titus 2:13).

There are other passages which confirm the deity of Christ, but the passages quoted provide sufficient biblical evidence to establish the doctrine.

The Holy Spirit

We also find that the Holy Spirit is a person and not an impersonal force. For example, he teaches and reminds (John 14:26), he guides (16:13) and speaks (Acts 8:29; 10:19; 13:2), and no impersonal power can do these things. He also intercedes (Romans 8:26), searches (1 Corinthians 2:10) and distributes gifts as he wills (1 Corinthians 12:11). He can be grieved (Ephesians 4:30), blasphemed (Matthew 12:31), lied to (Acts 5:3) and resisted (Acts 7:51). The Holy Spirit is associated with persons in Acts 15:28 and is identified as a person in Matthew 28:19.

Deity, as well as personality, is attributed to the Holy Spirit in the New Testament. He is omniscient (1 Corinthians 2:10-11), eternal (Hebrews 9:14), omnipresent (Psalm 139:7) and omnipotent (Luke 1:35; Romans 8:11). Peter tells Ananias that by lying to the Holy Spirit he had lied to God (Acts 5:3, 4). In 1 Corinthians 3:17 and 6:19 the phrases 'the temple of the Holy Spirit' and 'the temple of God' are used interchangeably to describe the body of the believer.

While many other biblical verses and passages could be cited in support, the foregoing references are sufficient to demonstrate that the doctrine of the Trinity is not a pagan, devilish teaching but one that is thoroughly grounded in the Bible. The deity of the Father, Son and Holy Spirit does not mean there are three gods, but rather that they are distinguishable persons, co-equal and co-eternal, within the one Godhead.

36.
The works of God

Having seen what God is like we will now underline what the Bible says about the works of God. We will consider four aspects of what God does, namely, the decrees of God, election, creation and providence.

1. The decrees of God

All that happens in the universe has been planned by God from eternity. Nothing happens by chance or accident. Throughout the centuries, God has worked according to his own absolute plan, which applies to all his creatures, not just to Christians or even to human beings, but also to animals and angels. The testimony of the Bible is that 'God works all things after the counsel of his will' (Ephesians 1:11).

It is difficult at times for us to understand why God works as he does in the world. There is much we cannot understand, for God's ways are past finding out (Romans 11:33; Isaiah 55:8-9). God is infinitely wise and plans all things perfectly. Nor will God fail to carry out his purposes. 'My purpose will be established' says the Lord,' and I will accomplish all my good pleasure' (Isaiah 46:10).

This does not mean that God wants us to sin. Not at all. God is holy and he 'cannot be tempted by evil, and he himself does not tempt anyone' (James 1:13). God permitted sin to enter the world yet is not the author of sin.

2. Election

Included in God's eternal decrees was his choice of those who should be Christians. Too often this is a theme which Christians argue about, and not always in a loving spirit. If you look at Ephesians 1:3-6 you will see that election was not a subject Paul argued about but one that he believed and accepted with gratitude and worship.

There are many questions to ask concerning election.

What does election mean? The word 'chose' in Ephesians 1:4 means to 'pick out' or 'choose out of'.

Who chooses us to become Christians? God! Ephesians 1:4 says, '...just as he [i.e. God the Father] chose us...' While we make our personal response to God in faith and repentance, this is only the result of God having first chosen us.

God was under no obligation to choose and save us. Certainly there was nothing in us to attract or deserve his love. God chose us for no other reason than that he was pleased to do so (Romans 9:15-16).

When did God choose us? 'Before the foundation of the world...', that is, in eternity.

How did God choose us? He chose us 'in him', that is, in Christ. In eternity, God the Father chose and placed his people in Christ as their representative and substitute. Christ it was who 'redeemed us from the curse of the law, having become a curse for us' (Galatians 3:13). Why choose us?

The answer in Ephesians 1:4 is 'that we should be holy and without blame before him in love' (AV). This begins when we receive a new nature in new birth (Ezekiel 36:26-27) and continues as the Holy Spirit makes us more like Christ (Romans 8:13). However, it is only when the Christian dies and goes to be with the Lord that he will be without sin.

Here is good news for you. God has never refused mercy to any who have turned to him in repenting faith. All who go to Christ will be welcomed: 'The one who comes to me', said Christ, 'I will certainly not cast out' (John 6:37). In fact, God commands all men everywhere to repent (Acts 17:30).

3. Creation

The Bible teaches that God created the whole universe (John 1:3: Colossians 1:16) including man himself (Genesis 1:26-27; 2:7, 21-22). Rather than developing from a chance evolutionary process, man is a special creation of God. Consider how complex the human body is. The human mind, for example, has been described as the best and most intricate computer the world has known. Or think of the way in which a fertilized cell grows into a perfectly developed foetus and then into a child (Psalm 139:13-16). 'It is he who has made us, and not we ourselves' (Psalm 100:3). Why did God create? The ultimate reason is for his own glory (Revelation 4:11).

4. Providence

It is not enough, however, to say that 'All things were created by him and for him' (Colossians 1:16, NIV). The Bible adds that 'In him, all things hold together' (Colossians 1:17). His power alone supports, preserves and directs creation. The world does not survive because of fate or chance; it is God who holds the universe in his hand. Left to itself, the universe could not survive and all life would perish. 'In him we live and move and exist' (Acts 17:28). In his wise, holy and righteous providence, God upholds, preserves and governs all creatures and all their actions. He makes all things work together for good to them that love God (Romans 8:28).

37.
Man: his creation and fall

What am I? Why do I behave as I do? Is there a purpose in living? These are some of the basic questions people are asking today. They are important questions, too. The true answers to these questions are given only by God and are found in the Bible. We will consider briefly what the Bible says about man.

What am I?

Although it is popular to believe that man has evolved over millions of years from primitive animal life, yet the Bible teaches that man is a unique creation of God. For example, before creating man, the triune God is described as entering into divine counsel: 'Let us make man in our image, according to our likeness...' (Genesis 1:26). On the other days of creation God said, for example, 'Let there be light,' or 'Let the earth sprout vegetation...' etc. However, on the sixth day God paused between two creative acts and the Holy Trinity enters into counsel before creating man. This illustrates man's uniqueness in creation.

Notice, too, that with regard to fish, birds and animals, etc., God created them 'after their kind' (Genesis 1:21), that is, in a way typical and exclusive to themselves only. By contrast, man was created in the likeness of God. In some respects man resembles the animals. Both animals and humans need food and rest. They also have in common the senses of hearing, seeing, smelling, tasting and feeling. Nevertheless, there is an essential difference between ourselves and animals. Humans, unlike the animals, are God-related; they are made in the image of God (Genesis 1:26-27; 9:6; James 3:9).

What does it mean to be 'in the image of God'?

Just as God has personality, a mind, a will and the power to love and hate, so man has these characteristics of personality. God also has a moral nature; he hates sin and loves what is pure. Being made in the likeness of God means that all humans, despite sin, have a moral sense of right and wrong. Furthermore, as God is spirit (John 4:24), man was created with a spiritual dimension so he can enjoy fellowship with God. Man is much more than a physical body or an aggregate of chemicals; he has a soul as well as a body (Matthew 10:28). Physical death is not the end of our existence as it is for animals; we shall live eternally after death in either heaven or hell.

We are now in a position to see some of the Bible's answers to our questions about human beings. What am I? I am a person created by God and radically different from the rest of creation. God's image is upon me and that is not true of animals. Is there a purpose for living? Yes, an important and satisfying purpose. God made man to enjoy fellowship with himself and to obey and glorify him (Ecclesiastes 12:13-14; Revelation 4:11).

Why obey?

Because we stand in a creature-Creator relationship to God, he has the authority to command us how we should live.

Adam and Eve were the first two persons God created. After Adam had been created, we are told that 'the Lord God *commanded* the man' (Genesis 2:16) not to eat the fruit of a particular tree. In this way God imposed his authority over man. God, of course, has every right to command us in this way. He is God. He is also our Creator. He rules the world he made. Despite sin, man remains under the authority of God and this is seen in many ways.

For example, God has given us consciences with a basic

awareness of right or wrong and a sense of obligation to obey
(Romans 2:14-15). God also exercises his authority over us through
magistrates and governments (Romans 13:1-4), parents (Ephesians
6:1-4), husbands (Ephesians 5:22-33) and employers (Ephesians
6:5-9). The authority of God covers every aspect of our lives. God
commands us what to do and how to live. Of course, people do not
obey God in their lives and the Bible calls such disobedience sin (1
John 3:4).

Where did sin come from?

When God created Adam and Eve, there was no sin in their lives.
They enjoyed and obeyed God in every detail. It was the devil, the
first to sin (John 8:44; 2 Peter 2:4), who tempted Eve to eat the fruit
of the forbidden tree. There was nothing in either Adam or Eve to
make them sin (Genesis 2:15-25; 3:1-13; 1 Timothy 2:14). Sin came
from without, yet Adam had the ability to obey or disobey God.

Adam our representative

What has Adam's sin got to do with me? Well, while Adam was an
individual, historical person yet God also made him the representative of the entire human race. When Adam obeyed, we obeyed;
when he sinned, we sinned, too. 'Therefore, just as through one man
sin entered into the world, and death through sin, and so death
spread to all men, because all sinned' (Romans 5:12).

38.
Man in sin

There is not a single human being who is without sin. That is what the Bible says: 'There is none righteous, not even one' (Romans 3:10); 'All have sinned and fall short of the glory of God (Romans 3:23).

What is sin?

It is important to understand what sin is. Sin is not confined to murder, rape or theft. In order to appreciate the nature and seriousness of sin, consider some of the words used in the Bible to describe sin.

Lawlessness or transgression

In 1 John 3:4 we are told that 'Sin is the transgression of the law' (AV). The word 'transgression' or 'lawlessness' here means crossing over the boundary line into a prohibited area. Whatever the motive, the law is broken. This is a picture of our attitude towards God. By nature, we are rebels against God, his laws and his Word. Sin disposes us to do what God prohibits. The Bible says, 'The carnal mind is enmity against God: for it is not subject to the law of

God, neither indeed can be' (Romans 8:7, AV). The sinner is opposed to God and refuses to bow before God or submit to his laws.

Debt

'Debt' is another word the Bible uses to describe sin. In the pattern prayer given to the disciples, the Lord Jesus taught them to pray, 'And forgive us our debts, as we also have forgiven our debtors' (Matthew 6:12). In what sense is sin a debt? It does not mean, of course, that we owe sin to God. That could not be true, for God hates sin (Habakkuk 1:13) and does not want us to sin (James 1:13-15; 1 Thessalonians 4:3). The word refers to the debt of obedience we owe to God. Perfect obedience is what God demands from us, but we are unable to pay God this debt we owe him. Sin is in that sense a debt and the 'wages of sin is death' (Romans 6:23).

Iniquity

This word means to twist or change the shape of something. After putting a piece of iron into the fire, for example, a blacksmith will hammer it into a different shape. A person suffering from rheumatoid-arthritis may find that his fingers become twisted out of shape. Sin, too, is something which distorts and twists our lives (Psalm 51:9).

Missing the mark

One word frequently used in the Bible to describe sin means 'to miss' (Psalm 32:1; Isaiah 44:22; Jeremiah 31:34). The word literally means to have missed something, that is, we have wilfully missed God's purpose for our lives, preferring to live selfish, sinful lives rather than to glorify God.

This word also has the related meaning of missing the mark. The picture is that of a marksman who aims for a certain target with his arrow or gun but misses or, perhaps, a person who fails to attain a pass mark in an examination. Similarly, sin for us means we have missed the mark of God's perfection and fallen well below the standards of his law. These standards are set out for us clearly in the Ten Commandments (Exodus 20).

There are three further things the Bible says about sin.

1. Sin is deeply rooted within us

Sin is not only something we do, like stealing or lying. These things, of course, are sinful, but we behave in a sinful way because we are sinful by nature. Let me put it in another way. Sin is not something we catch from other people, like influenza or smallpox. The reason is that sin is already within us. We were actually born in sin (Psalm 51:5). Our sins, then, stem from our sinful nature. 'For from within, out of the heart of men', said the Lord Jesus, 'proceed the evil thoughts and fornications, thefts, murders, adulteries, deeds of coveting and wickedness, as well as deceit, sensuality, envy, slander, pride and foolishness' (Mark 7:22-23). Sin comes from within our human nature. For this reason it is not enough to stop certain bad habits. That is like cutting off the top of a weed in the garden while the root is still left in the soil to grow again. God works differently. He goes to the root of all our troubles; he gives the believer a new nature and changes him from within. That is why the Lord Jesus told Nicodemus, 'You must be born again' (John 3:17).

2. Sin is extensive in our lives

Our actions, thoughts, desires, motives, will and affections are all influenced strongly by sin. 'The heart is more deceitful than all else and is desperately sick; who can understand it?' (Jeremiah 17:9). 'Heart' here refers to the entire person, including mind, will, affections and desires. Just as some kinds of rash spread over the body so sin has spread into all areas of our lives. There is no part of our lives which is free from sin.

3. Sin is punishable by God

God is holy (Isaiah 6:3) and cannot ignore or tolerate sin. All sin is punished by God. There are different ways in which God punishes sin but the climax is the sentence of unbelievers at death to hell (Matthew 25:41; Luke 16:19-31).

Is there hope for sinners? Yes. God has made a way of escape for us in Christ. God's own Son was 'pierced through for our transgressions... crushed for our iniquities... by his scourging we are healed' (Isaiah 53:5).

39.
The person of Christ

It was a profound and searching question that the Lord asked his disciples at Caesarea Philippi: 'But who do you say that I am?' Peter's answer was equally profound and true: 'Thou art the Christ, the Son of the living God' (Matthew 16:15-16). This was not speculation on Peter's part nor was it a merely subjective opinion. Far from it. The Lord Jesus commended the disciple for his answer but added, 'Flesh and blood did not reveal this to you, but my Father who is in heaven.' Not only did Peter speak the truth about the Lord Jesus Christ; it was God the Father who enabled him to make the confession concerning Christ's unique sonship with the Father.

As 'the Son of the living God', the Lord Jesus is unique but let us consider some of the biblical evidence for this fact.

His pre-existence

More than once, Jesus emphasized that he had come down from heaven (John 6:38). 'I am from above', he told the unbelieving Jews (John 8:23). He did not begin to exist at the time of his birth. In fact he claimed, 'Before Abraham was born, I am' (John 8:58). Abraham's brief physical life had come to an end but Jesus who existed long before Abraham still exists as the timeless 'I am'. While praying for his people, the Lord spoke of the glory he enjoyed with the Father 'before the world was' (John 17:5).

His virgin birth

Although betrothed to be married, Mary was still a virgin. She was not guilty of pre-marital intercourse. No, she was a virgin who could say honestly to the angel, 'How can this be, since I am a virgin?' (Luke 1:34). The astonishing news, however, was that a virgin was to conceive and bear a son without the co-operation of any man. No wonder she asked, 'How can this be?' Mary was told that her child would be conceived through the power of God: 'The Holy Spirit will come upon you, and the power of the Most High will over-shadow you...' (Luke 1:35).

The child born in a miraculous way to Mary was a special person. 'He will be great,' said the angel, 'and will be called the Son of the Most High...He will reign...for ever, and his kingdom will have no end...he shall be called the Son of God' (Luke 1:32-35). The Lord Jesus is distinguished from all others: he alone is the Son of God.

He forgives sin

The first words of the Lord Jesus to the paralysed man in Caper-naum were, 'Your sins are forgiven' (Mark 2:5). Some of the Jews who heard the words were critical for his words sounded like blasphemy. 'Who can forgive sins but God alone?' they replied. The answer of the Lord is significant in verses 9 and 10 and he healed the paralysed man so that they should 'know that the Son of Man has authority on earth to forgive sins'. The implication is clear: only God can forgive sins and, therefore, Christ in forgiving the paralytic underlined his own deity.

His equality with God

'I and the Father are one', claimed the Lord Jesus (John 10:30). More than oneness of purpose is intended here for the Jews were ready to kill Jesus 'because', they said, 'you, being a man, make yourself out to be God' (v.33).

He is Jehovah

Did you know that Jesus is actually called Jehovah, a name only applied to God in the Old Testament? For example, the prophecy of Isaiah 40:3 was fulfilled in the work of John the Baptist. John prepared the way for Christ, who was the one Isaiah called Jehovah or Lord (see, too, Mark 1:3). Again, the description of Jehovah in Psalm 102:25-27 is applied to Christ in Hebrews 1:10-12. Isaiah also saw the glory of Christ when he saw the vision of God in the temple (Isaiah 6:1; John 12:41). In Zechariah 2:9-11 there are two persons described as Jehovah and in the opening verses of chapter 3 these two persons called Jehovah speak to each other! The unique claim of God in Isaiah 48:12 is applied to himself by Jesus in Revelation 1:8 and 22:13.

Yes, Jesus was God but also man. He needed to be the God-man in order to fulfil his unique mission.

He was man

No human being or angel could save us; only God could do so. But in order to represent us before God and save us, God the Son needed also to be man (Hebrews 2:17). There is another reason, too. As God, Christ could not die; it was in his human nature that he suffered and died for our salvation.

He was God

It was necessary for the Lord Jesus to be God. First of all, no human being or angel was qualified to save us or capable of doing so. Secondly, as a divine person, Christ was without sin and did not inherit original sin as we do. Furthermore, to save *all* God's elect from *all* their sins in *all* generations by his substitutionary sacrifice was a task only God could fulfil. In addition, Christ had to overcome the devil, who is a powerful but evil angel. Finally, only as God could our Lord's sufferings have an infinite value. Being man, Christ was able to die in our place and to procure our salvation;

because he was God, his death has a value which is rich and infinite. It was as God, then, that the Lord Jesus humbled himself and stooped to become a man and a servant in order to die for our sins.

40.
The sacrifice of Christ

One day while John the Baptist was preaching, he saw the Lord Jesus walking towards him and told the people, 'Behold the Lamb of God who takes away the sins of the world' (John 1:29). Again the next day, John stood with two of his disciples, then pointed to Jesus and said, 'Behold, the Lamb of God' (John 1:36).

A sacrifice

John's description of Jesus as 'the Lamb of God' would have impressed his audience. In the temple at Jerusalem a lamb was sacrificed every morning and evening. They knew they could not worship or approach God without sacrifice, for sin is hateful to the holy God. He must always punish sin. Somehow this wrath of God has to be removed before the sinner can approach God and enjoy his mercy. This could only be done through sacrifice: 'Without shedding of blood there is no forgiveness' (Hebrews 9:22). Accordingly, one of the first things a person saw as he entered the temple was the altar of burnt offering. Here the blood of the innocent lamb was poured out and its flesh burnt. All who approached God had to come by the way of this altar and sacrifice. There was no other way to God. Once the animal had been sacrificed at the altar as a substitute and punishment for the person's sin, then he or she could approach the holy God and receive forgiveness.

The people also associated John's words with the killing of the Passover lamb in Egypt. When the Egyptian leader finally refused to release Israel, God responded by killing off all the first-born males in Egypt. There was, however, protection for Israel if they sacrificed a lamb and sprinkled its blood outside their homes. Only the mark of the blood kept these families safe from death (Exodus 12). The apostle Paul tells us this was a picture of Christ's sacrifice on the cross of Calvary: 'Christ our Passover... has been sacrificed' (1 Corinthians 5:7). It is only by the sacrifice of Christ that we can be saved from God's wrath and eternal death.

It was planned

All this was, of course, in the plan of God. Christ's birth and death were not an emergency plan suddenly put into operation by God. 'No', Peter says, 'he was foreordained before the foundation of the world' (1 Peter 1:20, AV). From eternity God had planned the death of Jesus (see also Acts 2:23).

All the details of his life, death and resurrection were also known in advance to the Lord Jesus Christ (Matthew 20:28; 16:21; John 10:11; 12:23-24; Matthew 26:26-46).

He was forsaken

It would be wrong to think that our Lord's suffering only began at Calvary. He suffered thoughout his earthly life and in various ways. The climax of his suffering, however, was on the cross. After his arrest and trial before a Jewish court. Pilate, the Roman governor, agreed to his death even though he knew Jesus had done no wrong (John 18:38). The governor's decision was simply an attempt to please his Jewish subjects. It was not long before the Lord Jesus was led away for crucifixion at Calvary. The soldiers mocked him and wove a crown of thorns to put on his head. While he hung on the cross, people laughed and ridiculed him. The physical pain involved in this form of death was considerable.

But why was Jesus dying on the cross? He was not a criminal. Why did he die then? The Bible tells us: 'For Christ also died for sins once for all, the just for the unjust, in order that he might bring us to God' (1 Peter 3:18). 'He was pierced through for our transgressions, he was crushed for our iniquities' (Isaiah 53:5). 'But the Lord has caused the iniquity of us all to fall on him' (Isaiah 53:6).

In his body, the Lord Jesus bore the punishment of our sin. His sufferings were spiritual as well as physical. That is the reason why he cried from the cross, 'My God, my God, why hast thou forsaken me?' (Matthew 27:46). In the few hours the Lord was on the cross, he bore the wrath of God against our sin. To do this, however, involved the Saviour in forfeiting in his human nature the comfort and awareness of his Father's love and presence.

'It is finished!'

Christ did not suffer and die in vain. On the cross, he became our sacrifice and thereby removed all our guilt and punishment. All our sin was dealt with once and for all at Calvary. There is no need of any further sacrifice. 'It is finished!' declared the Lord Jesus Christ, (John 19:30). He died once and his sacrifice was complete and sufficient (Hebrews 10:14). Through this one, unique, atoning sacrifice, Christ has reconciled believers to God (2 Corinthians 5:19-21).

Our response

Christ himself, and only Christ, is the door to God and heaven (John 10:7-11). No church, no movement, no man, not even our best efforts can reconcile us to God. 'No one comes to the Father', said the Lord Jesus, 'but through me' (John 14:6). Our responsibility is to receive in faith, and rest upon, Christ alone for salvation. Faith is simply the hand we stretch out to receive Christ and his righteousness. Such faith is a gift from God (Ephesians 2:8-9).

41.
The exaltation of Christ

Jesus Christ was already dead when the soldiers inspected his body. A soldier cut open Jesus' side with his spear to confirm that he was dead (John 19:34). The Roman centurion in charge of the soldiers was impressed by what he had seen and heard of Jesus and immediately after his death remarked to the people, 'Truly this was the Son of God' (Matthew 27:54; Luke 23:47). A man named Joseph obtained permission from Pilate to lay the body of Jesus in his own new sepulchre (John 19:38-42). The enemies of Jesus, however, were not satisfied. They placed soldiers to guard the sepulchre in case anyone tried to steal the body and then deceive people by saying that Jesus was alive (Matthew 27:62-66; 28:11-15).

The significance of the burial

The burial of Jesus was full of significance. For one thing, it was the fulfilment of a prophecy given 700 years earlier: 'His grave was assigned to be with wicked men, yet with a rich man in his death' (Isaiah 53:9). Our Lord also prophesied that he would be buried (Matthew 12:40). In his burial our Lord surrendered himself to death and the grave. Just before he died, Christ commended his spirit to the Father (Luke 23:46) and was under the care of his Father.

On the third day, something wonderful happened. Some of the

women went to the sepulchre but found the stone blocking the entrance had been rolled away and the body of Jesus was no longer inside. They were perplexed, Two angels then appeared to them and said, 'Why do you seek the living one among the dead? He is not here, but he has risen. Remember how he spoke to you while he was still in Galilee, saying that the Son of Man must be delivered into the hands of sinful men, and be crucified, and the third day rise again' (Luke 24:5-7).

The Bible teaches that there is an inseparable relationship between Christ's death and resurrection (see, e.g. Philippians 2:5-11). As our mediator, Christ met all the demands of the law, paid the penalty of sin and obtained for us, through his sacrifice, life eternal. For his obedience in achieving all this for us, the Father rewarded Christ, our mediator, by exalting him.

The Bible distinguishes four ways in which Christ, our mediator, is exalted.

1. The resurrection of Christ

This was the first stage in the Lord's exaltation but attempts have been made to deny the fact that Jesus was raised from the dead. Was it just a hoax? The suggestion is absurd. If the enemies had stolen his body as a hoax, why did they not produce it when they tried to stop the disciples preaching Christ's resurrection? Or would the disciples have been willing to die just for a hoax? But did the Lord only swoon, not die, then revive again in the cold sepulchre? Remember, however, that the soldiers, as well as the disciples and Jewish leaders, were satisfied that Jesus was dead. It was in the interest of the Jews to be sure that he was dead.

There is firm historical evidence to show that the resurrection of Jesus Christ really took place. It is not just a myth or a fairy story. Think of all the people who saw and heard Jesus after his resurrection. Some of them, like Thomas, refused to believe until they had convincing proof (John 20:25). Paul also marshals convincing evidence for the resurrection of Jesus (1 Corinthians 15:5-8). Peter, James and the apostles saw Jesus alone after his resurrection. On one occasion about 500 people met and talked with Christ. In other words, the physical resurrection of Jesus Christ is historical and true.

The resurrection establishes beyond all doubt the truth of the Lord's teaching as well as his claim to be God. He 'was declared with power to be the Son of God by the resurrection from the dead...' (Romans 1:4). By Christ's resurrection, the Father also indicated his approval of the Saviour's sacrifice for sin. Furthermore, the Lord Jesus promises to believers, 'Because I live, you shall live also' (John 14:19; 11:25-26).

2. The ascension of Christ

The ascension of Christ is recorded in detail in Acts 1:9-11 (cf. Luke 24:50-51). Remember it was necessary for the Lord to ascend to the Father. As our mediator he was rewarded and entered into his glory in heaven: 'Was it not necessary for the Christ to suffer these things and to enter into his glory?' (Luke 24:26). Christ had to enter heaven before the Holy Spirit could be poured out upon the church (John 16:7). When the Lord ascended, he also went as a forerunner to prepare a place for believers in heaven (John 14:2).

3. The session of Christ

When he ascended, the Lord Jesus was given a position of great honour at the right hand of God in heaven, and numerous Bible verses emphasize this point (Hebrews 1:3; 10:12; 1 Peter 3:22). What is he doing in heaven? As head of the church (Ephesians 4:15; 5:23; Colossians 1:18), he now actively rules over his church through the Word and Holy Spirit and also through pastors/elders whom he appoints to preach and rule in churches. Also it is from heaven that our Saviour builds and protects his church. This is not a difficult task, for all authority in heaven and earth belongs to the mediator (Matthew 28:18) and all powers are subject to him. Christ also prays for Christians (Romans 8:34) and sends the Holy Spirit to his church (Acts 2:33; John 16:7-15).

4. The return of Christ

The climax in the exaltation of Christ is yet to take place. Some time in the future, the Lord will return to this world. Christ has been once; that was 2,000 years ago. His purpose in coming to the world then was to save, and this he did by his death at Calvary. The next time the Lord comes, it will be to judge the world and to gather together and then glorify his church. There are many references to Christ's second coming in the New Testament and some of the more important ones are in Matthew 24-25; Acts 1:11; 3:20-21; 1 Thessalonians 1:10; 4:16-17; 2 Thessalonians 1:7-10; Hebrews 9:28 and 2 Peter 3.

How the Lord Jesus will return to the world

Personally

Jesus himself will return. He will not send a deputy or a messenger, not even an angel. 'The Lord himself will come down from heaven' (1 Thessalonians 4:16). 'This Jesus,' the angels told the disciples at the ascension, 'who has been taken up from you into heaven, will come in just the same way as you have watched him go into heaven' (Acts 1:11).

Visibly

The Lord Jesus emphasized this fact: 'They will see the Son of Man coming on the clouds of the sky...' (Matthew 24:30). His coming will not be secret or invisible, as the Jehovah's Witnesses teach. 'He is coming with the clouds, and every eye will see him...' (Revelation 1:7).

Gloriously

His coming will also be glorious. The clouds will be his chariot and the trumpet will sound as the archangel heralds his coming. Christians already in heaven will accompany the Lord, while the mighty angels will surround him and execute vengeance on Christ's enemies (Mark 13:24-27; 1 Thessalonians 4:14-16; 1 Corinthians

15:23-28, 52). Christ will be revealed as King of kings and Lord of lords and all human activity will stop. The affairs of nations will come to an abrupt end.

Suddenly

People will be surprised by the suddenness of this event; many will be unprepared. Christ stressed this point (e.g. Matthew 24:37-51; 25:1-13). Only God knows when the return of Christ will take place. 'But of that day and hour no one knows, not even the angels of heaven, nor the Son, but the Father alone' (Mark 13:32).

When the Lord returns he will raise the dead (John 5:28-29; 1 Thessalonians 4:16), judge all people (John 5:27; 2 Corinthians 5:10; Matthew 25:31-46) then make a new heaven and a new earth (2 Peter 3:13) where only righteousness exists.

42.
The Holy Spirit

In the section dealing with the Holy Trinity, we have outlined the biblical teaching that the one God exists eternally as the Father, Son and Holy Spirit. Here we will confine ourselves to three aspects of the Bible's teaching concerning the Holy Spirit, namely, his deity, personality and work.

1. *The deity of the Holy Spirit*

As God, the Holy Spirit has perfect knowledge of all things (1 Corinthians 2:10-11) and unlimited power, being capable of doing what is impossible for humans (Romans 8:11). Acknowledging that the Holy Spirit is everywhere in the universe as God, the psalmist asks, 'Where can I go from thy Spirit?' (Psalm 139:7). The Holy Spirit is also eternal (Hebrews 9:14). In some passages, the Holy Spirit is identified as God. Do you remember the story of Ananias and Sapphira lying to Peter about their money? Peter told Ananias that he had lied to the Holy Spirit (Acts 5:3) but in the next verse said he had lied to God! The sin of Ananias was that he had lied to God the Holy Spirit (cf. 1 Corinthians 3:16; 6:19-20).

2. *The personality of the Holy Spirit*

Although some cults and modernists teach that the Holy Spirit is a mere energy, or impersonal power, the Bible attributes personal faculties, abilities and functions to the Holy Spirit. The Holy Spirit has a mind (Romans 8:6), knowledge (1 Corinthians 2:11) and a will by which he acts (1 Corinthians 12:11). He also speaks (Acts 13:2), intercedes (Romans 8:26-27), witnesses (Romans 8:16), teaches (Luke 12:12; John 14:26) and he can be grieved (Ephesians 4:30) and lied to (Acts 5:3). All these abilities and personal characteristics can only be true of a person.

In addition, the Holy Spirit is mentioned in the Bible apart from power so that he cannot be reduced to an impersonal force or mere power of God. For example, while talking to Cornelius and his friends, Peter explained 'how God anointed [Jesus of Nazareth] with the Holy Spirit and with power' (Acts 10:38; cf. Romans 15:13; 1 Corinthians 2:4; 1 Thessalonians 1:5). It is wrong, therefore, to think of the Holy Spirit as a force or power that God uses; rather, the Holy Spirit is a divine person who has power.

3. The work of the Holy Spirit

The supreme work of the Holy Spirit is to glorify Christ: 'He shall glorify me' (John 16:14). This is always his objective; he works only for the honour and glory of Christ. That teaching which undermines and belittles both the divine person and the unique, substitutionary sacrifice of the Lord Jesus Christ cannot be attributed to the Holy Spirit.

In his objective work the Holy Spirit is involved in creation (Genesis 1:2; Job 33:4; Psalm 104:30), providence (Psalm 143:10; Genesis 6:3; Isaiah 34:16; Micah 2:7) and the writing of the Bible (2 Peter 1:21; 2 Timothy 3:16). The Lord Jesus Christ was also conceived in the womb of Mary by the Holy Spirit (Luke 1:35); it was the Holy Spirit who anointed and equipped the Saviour for ministry (Luke 4:18; Isaiah 61:1; Acts 10:38; John 3:34) and it was 'through the eternal Spirit' that the Lord offered himself on the cross to the Father (Hebrews 9:14).

The subjective work of the Holy Spirit includes his ministry of regenerating, sanctifying, energizing and keeping believers.

Regeneration

The word 'regeneration' in relation to the work of the Holy Spirit in our lives is used in Titus 3:5, 'the washing of regeneration and renewing by the Holy Spirit'. Other terms are used to describe this initial, miraculous work of the Spirit which raises 'dead' sinners to spiritual life and makes a natural man into a spiritual man. These terms are 'beget', to be 'born again' or 'bear and give birth', 'create' and 'quicken' or 'make alive' (John 1:13; 3:3-7; 1 Peter 1:23; 1 John 2:29; 3:9; 4:7; 5:1, 4, 18; James 1:18; Ephesians 2:5, 10.).

Sanctification

Sanctification refers to the continuous work of the Holy Spirit whereby he strengthens the new life already imparted in the new birth and gradually makes the believer more like Christ in mind, affections, will and behaviour (Romans 8:29; 1 Thessalonians 5:23).

Sometimes sanctification describes a once-for-all action in breaking the power of sin in an individual life (Romans 6: 1-7:6; 1 Corinthians 1:2; 6:11; Acts 20:32; 26:18, etc.) and, on other occasions, it is described in the Bible as a slow but progressive work in which the believer actively fights against sin and strives to be more holy. The believer's efforts, however (Colossians 3:5-4:6; 2 Corinthians 7:1), are possible only through the power of the Holy Spirit (Romans 8:13) and union with Christ (John 15; Romans 6:1-7:6).

The Holy Spirit thus indwells all believers (1 Corinthians 3:16; 6:19; Ephesians 2:22), helps them to pray (Romans 8:26-27), gives understanding of the Scriptures (Ephesians 1:17; 1 Corinthians 2:10-16) and power in the preaching of the Word (1 Corinthians 2:4; 1 Thessalonians 1:5).

43.
Becoming a Christian

How can I become a Christian? What must I do? You may be anxious to know the answer to this important question. The Bible's answer is 'Believe in the Lord Jesus, and you shall be saved' (Acts 16:31). But how can I do this?

God draws us

The Bible teaches that we cannot respond to God and believe unless God first helps us. 'No one can come to me unless the Father who sent me draws him...' (John 6:44). The position is clear. Unless God draws a person then it is impossible for him to go to Christ and trust in him as Saviour. Why is this? The Bible's answer is sin, for sin makes all our lives wrong and cuts us off from God. Even worse, sin has made us rebels and enemies of God (Romans 8:7). Rather than wanting to love or obey God, the sinner resists and opposes God. By nature, too, we are 'dead in trespasses and sins' (Ephesians 2:1). Just as a dead man cannot hear or respond to anyone in this world, so in relation to God the sinner is 'dead' in a spiritual sense and cannot hear or respond to God. What does God do to draw us to Christ?

God's call

Consider, for example, the way in which people became Christians in Corinth during the ministry of the apostle Paul. For three successive weeks, Paul preached the Word of God in the synagogue and some believed on the Lord Jesus Christ. Notice what happened to them. They first heard the Word of God and afterwards believed. Hearing the Word is important for God gives faith through his Word (Romans 10:17; Acts 18:1-11).

But how could these people in Corinth believe if they were themselves helpless and rebellious? Paul tells us what God did for them: 'God is faithful, through whom you were called into fellowship with his Son, Jesus Christ our Lord' (1 Corinthians 1:9). God 'called' them to Christ. The word 'called' here is a strong word. When God calls in this way he enables the sinner to answer the call of the gospel by giving him a new heart and a new spirit (Ezekiel 36:26), so that he is brought from spiritual death to spiritual life (Ephesians 2:5; Colossians 2:13).

The raising of Lazarus after he had been dead for four days illustrates God's power in making us Christians. Standing outside the sepulchre where Lazarus was buried, the Lord Jesus shouted, 'Lazarus, come forth' (John 11:43). As a dead man, Lazarus could not even hear the words of Jesus nor could he co-operate with him in any way. Clearly it was not enough for the Lord to speak to Lazarus. The dead man had to be made alive first and only then could he respond to the words of Jesus. When he spoke to Lazarus, therefore, the Lord also gave him physical life so that he could walk out of the sepulchre in response to Jesus and in exercise of that new life.

This story can be used as an illustration of the way in which the Lord makes us Christians. Although, unlike Lazarus, we are alive physically, in a spiritual sense we are dead. Our need, therefore, is for spiritual life. This the Lord provides by the Holy Spirit when he puts new spiritual life within us. God the Spirit performs this miracle and as a result we are able to walk out of the sepulchre of sin and death and walk to Christ in trust and obedience. The Lord Jesus described it as being 'born again' (John 3:3) and without this new birth, no one can become a Christian.

Conversion

To use the illustration of Lazarus again, notice that after he was raised to life, Lazarus began to walk out of the sepulchre in obedience to the words of Jesus. Something similar happens to us when God raises a person to spiritual life in the new birth, for we are then able to go to Christ in repenting faith.

Conversion consists of repentance and faith.

Repentance

Repentance is frequently taught in the Bible (Job 42:6; Isaiah 55:7; Mark 1:15; Luke 13:3-5; Acts 2:38; 17:30; 26: 20;2 Peter 3:9, etc.). In repentance the sinner turns away from his sin and turns to God in trust and obedience; such repentance involves a radical break with sin.

Faith

Faith is to be exercised personally in the Lord Jesus Christ (Acts 16:31). Such faith involves trust in the person of Jesus Christ the Son of God as we rely upon him alone for mercy and forgiveness (John 1:12; 7:37).

There are many examples of conversion in the New Testament which you can read about (e.g., Luke 19:1-10; John 4:1-39; Acts 2:37-42; 8:26-40; 9:1-22; 10:1-48; 16:13-15, 27-34).

44.
The church

God has appointed individuals to be born and brought up within a family unit. Although there are sad exceptions, the family unit normally provides the love and security an individual child or adult needs. In a similar way, the Lord places Christians in the family of his believing people; other Christians are not simply friends but brothers and sisters in Christ. This family of God is what the Bible means by a 'church'.

A church is not simply a building, whether Roman Catholic or Protestant, nor is it simply a group of people who hold religious services. The true church of God means much more: it is a group of people who believe personally in the Lord Jesus Christ as Saviour and Lord (1 Corinthians 1:2; Colssians 1:3-8; 1 Thessalonians 1:1-10).

In the New Testament, the important Greek word translated 'church' is *ecclesia* and its dominant meaning is the assembly or gathering of people together. The Old Testament background to *ecclesia* is important and confirms this interpretation. Passages like Deuteronomy 9:10; 10:4; 18:16 are significant as they refer to God's people meeting formally together before the Lord on 'the day of assembly' *(qahal)* to worship. *Ecclesia* is used many times in Acts and in the epistles to describe a specific church in a locality, whether at Jerusalem, Antioch, Ephesus, Cenchrea, Corinth, Laodicea or Thessalonica, etc. (Acts 8:1; 11:26; 14:27; 15:3-4, 22; 20:17, 28; Romans 16:1; Revelation 2:1, 8, 12, 18; 3:1, 7, 14).

The church is a gathering

By means of the preaching of the gospel and the regenerating work of the Holy Spirit, men and women are brought as sinners to trust and obey the Lord Jesus Christ; it is such people who form the church within a locality.

On the day of Pentecost, 3,000 people were converted through the preaching of the apostle Peter and immediately integrated into the life of the church at Jerusalem (Acts 2:41-47). As God blessed the preaching of the apostle Paul in different cities and countries, local churches were established (Acts 14:23 etc.) and these were all gathered churches of believers.

Another example is the church at Philippi. During his second missionary journey, Paul preached in this city between A.D. 50 and 54 and as yet there was no church there. How did the church commence there? Paul preached to a small group of women who belonged to the Jewish religion. While listening to Paul preaching the gospel, Lydia believed on Christ (Acts 16:14). That was not all. Her family also trusted the Lord and afterwards as believers they were all baptized in the river. It was not the water nor the act of baptism that made them Christians nor was it anything that Paul did. Paul only pointed them to Christ, but as he did so the Lord worked to change them into new persons in Christ. Lydia and her family were believers before being baptized in obedience to the Lord's command (Matthew 28:19-20).

Other people were also converted in Philippi. There was a slave girl as well as the jailor and his family (Acts 16:16-34) who all believed on the Lord Jesus Christ. This is how the church began in the city. According to the Bible, only converted men and women belong to the church of God.

The church provides fellowship

God's purpose for Christians is that they should meet together regularly for worship and prayer (Hebrews 10:25; Acts 2:42-47; 4:23-32). As Christians they are the church or body of Christ (Romans 12:4-6; 1 Corinthians 12:12-27; Ephesians 4:4-16) and they need one another.

The church is governed

Christ is the head of the local church in at least three ways. He is the federal (Romans 5:12-21; 1 Corinthians 15:22), organic (John 15:1-11; Ephesians 4:15-16) and ruling head of the church (Ephesians 5:23-32). He rules his people by the Bible and the Holy Spirit; he is also pleased to appoint pastors/elders to teach the Bible and rule in churches (Acts 20:28; 1 Timothy 3:1-7; etc).

One essential characteristic of a church, therefore, is the preaching of the Bible. If a local church or denomination fails here, it ceases to be a true church of God. Truth is of vital importance (John 8:31, 47; 1 Timothy 3:15; Galatians 1:8-9) for the Lord rules over his people by the word of truth.

The church's responsibilities

As our head, Christ tells us of our responsibilities within his church. Believers should be baptized (Matthew 28:19-20; Acts 2:41), regularly observe the Lord's Supper (Matthew 26:26-28; 1 Corinthians 11:23-34), contribute financially to the support of the church (Proverbs 3:9-10; 1 Corinthians 16:2), love and care for other believers in practical ways (1 Corinthians 12:25; Matthew 25:36; James 1:27, Hebrews 13:1-2; Galatians 6:1-6), live holy, consistent lives both at home, work and in society (Ephesians 5:22-6:9; Colossians 3:18-4:1; 1 Peter 2:13-25). In all these ways we give evidence that Christ is our Saviour and that he is ruling our lives and our churches.

Christ is building such churches and preserving them in the world until he returns and all the elect from every nation have been saved (Matthew 16:18; Acts 2:47). It is a privilege to belong to the glorious church of Christ.

45.
Death and the after-life

One day we shall all die. A sudden heart attack perhaps, or an accident, and we may have to leave this world without warning. For others, death will come after a long, painful illness, but no matter how, we shall die. The Bible says, 'It is appointed for men to die once' (Hebrews 9:27). At best, our life here is brief. That is why the Bible says our life is like a puff of smoke 'that appears for a little while and then vanishes away' (James 4:14; cf. Job 14:2).

Have you thought what happens when a person dies? At death, only our physical life comes to an end, but our soul or spiritual dimension continues to live. But what happens to us? Where do we go? It really depends whether we are Christians or not. Christians will go to heaven at death, while unbelievers will go into hell. We do not all go to the same place (Matthew 7:13-14; John 5:28-29). God does not save everyone; he saves only those who become Christians before they die. There is no second chance once we have died (Luke 16:26-31). That is why people are urged to 'seek the Lord while he may be found' (Isaiah 55:6), for while we are still in this world the Lord offers his grace and salvation to us; it is our duty to repent and believe on the Lord Jesus Christ (Hebrews 2:1-3; Acts 17:30-31). If we die without saving faith, the doors of heaven will be closed to us, but we shall only have ourselves to blame, for God is 'not wishing for any to perish but for all to come to repentance' (2 Peter 3:9). After death it will be too late.

Heaven

God is 'our Father who [is] in heaven' (Matthew 6:9). In fact, heaven is where God is; it is God who makes the place so glorious. Angels and believers worship and serve the triune God (Isaiah 6:3; Revelation 5;7), while believers on earth look forward to going to heaven when they die because there they will see the Lord (Isaiah 33:17; 1 John 3:2) and be like him. Believers look forward with joy to being with the Lord in heaven (2 Corinthians 5:8, Philippians 1:21-23).

Heaven is also a perfect place; no sin is allowed to enter (1 Corinthians 6:9-11; Hebrews 12:14; Revelation 21:27) and there will be no pain or sorrow or death there (Revelation 21:3-4). There will be no devil or sin to resist in heaven; this is part of the significance of the words: 'Blessed are the dead who die in the Lord from now on... that they may rest from their labours' (Revelation 14:13). Only believers, however, will enter heaven, namely, those who are 'in the Lord' by effectual calling and faith.

Hell

While we sometimes speak of experiencing 'hell' in this world as a result of some suffering or unhappy experience, hell is a place where unbelievers go when they die and where they are punished by God for their sin.

Four Hebrew or Greek words are translated as 'hell' in the Authorized Version of the Bible. These words are *Sheol, Hades, Tartarus* and *Gehenna.* The Hebrew *She'ol* usually denotes the state of death into which all are brought (1 Samuel 2:6; Job 14:13-14; 17:13-14; Psalm 89:48) or the more restricted meaning of 'grave' (Job 7:9; Genesis 37:35). The word is used in Psalm 9:17 of future punishment and it may also have this sense in Deuteronomy 32:22. Similarly *Hades* is used in more than one way in the New Testament. Sometimes it only means the grave or physical death (e.g. Acts 2:27; Revelation 6:8), but in other contexts Hades clearly refers to eternal punishment. An obvious example is Luke 16:23, where the rich man is described as being 'in hell... in torments'.

Gehenna is another word used in the New Testament generally to describe the location of unbelievers, body and soul, after the judgement day (e.g. Matthew 10:28, Mark 9:43-47) in hell.

What is hell like?

In hell, sinners are *separated from the Lord and his mercy*. They 'will pay the penalty of eternal destruction, *away from* the presence of the Lord...' (2 Thessalonians 1:9). Our Lord, at the last day, will say to the unbelieving, 'I never knew you; depart from me, you who practise lawlessness' (Matthew 7:23). Later, in Matthew 25:41, the Lord Jesus says, 'Depart from me, accursed ones, into the eternal fire...' Such separation involves 'eternal punishment' in verse 46.

The Bible also emphasizes the fact that sinners are *punished eternally* in hell by God. In Matthew 25:46 the Lord Jesus describes their fate as that of 'everlasting punishment'. *Kolasis* is the Greek word translated 'punishment' and the Watchtower translation of it as 'cutting-off' is wrong. In its verbal form the word is used in Acts 4:21, where the Sanhedrin tried unsuccessfully to obtain evidence whereby they could justly punish the apostles. They did not intend or wish to annihilate them! The word is also used in 2 Peter 2:9 where the unjust are described as being reserved in punishment until the final judgement. 'Punishment', and not 'cut-off', is the correct translation of *kolasis* in Matthew 25:46.

Another important Greek word in the New Testament is *apollumi*, which is translated 'destroy' in Matthew 10:28 and as 'lose', 'perish' or 'destroy' in other contexts, but nowhere does it mean annihilation. There are several clear references where the word cannot mean annihilation (e.g. Matthew 8:25; Luke 5:37; 19:10; 2 Peter 3:6; Hebrews 1:11-12).

How are sinners punished in hell?

Our Lord tells us that the soul and, eventually, the body are both punished (e.g. Matthew 10:28; Jude 7; Mark 9:43-48). The last of these references may refer to a condemning conscience which persists throughout eternity. Punishment in hell is also described as 'everlasting fire' or 'eternal fire' (Matthew 18:8; Jude 7), 'the fire' that 'is not quenched' (Mark 9:48) and 'flaming fire' (2 Thessalonians 1:7).

We are told that 'The smoke of their torment goes up for ever and ever' (Revelation 14:11; 19:3). Dives was also 'in torment' and 'in agony in this flame' (Luke 16:23-24), while the devil and his host 'will be tormented day and night for ever and ever' (Revelation 20:10). The references to fire are probably figurative, pointing to the wrath of one who is himself 'a consuming fire' (Hebrews 12:29). Unspeakable suffering and misery await unbelievers in hell and these will continue for ever. The Greek word *aionios* in the phrase 'eternal punishment' (Matthew 25:46) is also used in the same verse to describe the duration of everlasting life in heaven. This word and its related forms are used seventy-one times in the New Testament. While it sometimes denotes an age or indefinite period of time, it is used in the majority of cases in the sense of everlasting. In Romans 16:26 and 1 Timothy 1:17, for example, the word expresses the eternity of God and on fifty-one occasions it describes the unending bliss of the redeemed in heaven.

No wonder that God commands people to repent, for 'It is a terrifying thing to fall into the hands of the living God' (Hebrews 10:31). We are indeed fools if we die without preparing to meet God.

To illustrate the point, the Lord Jesus told a story about a farmer. The man worked hard. All his time and energies were given to the farm. After a while he became very successful. One year his crops were so good that he had to extend the farm. The old barns were pulled down and bigger ones built in their place. He was happy. Why shouldn't he be? Now he had sufficient food and money to keep his family for years. His success seemed to make his future secure. The man felt he had no need of God. To him, death and judgement were far away. 'Eat, drink and be merry' was now his philosophy of life and he intended to have a good time. Unknown to him, however, that evening he was going to die. 'You fool!' God said to him, 'This very night your soul is required of you; and now who will own what you have prepared?' (Luke 12:19-20).

A fool — yes! He was unprepared to meet God. But you need not be a fool. The Lord is ready to receive you. He will not turn anyone away. He is able to save you and put you in a right

relationship with God. He is the only one who is able and qualified
to reconcile us to God. The doors of heaven are open to you today.
Why be a fool? Repent and believe on the Lord Jesus Christ.

Appendices

Appendix I
Humanism

Humanism has a long and respected history reaching back before the incarnation of Christ to fifth-century Greece, when philosophers began to free sciences like natural history, medicine and astronomy from superstition and mythical beliefs. Great emphasis was placed on the intellect, and reasoning was regarded as the only legitimate way of obtaining true knowledge. Philosophers such as Protagoras and, later, Socrates, Plato and Aristotle made a major contribution to modern knowledge. Aristotle, for example, has been described as 'one of the greatest biologists the world has ever known'.[1] In Western Europe for almost a thousand-year period, up to A.D. 1400, theology dominated European thought and the scholars were mostly found in Roman Catholic monasteries. With the Renaissance, humanism again emerged and developed largely through the rediscovery of ancient Greek and Roman literature, so that both mediaeval theology and the authority of the church were gradually questioned and then rejected. Great advances made in art and sculpture (e.g. Michelangelo and Leonardo da Vinci), anatomy, astronomy (Copernicus and Galileo) and physics, and the success of the inductive method (i.e. conclusions drawn from observation and experiment) in the sciences gave men a new self-confidence as well as a high regard for reason. It was in the Renaissance that the word 'humanist' was first used to express the concern of scholars with humanity, but inevitably a conflict emerged between Renaissance leaders and the Roman church as greater emphasis was placed on man rather than on God, on nature rather than the supernatural and on the sciences instead of the Bible or church tradition.

During the Enlightenment of the seventeenth and eighteenth centuries humanism tended to dominate Western philosophy and science, as well as the arts, while Christendom was troubled by Deism, which was an attempt to apply humanistic principles to Christianity. While acknowledging the existence of God as Creator, Deists denied doctrines such as special revelation (i.e., the Bible), providence, human sin, salvation from sin and hell through the one, perfect sacrifice of Christ, and they also rejected the notion of miracles. During the second half of the nineteenth century a 'landslide of unbelief' occurred as science appeared to many to make God and the Bible irrelevant to modern life. Charles Darwin's *Origin of Species,* published in 1859, was seized upon by many as disproving Christianity and by the end of the century some theologians and churches had yielded to Darwin's theory of evolution, with the proviso that at a prior stage God had initiated the whole process of life and development. Alongside the rise of biblical criticism, which radically undermined faith and biblical teaching, humanist groups were formed in England to propagate rational views. For example, a group of secularist movements formed the Ethical Union in 1896 and in 1899 the Rationalist Press was established; these two groups united in 1963 to form the British Humanist Association under the leadership of Sir Julian Huxley and, later, Professor A. J. Ayer, the Oxford philosopher. Many influential people in Britain belong to the association and they work as an effective pressure group within Parliament, the media and education generally, with over 100 local groups now throughout Britain. Some of the reforms they want include the removal of all Christian and religious bias from society, the disestablishment of the Church of England and the repeal of the 1944 Education Act with its mandatory provision of worship and religious education in schools. They are also eager to develop a totally humanistic morality based only on a regard for human welfare. Humanists also support humanitarian work like UNESCO and OXFAM etc. as well as various peace organizations, such as the United Nations.

What Humanists believe	*What the Bible teaches*

God

Most humanists deny the existence of God and reject religious beliefs as irrational and meaningless.

'The fool says in his heart, "There is no God"' (Psalm 14:1).

'Without faith it is impossible to please [God], for he who comes to God must believe that he is, and that he is a rewarder of those who seek him' (Hebrews 11:6).

'You believe that there is one God. Good! Even the demons believe that — and shudder' (James 2:19, NIV).

Revelation

No special revelation or illumination is required and there are no 'true', authoritative answers to man's questions and problems.

'Can you discover the depths of God? Can you discover the limits of the Almighty? It is high as the heavens... deeper than Sheol, what can you know?' (Job 11:7-8).

'Where is the wise man? Where is the scribe? Where is the debater of this age? Has not God made foolish the wisdom of the world? For since in the wisdom of God the world through its wisdom did not come to know God, God was well-pleased through the foolishness of the message preached to save those who believe' (1 Corinthians 1:20-21).

'A natural man does not accept the things of the Spirit of God; for they are foolishness to him, and he cannot understand them, because they are spiritually discerned' (1 Corinthians 2:14; cf. Romans 1:20-22; Hebrews 1:1-2).

Authority

Everything is judged by the standard of man's own reasoning, experiences and pleasures. Nothing which conflicts with reason should be believed or practised.

'Whatever I command you, you shall be careful to do; you shall not add to it nor take away from it' (Deuteronomy 12:32).

'[Jesus] answered..., "It is written, 'Man shall not live on bread alone, but on every word that proceeds out of the mouth of God'" (Matthew 4:4).

'Heaven and earth will pass away, but my words will never pass away' (Mark 13:31)

'Thy word is truth' (John 17:17).

Creation

The world and human beings evolved over millions of years.

'In the beginning God created the heavens and the earth' (Genesis 1:1).

'All things came into being through him [Christ]; and apart from him nothing came into being that has come into being' (John 1:3).

Providence

Within a chance, evolutionary process human beings alone are responsible for their own destiny and happiness.

'He does according to his will in the host of heaven and among the inhabitants of the earth' (Daniel 4:35).

'God in whose hand are your life and breath and your ways' (Daniel 5:23).

'For in him we live and move and exist' (Acts 17:28).

Man

Man is inherently good and self-sufficient.

'There is none righteous, not even one; there is none who understands, there is none who seeks for God... there is none who does good, there is not even one...' (Romans 3:10-12).

Salvation

Being basically good, man has no need of Christ or of his sacrifice. Economic, social and personal problems can be resolved by means of education and science.

'There is salvation in no one else; for there is no other name under heaven that has been given among men, by which we must be saved' (Acts 4:12).

'The wrath of God is revealed from heaven against all ungodliness and unrighteousness of men' (Romans 1:18).

'Our God is a consuming fire' (Hebrews 12:29).

'Hide us from the presence of him who sits on the throne, and from the wrath of the Lamb, for the great day of their wrath has come, and who is able to stand?' (Revelation 6:16-17).

Morality

There are no absolute standards of right or wrong, so morality is based on a regard for human well-being. Some values in society, such as love, honesty and justice, have proved acceptable over the centuries but no values are beyond criticism.

'Fear God and keep his commandments, for this is the whole duty of man' (Ecclesiastes 12:13, NIV; cf. Exodus 20:1-17).

Life after death

Instead of an after-life, humanists offer the ideal and challenge of fulness in this life only. People should not evade the fact of death 'by taking refuge in comfortable illusions', such as God and heaven.

'These will go away into eternal punishment, but the righteous into eternal life' (Matthew 25:46).

'The poor man died and he was carried away by the angels to Abraham's bosom; and the rich man also died and was buried. And in Hades... being in torment...' (Luke 16:22-23).

'I [have] the desire to depart and be with Christ, for that is very much better' (Philippians 1:23).

Appendix II
Useful addresses and contacts for further reading and research

Spiritual Counterfeits Project
Box 4308
Berkley
Calif. 94704
U.S.A.
SCP publish a magazine and newsletter as well as detailed information on individual groups.

An annotated bibliography and a newsletter about new religions are available from the Research Working Group on New Religious Movements:
Institute of Social and Economic Research
University of Manitoba
Winnipeg
Manitoba
Canada R3T 2W2

Good informative materials are also available from:
Institute for Contemporary Christianity
Box A
Oakland
NJ 07436
U.S.A.

Christian Research Institute
P.O. Box 500
San Juan Capistrano
California 92675
U.S.A.

Two interesting American news-sheets on cult activities in the
USA:
The Advisor (American Family Foundation)
P.O. Box 343
Lexington
Ma. 02173
U.S.A.

News (Citizens' Freedom Foundation)
National Office
P.O. Box 1246
Springfield
Virginia 22151
U.S.A.

Centre for New Religious Movements
King's College
Strand
London
WC2R 2LS
The centre collects data and produces a journal on new religious
movements.

Deo Gloria Outreach
7 London Road
Bromley
Kent   BR1 1BY
England

Family Action Information and Rescue (FAIR)
BCM Box 3535
P.O. Box 12
London
WC1N 3XX

FAIR is supported by Christians and members of other religions as well as atheists, but it provides a great deal of useful, relevant information on cultic activities and responses by churches, groups and individuals in *FAIR News*.

Awareness is a quarterly journal for those who want to be kept informed on current activities of the various cult groups throughout the world. It publishes up-to-date news and carries articles on the doctrines and teaching of a wide range of cults, with testimonies from former cult members.

The editor is Eric Clarke, who is now Director of Christian Information Outreach, *Awareness* has approximately twenty pages; the first issue appeared in August 1982. Write to:
Christian Information Outreach
92 The Street
Boughton
Nr Faversham
Kent
ME13 9AP
England

Emerge (Ex members of Extremist Religious Cults)
BCM Box 1199
London
WC1N 3XX

Reachout Trust
P.O. Box 43
Twickenham
TW2 TEG
Middlesex
England

References

Introduction
1. See, e.g., *Concilium*, 161, New religious movements, T. & T. Clark; A. R. Brockway and J. P. Rajashekar, eds, *New religious movements and churches*, World Council of Churches Publications, 1987.
2. *Christianity today*, 23 October 1981, p.26; *A guide to cults and new religions*, pp.9-24, IVP, 1983.
3. *Understanding cults and new religions*, Eerdmans, 1986, pp.111f.
4. *Wayne State University Bulletin*, Summer 1982.
5. *Religion in sociological perspective*, Oxford University Press, 1982, pp.111-13.
6. *The lure of the cults*, IVP, 1983.
7. *Concilium*, 161, p.9.

Chapter 1: Modernism
1. Deists in the eighteenth century were people who accepted the existence of God but rejected the revealed message of the Bible.
2. Higher Criticism assesses theories concerning the compilation of Bible narratives from alleged sources, such as 'Q' in the synoptic Gospels, or J E P in Genesis, etc.
3. The first five books of the Old Testament.
4. John Urquhart, *Inspiration and accuracy of Holy Scripture*, p.iv.
5. *Ibid.*, p.iii.
6. *Ibid.*, p.89.
7. Quoted by A. C. Thiselton in *The two horizons*, Paternoster, pp. 207, 214.

8.   Hannah Tillich, *From time to time*, Stein & Day, 1973, pp.222-224.
9.   The Universities and Colleges Christian Fellowship (UCCF, previously known as IVF) is an evangelical organization committed to propagating biblical truth in the colleges and gathering Christian young people together in Christian Unions for the purpose of fellowship and witness.
10. The Evangelical Movement of Wales has known considerable blessing on its work, e.g. annual youth camps, conferences, preaching meetings, ministers' fellowships and literature, etc.
11. Donald Miller, *The Case for liberal Christianity*, SCM, 1981, p.37.
12. *Ibid.*,p.38.
13. John A. T. Robinson, *But that I can't believe*, Collins, 1967, p.86.
14. *Ibid.*, p.14.
15. *Ibid.*, p.25.
16. *Ibid.*, p.31.
17. *Ibid.*, p.32.
18. *Ibid.*, p.79.
19. *Ibid.*, p.41.

Chapter 2: Roman Catholicism
1.   D. M. Lloyd-Jones, *Maintaining the evangelical faith today*, IVF, 1951, pp.10-11.
2.   W. Hendriksen, *Matthew*, Banner of Truth Trust, p.301.

Chapter 3: The Quakers
1.   John R. Hughes, *The background of Quakerism in Wales and the Border*, 1952, p.39.
2.   Quoted by George H. Gorman, *Introducing Quakers*,FHSC, 1979, p.10.
3.   *Ibid.*,p.25.

Chapter 4: Seventh-Day Adventists
1.   G. J. Paxton, *The shaking of Adventism*, Zenith Publishers, 1977, p.55.
2.   *Spectrum* 9:31.
3.   Published by Evangelion Press, 1980.
4.   *Spectrum* 11:36
5.   *Ibid.* 13:7
6.   *Adventist Review*, 4 September 1980; cf. *Ministry* 53, October 1980 and *Spectrum* 11:2-26, November 1980.
7.   *Christianity Today*, 10 October 1980.

8. *Ibid.*, p.87.
9. Zondervan, 1960.
10. *Ibid.*, pp.236-7.
11. An excellent study book on the history and development of Adventism is Gary Land, ed., *Adventism in America*, Eerdmans, 1986.

Chapter 6: Churches of Christ
1. *Light to London*, vol. 8, Winter issue, January 1989, pp.4-5.; Douglas Jacoby, 'Where it all went wrong; a survey of church history,' (p.5, 'The fifth century').
2. Ed. Peter Brierley, published by Marc Europe/Evangelical Alliance/ Bible Society.
3. *Light to London*, vol. 6, no.7, July 1987, p.3, Douglas Jacoby, 'Immersion for salvation'.

Chapter 7: Unitarian churches
1. *The Unitarians*, pp.2-3.

Chapter 8: 'Jesus only'
1. In the early church period this teaching was known as Modalism, Modalistic Monarchianism and Sabellianism. Sabellius lived in the third century A.D. and taught in Rome about A.D. 215. His teaching was condemned in Rome but flourished in other areas, especially in Egypt and Libya. Sabellius argued that the Father, Son and Holy Spirit are all one and the same although manifested in different forms at different times.
2. Gordon Melton, *Encyclopedia of American Religions*, McGrath Publishing Co., 1978, vol. I, p.288.
3. Led by Raymond P. Virgil, this is a small group with its head office in Pueblo, Colorado; its work is among Spanish-speaking Americans.
4. The first local congregation was established in Honolulu in 1923/4 by the Rev. and Mrs Charles Lochbaum. Their influential radio ministry was launched in 1969.
5. Plans to form this group were first made in 1933 but implemented about ten years later. The group is pacifist by conviction and congregational in its church government; its main aim is to encourage fellowship between 'oneness' Pentecostal churches, particularly those refused fellowship by trinitarian Pentecostal churches.
6. This group was established in 1952 after a merger of three separate

'Jesus only' groups. Doctrinally, this group is in almost complete agreement with the larger United Pentecostal Church; it also has an active missionary work in Uruguay and Colombia.

7. Formed in 1919 by G. T. Haywood, this is the oldest 'oneness' Pentecostal denomination. Since 1924 its work has been restricted to coloured people, and it is now active in countries like Nigeria, Jamaica, Ghana, Egypt and Britain. The headquarters of the group is in Indianapolis.

8. They are led by a bishop and observe the sabbath on the seventh day of the week. Their name arises from the conviction that Jesus is the 'new and proper name of God, Christ and the Church'.

9. A former black minister in the Methodist Episcopal Church, Alabama, W. T. Phillips, formed the Ethiopian Overcoming Holy Church of God in 1919; the name was changed in 1927.

10. An early 'oneness' group established in 1919 by R. C. Lawson.

11. This was formed in 1957 by members of various congregations within the Church of Our Lord Jesus Christ of the Apostolic Faith who wanted a more democratic form of church government.

12. The Rev. A. D. Bradley was warned by the bishops of the Church of God in Christ in 1927 to stop preaching the 'Jesus only' heresy. When Bradley refused to comply, he helped to establish this new group and became its first presiding bishop.

13. Founded by the Rev. Donald Abernathy in 1963 in California. They identify Jesus with the Father, prohibit the use of medicine or surgery and have strict rules concerning dress for both men and women.

14. Two groups formed this new body in 1945. The head office and publishing house are in St Louis; their magazine, *Pentecostal Herald,* has a wide distribution. They undertake missionary work in twenty-one countries, including Great Britain.

15. John Montgomery, for example, shows conclusively how the Churches of God denomination in Ulster changed from a trinitarian to a 'oneness' doctrine about 1955 through the influence of Gordon Magee. An Ulster man who had emigrated to the United States, Magee embraced the 'Jesus only' teaching and felt he should share this 'new revelation' with the Churches of God in Ulster. See his *Evangelical or heretical; an examination of the Church of God in Ulster,* Burning Bush Publications, 1985, p.64

16. Quoted by James Bjornstad in duplicated notes dated 16 December 1983 and entitled *The oneness and threeness of God',,* p.9.

17. *Truly Pentecostal?, A critique of the United Pentecostal Church,* (leaflet), p.2.

18. *Calvin's Commentaries, Acts of the Apostles,* Eerdmans, 1949, vol. 1, p.120.

Chapter 10: Christian Science
1. *Eternity,* August 1979.

Chapter 12: Jehovah's Witnesses
1. A. Hoekema, *Jehovah's Witnesses,* Paternoster, p.26.
2. R. Franz, *Crisis of conscience,* Commentary Press, 1983, p.375.
3. E.C. Gruss, *We left Jehovah's Witnesses,* Baker Book House.

Chapter 15: Unification Church
1. *The Times,* 30 April 1978.
2. *The Rising of the Moon,* IVP, p.7.
3. *The Times,* 30 April 1978.
4. Jacqui Williams, *The Locust Years: Four Years with the Moonies,* Hodder & Stoughton, 1987.

Chapter 16: Family of Love
1. Kenneth Frampton, *Beware - the Children of God,* p.3.

Chapter 17: The Way International
1. Way literature claims that Wierwille also studied at Moody Bible Institute, but this is doubtful, especially in view of the fact that Moody has no record of his registration with them.

Chapter 18: Scientology
1. *Readers Digest,* May 1980, p.141.
2. *Christianity Today,* vol. 27, no. 4, p.31.
3. *Ibid.,* vol. 29, no. 10, p.51. The award was thirty-nine million dollars. The court ruled that Julie Christofferson had been defrauded by the Church of Scientology when she did not receive the self-improvement she was promised.
4. *Daily Express,* 7 August 1986, pp.1, 18-19.
5. *Newsweek,* 6 December 1982, p.8.
6. *Christianity Today,* vol. 27, no.4, p.32.
7. *The Times,* 29 January 1986, p.12.
8. *Daily Telegraph,* 25 February 1986, p.9.

Chapter 19: Freemasonry
1.   During 1985 the Methodist Church in Britain warned its members that 'There is a great danger that the Christian who becomes a Freemason will find himself compromising his Christian beliefs or his allegiance to Christ.'
2.   Stephen Knight, *The Brotherhood,* Grafton Books, 1985, p.240.
3.   Walter Hannah, *Darkness Visible,* Augustine Publishing Co.
4.   Knight, *The Brotherhood,* p.246. Knight has a most helpful section detailing the history of the attitude of the Roman Catholic Church towards Freemasonry (pp.245-54), as well as the present confused position in which English Catholic bishops are more tolerant of Freemasonry than some of their colleagues in other countries.
5.   David Yallop, *In God's Name, An Investigation into the Murder of Pope John Paul I,* Corgi Books, 1984.
6.   Knight, *The Brotherhood,* pp.211-215.
7.   Quoted in *The Brotherhood,* pp.131-2.
8.   *Ibid.,* p.188
9.   *Daily Post,* 27 May 1985, p.7. See also Narayan's book entitled *Barrister for the Defence.*
10. Knight, *The Brotherhood,* pp.49-63.
11. *Daily Telegraph,* 29 August 1984, p.13.
12. Knight, *The Brotherhood,* p.86.
13. *Ibid.,* pp.113-4.
14. *Banner of Truth* magazine, June 1986, Issue 273, pp.15-22.
15. Hannah, *Darkness Visible,* p.18.
16. *Ibid.,,* p.30.
17. *The Monthly Record,* March 1987, pp.132-3.

Chapter 20: EST
1.   *Questions people ask about the training,* 1981, p.1.
2.   John Weldon with Mark Albrecht, *The Strange World of EST,* Spiritual Counterfeits Project, 1982, p.1. Also *New Age Journal,* no. 7, pp.18-20.
3.   *Questions people ask...,* p.2.
4.   *Ibid.,* p.3.
5.   'EST - The new life-changing philosophy that makes you the boss', *New Times,* 18 October 1974.
6.   *Ibid.,,* p.5.
7.   *East-West,* p.5.
8.   *EST - Four days to make your life work,* Pocket Books, 1976, p.131.
9.   Werner Erhard, *If God had meant man to fly...,* 12974, p.2.
10. 'EST - The new life-changing philosophy...'

Chapter 21: Exegesis
1. Quoted by *Daily Mirror*, 19-20 March 1980 and also in *News and Views*, (Deo Gloria Outreach) no. 3, June 1980, p.3.
2. An excellent historical survey and assessment of the self-improvement movement is provided by the *Spiritual Counterfeits Project Journal* in vol. 5, no. 1, entitled, 'Empowering the self: a look at the Human Potential Movement'.

Chapter 22: The Occult
1. *Christianity Today*, 6 February 1981, p.92.
2. Kurt Koch, *Between Christ and Satan*, p.72.

Chapter 24: Theosophy
1. *Banner of Truth*, 1980, Issues 203-4, pp.10-11.

Chapter 25: Eckankar
1. Ronald Endroth and others, *A Guide to Cults and New Religions*, IVP, 1983, p.60.

Chapter 26: The New Age Movement
1. J. Gordon Melton, *Encyclopedic Handbook of Cults in America*, p.110.
2. *Ibid.*, p.108.
3. Quoted by Jane Grumbridge in a duplicated article entitled 'The New Age' (1983). This article was made available to me by Family Action Information and Rescue (FAIR).
4. *Ibid.*, p.4
5. *Ibid.*, p.2

Chapter 28: Hare Krishna
1. Figures taken from the *UK Christian Handbook*, 1989/90 edition, MARC Europe.
2. *Bhagavad-Gita as it is*, ch. 18, text 66, p.835.

Chapter 30: Transcendental Meditation
1. *The Times*, 16 April 1980.
2. Pat Means, *The Mystical Maze*, p.134.

3.   Maurice Burrell, *The Challenge of the Cults,* IVP, 1981, p.93.
4.   *Meditations of Maharishi Mahesh Yogi,* Bantam Books, 1973, pp.17-18.
5.   *Ibid.,* p.59.
6.   *Ibid.,* pp.177-8.

Chapter 32: Rajneesh Foundation
1.   *Shree* is often translated as 'Sir'.
2.   *Christianity Today,* 23 April 1982, p.39.
3.   *Ibid.*
4.   *Ibid.*
5.   *Ibid.,* p.40.
6.   *Newsweek* and *Time,* October 1981.

Chapter 35: The Holy Trinity
1.   E. C. Gruss, *Apostles of Denial,* p.127.

Appendix I: Humanism
1.   T.M. Kitwood, *What is Human?,* IVP, p.14.

Index

Index

This index does not include biblical characters or doctrines.

Apocrypha, 33-4
Apostolic Oneness Movement —
    see 'Jesus only'
Armstrong, Herbert W., 125-32
Astrology, 190

'Bab', 222-4
Baha'i, 222-8
    background, 222-4
    modern history, 224
    teaching, 225-8
Baker-Eddy, Mary, 93-9
Barnhouse, Donald Grey, 56
Berg, David, 148-52
Besant, Mrs Annie, 202-3, 204
Bhagavad-Gita, 229, 230
Blavatsky, Madame Helena P.,
    201-2, 203
British Council of Churches, 74
Buchman, Frank, 62-7
Buddhism, 249, 254

Campbell, Thomas and
    Alexander, 70
'Campbellites': (Churches of
    Christ) 68-73
    causes for concern, 68-70
    current divisions, 71-2
    historical background, 70-71
    teaching, 72-3

Children of God — see Family of
    Love
Christadelphians, 87-92
    origin and development, 87-8
    statistics, 88
    teaching, 88-92
Christian Science (Church of
    Christ, Scientist), 93-9, 215
    early history, 93-4
    statistics, 94-5
    teaching, 95-9
Cults
    appeal, 10-11
    challenge, 12
    classification, 11-12
    definition, 10

Daily Mail, 141-3
D'Aubigny, Robert, 183
Divine Light Mission, 215, 247-
    50
    founder, 247-50
    teaching, 249-50
    today, 248

Eckankar, 207-12,
    false claims, 207-8
    founder, 207-8
    teaching, 209-12
Erhard, Werner, 177-82

EST (Erhard Seminars Training),
        177-82
    challenge to the gospel, 179
    claims, 178-9
    founder, 177-8
    teaching, 179-82
Exegesis, 179, 183-4
    dangerous techniques, 183-4
    founder, 183

Family of Love (formerly the
        Children of God), 148-52
    formation, 148
    leader, 148-9
    statistics, 149
    teaching, 149-52
Ford, Desmond, 54-6
Fox, George, 46-8
Fox, Margaret and Kate, 193
Franz, Frederick, 114
Franz, Raymond, 114
Freemasonry, 167-74
    background, 169-70
    incompatibility with
        Christianity, 171-2
    membership, 167-9
    teaching, 173-4
Friends, Society of — see
        Quakers

Gnosticism, 220

Hare Krishna (International
        Society for Krishna
        Consciousness), 218, 229-34
    current scene, 230
    founder, 229-30
    routine, 230
    teaching, 230-34

Hinduism, 242-4, 246, 249, 250,
        254
Hubbard, L. R., 159-63
Humanism, 311-15
    history, 311-12
    teaching, 313-15

International Society for Krishna
        Consciousness — see Hare
        Krishna
Irvine, Doreen, 188
Islam, 249
    Shi'ites and Sunnites, 222-3

Jehovah's Witnesses, 110-24
    definition, 110-11
    disillusionment among ex-
        members, 114-15
    leaders, 111-13
    origins, 111-12
    scandals, 112-13
    statistics, 114-15
    teaching, 116-24
Jesuits, 31
'Jesus only,' 80-84
    background, 81-2
    teaching, 82-4

Koch, Kurt, 190, 192
Knorr, Nathan Homer, 113
Koran, 225

Lodges, 167, 170, 172

Magic, 190-91
    black, 190-91
    white, 191
Martin, Walter R., 56
Meyer, F. B., 63

Miller, William, 52-3
Modernism, 15-28
  bibliography, 27-8
  definition, 16
  history, 16-17
  protests against, 18-19
  stranglehold on Christendom, 19-21
  teachings, 22-7
Moon, Rev. Sun Myung, 139-47
Moonies — see Unification Church
Moral Re-Armament, 62-7
  beginnings, 62-3
  expansion, 63-5
  statistics, 64-5
  teaching, 65-7
Mormons, 100-109
  Book of Mormon, 102-3, 104
  history, 101-2
  statistics, 100
  teaching, 103-9
Moslems — see Islam
Muhammad, 222, 223, 225, 227, 250

New Age Movement, 215-21
  Eastern influences, 215-16
  leaders, 216-17
  regard for nature, 218
  teaching, 219-21

Occult, 187-92
  definition, 189
Oxford Group, 64

Penn, William, 47, 48
Penn-Lewis, Mrs, 62
Pope, 29-32, 34-35

Protestant churches and modernism — see Modernism

Quakers, 46-51
  beginnings, 46-7
  concern, 48
  inward illumination, 48
  persecution, 47
  statistics, 47-8
  teaching, 49-51

Rajneesh Foundation, 251-6
  claims, 252-3
  founder, 251-2
  origins, 251-2
  teaching, 254-6
Rastafarians, 133-5
  background, 134
  practices, 134
  teaching, 134-5
Roberts, Robert, 88
Roman Catholicism, 29-45
  changes, 31
  Jesuits, 31
  mass, 29, 39
  teaching, 33-45
Russell, Charles Taze, 110-13
Rutherford, 'Judge', 110, 112, 113

Satanism, 188, 191-2
Scientology, 158-63
  background, 160
  dangers, 158-9
  leader, 159-62
  teaching, 162-3
  wealth, 159
Selassie, Emperor Haile, 134, 135

Seventh Day Adventists, 52-61,
    111, 125
    beginnings, 52
    controversy, 54-6
    history, 53
    relations with evangelicals,
    56
    statistics, 57
    teaching, 58-61
Smith, Joseph, 101-2, 103, 104
Society of Friends — see Quakers
Spiritism, 189, 193-200, 215
    origin, 193-4
    statistics, 194
    teaching, 195-200

Theosophy, 201-6, 215
    later developments, 203
    leaders, 201-2
    Pink, Arthur, 202-3
    resemblance to Spiritism and
    other cults, 201
    teaching, 203-6
Thomas, John, 87-8
Tibetan Book of the Dead, 19
Tkach, Joseph W., 127-8
Transcendental Meditation, 215,
    240-46
    British headquarters, 240
    false claims, 242
    Hindu elements, 242-3
    leader, 240-41, 243-4
Twitchell, Paul, 207-12

Unification Church (Moonies),
    139-47
    court case, 141-2
    founder, 139-41
    teaching, 144-7
Unitarian churches, 74-9
    definition, 74-5
    statistics, 74
    teaching, 75-9

Vedas (Hindu Scriptures), 243
Vedic rites, 242-3, 246

Way International, 153-7
    beginnings, 153-4
    teaching, 155-7
    way of working, 154-5
White, Mrs Ellen, 53-6, 58, 60
Wierville, V. P., 153-4, 157
Witchcraft, 187, 191
World Congress of Faiths, 74
Worldwide Church of God, 125-
    32
    developments, 127-8
    growth, 126
    teaching, 128-32
    founder, 125-7

Yoga, 235-9
    definition, 235
    indispensable practices, 236-
    8
    teaching, 238-9
Young, Brigham, 100, 102